# CHOREOGRAPHY OBSERVED

JACK ANDERSON

# Choreography Observed

UNIVERSITY OF IOWA PRESS / IOWA CITY

TO GEORGE DORRIS

University of Iowa Press, Iowa City 52242
Copyright © 1987 by the University of Iowa
All rights reserved
Printed in the United States of America
First edition, 1987

Book and jacket design by Sandra Strother Hudson
Typesetting by G & S Typesetters, Inc., Austin, Texas
Printing and binding by Edwards Brothers, Inc., Ann Arbor, Michigan

Library of Congress Cataloging-in-Publication Data

Anderson, Jack, 1935–
Choreography observed.

Includes index.
1. Choreography.   2. Choreographers.   3. Dancing.
4. Dancers.   I. Title.
GV1782.5.A53   1987      792.8'2      87-6021
ISBN 0-87745-172-9

Title page: the Royal Danish Ballet in
August Bournonville's *Konservatoriet*. Photo courtesy
of the Royal Danish Ballet.

# CONTENTS

# INTRODUCTION
# AND ACKNOWLEDGMENTS

*I* saw my first dance performance in 1950; I published my first dance review a decade later. Over the years, I have written about dance for numerous publications, including daily newspapers, specialist monthlies, and critical quarterlies. When I began to assemble this collection of reviews and essays, I decided it ought to possess some sort of focus so that it would be more than a miscellany. Therefore, I have chosen to emphasize choreography, for that is the aspect of dance that fascinates me most.

However, I should like to make clear at the outset that this book does not attempt to be a survey of all important choreographers, past or present; it is an anthology of criticism, not a text in dance history. Therefore, the absence of essays about certain famous choreographers should not be taken to mean that I find those artists unimportant. I have not been able to write at length about some major choreographers. Others are not represented here because, although I have written about them, I now find my reviews of them less interesting than those I have written on the choreographers I have chosen to include.

In gathering reviews, I have tried to leave them unchanged. However, since all publications do not follow the same stylesheets, some modifications have been made. Spellings, dates, and punctuation have been regularized. Discussions of nonchoreographic matters have been trimmed; but, since choreography does not exist in a vacuum, there will be passing references to music, stage design, and specific dancers. Statements of purely journalistic information have been dropped when they are now irrelevant (e.g., "the program will be repeated next Tuesday") or clarified when they are vague (e.g., specific dates have been added where the original text may simply say "last night").

Though I have made stylistic adjustments, I have resisted the temptation to tamper with my opinions and analyses. Yet it should be remembered that critics may change over the years. So, in a sense, may dances:

they may seem different when different casts offer varying interpretations of them; the contexts in which dances are seen may also affect their impact. Because a piece of criticism is a specific reaction at a specific point in time, I would urge readers not to ignore the date of publication which has been placed at the end of each article.

For all writers, editors can be blessings, and I have been blessed to work with several fine ones. It was the late Estelle Herf of England's *Ballet Today* who gave me my start in dance journalism. I was fortunate to have had Lydia Joel as editor when I began to write for *Dance Magazine,* and Doris Hering and, later, Tobi Tobias served as my helpful review coordinators there. It continues to be my good fortune that Mary Clarke is my editor at the *Dancing Times* of London. Arlene Croce proved to be an exemplary editor at *Ballet Review.* Anna Kisselgoff has encouraged me at the *New York Times,* and I extend thanks to all the *Times* cultural editors and culture copy-desk staff members who have advised me. I am particularly grateful for the editorial guidance of Allen Hughes and the late Seymour Peck.

Several years of pestering by Paul Zimmer of the University of Iowa Press eventually goaded me to put this book together. George Dorris has provided constant support along the way. And the dance writings of the late Edwin Denby continue to be an inspiration.

# ONE
# Thinking about Choreography

*Cynthia Harvey, Mikhail Baryshnikov, and members of the American Ballet Theatre in Swan Lake. Photo: MIRA.*

*C*horeography keeps slipping away. Once a dance has started, it cannot be stopped or slowed down; once a dance has ended, it is hard to summon back. Many dances have not been notated or filmed, and survive only in the memories of their interpreters, and memories, of course, are fallible. And since notation systems can seem abstruse, there are people in the dance world who prefer to leave their mastery entirely to specialists.

Given its elusiveness, choreography is often hard to think about—and to talk about, as well. Yet it deserves serious discussion, for it is the stuff of which dances are made. Even the most brilliant dancers must have something to dance before they can dazzle.

Because there exists nothing in dance as universally accepted as, say, the play script or the musical score, the textual problems of choreography can be quite different from those of drama or music. The very nature of the choreographic text is itself a major problem, and dancegoers and dance producers divide into several factions on this issue. For instance, there are those who believe that the steps of a dance work must always be preserved. On the other hand, there are those who countenance changes in steps, provided that the theatrical effects of those steps remain unaltered by the substitutions. Still others assume that steps can be changed at will to suit the whim of the dancer—that choreography is essentially an excuse to show off the dancer. And many other points of view also exist.

Whatever steps specific works may contain and however much or little they may be altered from performance to performance, all dances are revelations in space and time. Just what they reveal depends upon the taste and aesthetic inclinations of individual choreographers. Many dances are simply studies in pattern and energy. However, choreographers, through movement, may also seek to present ideas, depict dramatic characters, or

*elicit specific emotional responses from the viewer. It could be said that
every dance is a little world all its own. At times, such little worlds may be
of interest solely for their own sake. At other times, however, they can serve
as microcosms of the great world in which we live.*

# CONFESSIONS OF A
# CHOREOGRAPHY-WATCHER

*L*et me confess: I am a choreography-watcher. Although I love many
things about dance, I go to dance performances primarily because I
want to see fine choreography. Of course, I like seeing fine dancers, too. Yet it is choreography that interests me most.

This may seem an extreme view. It is also, I admit, a deliberately
exaggerated one, a critical stance adopted to help make clear how and
why this book of reviews has been put together. Yet I have a hunch that
many dancegoers are basically either choreography-watchers or dancer-
watchers. To classify spectators in this fashion is neither to proclaim one
category necessarily superior to the other nor to suggest that dancegoers
cannot alter their interests, sometimes from performance to performance, sometimes even from work to work during the course of a single
performance. Nevertheless, I still think it possible to say that—at least
on some occasions—audiences at dance performances may be made up
of choreography-watchers and dancer-watchers.

When fans flock to see certain internationally acclaimed artists—some
even following such stars as Rudolf Nureyev and Mikhail Baryshnikov
on cross-country tours—they are being dancer-watchers. So are the
balletomanes who regularly attend the international competitions for
young dancers in such places as Moscow; Varna, Bulgaria; and Jackson,
Mississippi. In contrast, the scores of dancegoers from many countries who journeyed to Copenhagen in 1979 to attend a festival by the
Royal Danish Ballet did so not only to admire the charms of the Danish

dancers: most were there because the festival was devoted to the works of a single historically important, and much beloved, choreographer, August Bournonville. Other choreography-watchers are those who seek out productions of unusual or rarely revived works by American regional companies.

Historical precedents exist for both categories. When the novelist Stendhal compared the early-nineteenth-century choreographer Salvatore Viganò to Shakespeare, he was being a fervent choreography-watcher, whereas the flowery tributes written by the poet and critic Théophile Gautier to the ballerinas of the Romantic era are aesthetic love letters from a dancer-watcher.

One thing that makes choreography fascinating to contemplate for its own sake—apart from the merits of the specific performers who may be interpreting it—is the way choreographers employ time, space, and motion so that each dance becomes a little world all its own. The events that occur in that world may be influenced by many factors, ranging from the choreographer's personal taste to the prevailing critical or public taste of the time. Theoretically, one could say that, from all the possibilities for motion that exist, choreographers select the movements they consider most appropriate for a given work. However, in actuality, choreographers rarely have such total freedom. Sometimes choreographers are restricted by the limitations tradition has established for a specific dance form: for instance, in its purest manifestations the Indian form known as Bharata Natyam can be danced only by women; in Western ballet, men ordinarily do not dance on pointe. At other times, creative choices may be dictated by the abilities of the dancers at a choreographer's disposal.

Nevertheless, choreographers usually do have a multitude, if not an infinitude, of choices, and in contemporary Western ballet and modern dance they also have the freedom to follow or defy tradition. In each dance we watch, we behold interplays of energy appealing simultaneously to the senses and to the mind. The kinetic sense is stimulated by the dynamics of a dance, by its passages of speed and slowness, by its contrasts between tension and relaxation or weight and weightlessness.

Our visual sense responds to the shapes the dancers make as they pass through space and time.

Yet we do not merely see a dance, we also think about it—both in retrospect and as it proceeds. The mind is always at work sorting out and organizing what the eye is watching. And as a result of that sorting out, we come to some conclusions about a dance's overall significance. Presumably, the choreographer may also have certain notions as to the dance's intended significance and has so arranged the steps to make that significance clear. Yet dances may suggest meanings that were not consciously placed there by their creators. When Marius Petipa choreographed *The Sleeping Beauty* in St. Petersburg in 1890, he surely intended to retell a familiar fairy story. But did he also *consciously* intend to make his ballet a glorification of aristocratic manners and of monarchy itself? Perhaps. Perhaps not. Yet audiences for generations have pronounced it regal.

The kinds of things a dance may convey differ from culture to culture and period to period. Much ballet and modern dance has been dramatic or thematic. Movements are used to tell a story, explore a theme, or express an emotion. These may include both movements that audiences of a particular period almost automatically associate with certain meanings (e.g., placing hand on heart means "I love you") and movements that acquire their meanings through the way they are combined or juxtaposed with other movements. The emotions a dance expresses may be unusually strong ones, but they need not be—and most often, presumably, are not—emotions the choreographer or dancer is literally feeling at the time of the work's creation or performance. Otherwise, Martha Graham could only have effectively danced her tragic *Lamentation* at times when she herself was consumed with grief.

This point may seem obvious. Yet it may be worth fussing over. When we watch performances, we may be so impressed by the apparent union of dancers with their choreography that we may forget that dancing and choreography are separable entities. Spectators overwhelmed by the stage presence of certain dancer-choreographers may be especially inclined to forget this, and some have even argued that because such modern dance pioneers as Isadora Duncan, Ruth St. Denis, and Mary Wigman are now dead, their dances are fundamentally unrevivable, even when their steps are known. But by distinguishing between the dancer and the dance, it becomes possible to argue that, even though its creator may have died, a given dance may still possess evocative or striking steps that can be effectively reproduced by other performers.

In addition to dramatic or thematic works, choreographers in our own century have created plotless or so-called abstract dances. Here no specific story is told and no message is preached. Yet such dances are in no way devoid of significance. Some appeal to the pleasure we take in contemplating pattern. Others contrast states of order and disorder. And since all are performed by human beings, they contain images of men and women in harmony or conflict. Because they present us with visions of chaos or design, many fine abstract dances seem to possess moral, social, and even spiritual significance. Because we can respond to the changing degrees of tension and relaxation in the steps of a dance, even if those steps are not pantomimic or representational, every little movement may very well convey a meaning of its own.

At some point in their theatregoing careers, dance lovers may find themselves pondering a momentous question. Baldly put, the question is this: *Do you believe that any way of dancing, apart from its usage in specific works, is somehow a good in itself?* Care should be taken in formulating a reply, for all sorts of consequences will proceed from whatever answer is given, be it affirmative or negative.

Many of the early modern dancers were convinced that their form of dance could help bring about both social and artistic liberation. Apologists for ballet have been equally vehement. Lincoln Kirstein, the poet, critic, and polemicist who directs the New York City Ballet, has felt impelled to employ religious imagery in his defense of ballet. He has compared the passing on of balletic tradition to Apostolic Succession and has branded modern dance as heresy. Two provocative British writers, Adrian Stokes and Rayner Heppenstall, expressed similar views in the 1930s.

Given classical ballet's undeniable accomplishments and its carefully ordered and constantly developing system of training, such arguments are tempting. Like anyone who has seen some of our regional ballet companies, I know that, even if choreographic inspiration may not be of the highest in certain productions, classical style and technique can, to quote Stokes, work "as a disinfectant against vulgarity." Yet my own answer to my question is a cautious "no." Any dance form, technique, or style can be good on specific occasions—just as, on other occasions, it may be inappropriate.

Having given such a reply, I realize that I am letting myself in for what Heppenstall called "the welter of nasty Nonconformist sects." But I also hope I am letting myself in for a healthy pluralism. I believe that our century's choreographic achievements have demonstrated that not only classical ballet but several other types of dance can fill the stage with beautiful immediacy. The tensions between these ways of dancing—or their occasional hybridization—can be of creative value, preventing the practitioners of any single way of dancing from sinking into complacency. Rather than trumpet classicism (or, for that matter, some variety of modernism) for its own sake, I would advocate pragmatism and seemliness: a way of dancing is valid only insofar as it can convince one of its validity in actual performance. All ways of dancing are forever on trial.

Just as it is possible to categorize dancegoers on the basis of their interests, so one can establish subdivisions in the category of choreography-watchers. For instance, there are—among other possibilities—choreography-watchers who favor choreography that includes and those who favor choreography that excludes. Comparable preferences also exist among lovers of other arts. Exclusionists often like to set up artistic boundaries, to define the limiting conditions of each artistic medium, and to determine what is proper within each medium. Exclusionist choreography-watchers frequently extol what they call "pure" or "absolute" dance, and they may scorn works for containing material they consider inappropriate to the art form: for instance, some fanatical proponents of "abstract" ballet dismiss narrative dance as inherently inferior. And some exclusionists worry much over decorum and propriety.

If exclusionists like to see what art can leave out, inclusionists are fascinated by the sorts of things—even the disparate or contradictory things—that can be let into art, and they may not mind it when an artist appears to be straining against the perceived boundaries of a medium. Inclusionists do not mind "impurity"; they may welcome the mixing of media—provided that, in these mixtures, arts are either harmoniously combined or effectively contrasted. Inclusionism is certainly not just a matter of preferring narrative to plotless dance, representational to abstract painting, or decorated to open stage spaces. To an inclusionist, what matters is not necessarily the style or genre of a work, but its richness. Thus, the abstract ballets of George Balanchine may be as rich in emotional implications as they are in technical ingenuity, whereas an abstraction by a lesser ballet master may seem only an arrangement of classroom steps.

I am surely an inclusionist when it comes to dance, and I hope my reviews convey some of the things I find exciting about the choreography I see. I also find I harbor a certain distrust of exclusionist critical theories, especially when advanced by pedants. Those who state them most dogmatically sometimes imply that they believe art has systematically developed over the centuries until it has attained whatever state the theorist considers desirable (thus, painting has "logically" gone from representation to abstraction, dance from narration to abstraction, and music from tonality to serialism). The notion that theorists can logically determine what is aesthetically imperative at any point in history strikes me as presumptuous and even insulting to artistic creativity. Moreover, reductionist theories occasionally give the disquieting impression that the theorist believes that, now that art has reached a certain state, *nothing* significantly different can come next: consider the lamentations of some lovers of abstract painting at the rise of Pop Art or the New Realism, or the wailings of atonalists over music's New Romanticism. Rather than fitting art into an all-encompassing theory, I prefer to make tentative observations as I watch art squirm about in its often surprising way.

To be sure, my experience as a dancegoer has led me to suspect that there are certain things dance cannot easily do: thus, it is difficult for choreography to relate events that have supposedly occurred in the past or to depict complicated social relationships ("There are no sisters-in-law in ballet," Balanchine reportedly said); and though dance can vividly show the effects of ideas in action, it cannot easily argue intellectual positions (Agnes de Mille is the granddaughter of a distinguished economist and remains sympathetic to his theories; yet, to my knowledge, she has never attempted to choreograph a ballet demonstrating the validity of Henry George's concept of the single tax). Nevertheless, I still consider it conceivable that, should their passions and imaginations be sufficiently stirred, talented choreographers might one day create effective ballets about both sisters-in-law *and* the single tax.

Whereas casual dancegoers can get away with saying, "Gee, that was nice," or "Ugh!" after a performance, critics are required to be more articulate. Criticism may discuss many issues. But all criticism involves what, for alliterative convenience, I shall term "evocation" and "evaluation."

Through evocation, a critic conveys a sense of what happened at a performance. If choreography is to be the focus of a review, then a critic must suggest what a dance work was like: was it dramatic? abstract? sad? happy? tumultuous? serene? Moreover, since dance is an art of motion, a critic should attempt to provide readers with some idea of the kinds of movements and patterns the choreographer employed: were steps harsh and slashing or smooth and flowing? did dancers hug the earth or leap through the air? did they cover the stage with their steps or was everyone confined in a restricted area?

The kind of language critics employ in evocation may be affected by the publications for which they write and the space allotted them. Thus, technical terms for dance steps may be used by a writer for a specialist dance publication, whereas a writer for a daily newspaper might avoid them, fearing they will be incomprehensible to that paper's readers; and, obviously, a 1,000-word piece can contain more evocative detail than a piece of 300 words. Yet a critic might consciously reject using technical terms even for a specialist publication, believing that, though they may convey the choreographic outline of a passage, they may fail to suggest its mood or emotional impact; and even when they have almost unlimited space, critics may keep evocative passages to a minimum either because a particular dance may be based upon only a few basic steps or because the critics consider the ideas they wish to present about the dance more important than a catalogue of steps.

However, a review should contain at least some evocative writing so that readers may learn just what went on in the dance. In any case, whether it is extensive or minimal, evocation is essentially descriptive.

But critics do more than describe—they evaluate: they analyze, interpret, and come to some conclusions about the works they see. They ask themselves questions, including such simple and obvious ones as "Did I like this dance? Did I think it significant? Why or why not?" The process of evaluation disturbs some dancers, and I have heard dance students wonder, "Why must critics evaluate? Why don't they just describe and let readers make up their own minds? Why can't critics be objective?"

"Objective." It is sometimes difficult to determine precisely what people mean by this word. On the one hand, it can mean being free of prejudice. Certainly, all critics should strive to be objective in this sense. But occasionally it seems that some dancers, in asking critics to be objective, are asking them to be totally descriptive and to avoid evaluation altogether. Much attention is paid to description in contemporary dance criticism, and virtually every workshop in dance writing stresses the ability to write evocatively. Perhaps this is only to be expected: writers must find a way to verbalize their perceptions of a nonverbal art; dancers and choreographers, lacking a universally accepted notation system, may be especially eager to insure that at least something about a dance is documented.

But description alone is not criticism; it may not even be interesting: an endless list of steps, however accurately described, could easily weary readers. And such catalogues, even at their lengthiest, would probably still offer a less comprehensive account of a dance than could be provided by the dance notation systems that do exist. Evocation without evaluation is useless, even meaningless, for it can make all dances sound equally important—or unimportant.

Evaluation need not involve hurling thunderbolts of approbation or condemnation. In evaluating a dance, a critic examines it to determine what sort of work it is and what has made it effective or ineffectual. The judgments reached are purely personal ones—how could they be otherwise?—but if the evidence leading to them can be found in the dance itself and not just in the critic's imagination, and if the arguments a critic marshals are lively, then evaluation can be stimulating indeed. The ideas of some critics may be so provocative that readers find these critics illuminating even though they may disagree with them. Being the result of one person's mind reflecting on an aesthetic experience, all criticism is ultimately subjective. Even a totally descriptive account of the key movements in a dance could be called a subjective piece of writing, since to decide what those key movements are is, in effect, to interpret that dance in some way.

Whether critics or casual dancegoers, we all evaluate the performances we attend. That is why friends gather in bars or coffee shops after the theatre to argue far into the night. The fact that we are willing to evaluate and argue may even be a sign that we find performances important to us.

Dance in general—and choreography in particular—has been important enough to me that, for about a quarter of a century, I have been willing to mull over, analyze, evaluate, and argue about it in print. I have attended many dull performances. Yet because dance as an art has not lost its capacity to delight me, I keep coming back to it and keep writing about it. In that quarter century I have seen choreographers accomplish so many kinds of surprising things that I know that, although every review must have a last word, there can be no final word in criticism.

# WILL CHOREOGRAPHY EVER BE RESPECTED AS AN ART FORM?

*L*et's not mince words, but say what has to be said as bluntly as possible. So here goes: dance, as an art form, is too often an absolute mess. There, now, it's been said.

Almost immediately, I suspect, there will be angry sputters and fans will start waxing eloquent over the marvelous performances of Miss X or Mr. Y. Or they'll extol the glories of the Ballet Such-and-Such or the So-and-So Modern Dance Company. A few may even praise someone's choreography. But to those who do, a question should be put: how can you be sure that you'll ever see that choreography again?

Dance may be an art of magnificent spectacle, but it is an art surprisingly lacking in any sizable and coherently organized body of choreographic literature that can be compared with the extant bodies of musical or dramatic literature. Precious few examples of historically important choreography can be seen anywhere. The creations of the eighteenth- and early-nineteenth-century reformers—including those of Jean-Georges Noverre, Gaspero Angiolini, and Salvatore Viganò—are totally lost. No complete ballet exists by Jules Perrot. Not many exist by the prolific Marius Petipa. And while the Danes are proud of their great nineteenth-century choreographer, August Bournonville, only eight ballets and a few divertissements of his more than sixty compositions remain.

What is particularly shocking is our willingness to permit choreographic deterioration to continue, for we often don't know how to deal with the choreography we do possess. Though we live at a time when we can preserve choreography through films and notation, works—both notated and unnotated, filmed and unfilmed—are constantly being altered. A dancer friend recently told me that he had just seen thirty-two *Don Quixote* pas de deux at a ballet festival. No two were choreographically identical and not one of them totally resembled the pas de deux that was standard when my friend was a student.

Even though legitimate variants of a work may exist and virtuoso dancers, like virtuoso singers, may under certain circumstances add ornaments to the showpieces they perform, the idea that there can be at least thirty-two different versions of *Don Quixote* is an appalling one, for it implies that we are not really sure of what choreography involves.

Just what is a ballet or a modern dance work? Is it a sequence of specific steps? Or do specific steps not matter so long as a certain style or atmosphere is preserved? Or is a ballet anything that one does to a familiar plot or piece of music? No actor or critic would regard Aeschylus's *The Libation Pourers*, Sophocles' *Electra*, and O'Neill's *Mourning Becomes Electra* as the same play, even though they tell the same story. Yet, in discussing *Swan Lake*, productions that try to preserve traditional choreography, productions that combine traditional choreography with new choreography, and productions that consist almost entirely of new choreography are regularly lumped together by dancers, writers, and audiences without qualification. So what, then, constitutes *Swan Lake?* Simply some Tchaikovsky music to which anything goes?

Just how chaotic dance is becomes particularly apparent when one turns to the musical scene. One of the most exciting recent developments in music is the increased concern for period instruments and performing techniques. We have long been able to hear Bach on a harpsichord. But now we can also hear Mozart, Beethoven, and Schubert on the fortepianos of their own times. In contrast, dancers often adapt old works to fit the general performance standards that prevail today, even though the results can resemble Leopold Stokowski's overblown orchestrations of Bach.

Some older dancers view alterations philosophically, claiming that "just as times change, so dance must change along with the times." Yet some of these same dancers will berate students for having no sense of period style, seemingly unaware that radical choreographic changes in older works may make the mastery of period style difficult. And seldom do dancers stop to think that there can be changes for many different reasons, not all of them equally valid. There can be changes in a work made by the choreographer after the premiere, changes made by someone else after the choreographer's death but at a time when the style of the work is still considered current, changes made long after the choreographer's death but in an attempt to imitate the original style, and changes made in a totally new style. Each type of change should raise different scholarly and practical questions.

However, apparently believing that art can grow by accretion, some observers dismiss these fine points and argue that the changes made in an old work by each successive choreographic generation represent the accumulated wisdom of the art. But such a view is tenable only if one believes that art automatically progresses, whereas, to this mind, the notion of automatic progress is as dubious in aesthetics as it is in morals.

Some observers also argue that the works preserved from any period are that period's masterpieces. Good choreography survives, they claim, bad choreography dies. But this view rests upon another odd assumption: the belief that standards of taste never vary. Given our adulation of Bournonville and Isadora Duncan, it is sobering to be reminded that there were times when those choreographers were considered passé. In fact, Duncan's choreography has lived on only through the efforts of a few fanatics who not long ago were dismissed as mere eccentrics.

The reason why we take a cavalier attitude toward choreography may be that, despite our pious protestations to the contrary, we still do not consider dance a truly great and serious art. We have been so brainwashed by prudes, who call dance immoral, and pedants, who call it trivial, that we find it difficult to regard dance as potentially equal to poetry or music.

Fortunately, new attitudes may be developing. Interest in dance notation has increased, and the existence of choreographic texts will do much to make dance less messy. The recently established Society of Dance History Scholars is only one of several organizations dedicated to historical research in dance. The critic and historian Selma Jeanne Cohen has written *Next Week, Swan Lake* (Wesleyan University Press, 1982), a book that seriously grapples with the problems of the aesthetic identity of a dance. And the 1982 conference of the Dance Critics Association was devoted to problems of reconstructions and revivals.

At that conference, Muriel Topaz, executive director of the Dance Notation Bureau, read a statement so provocative that some of it is worth quoting here. According to Topaz,

> The basic issue that we confront together, as critics, historians, notators, dancers, and choreographers, is simple: Is choreography an art form? Is choreography an evanescent form existing only in the bodies and personalities of the initial performers, or does it, like all other performing art forms, have a substance, a compositional integrity that transcends the initial performance . . . ?
>
> If the choreographic art exists, then it must do so as more than a vehicle for the performer, no matter how virtuosic, stylistically pure, or finely honed. If the choreographic art exists, it must have observable formalistic content, structural components, and a reality which lends itself to analytic scrutiny. And, if it exists . . . it must survive changing tastes, changing technical training, and changes in the eye of the beholder.

One can only say amen. Dancers love to quote Yeats's line about the difficulty of distinguishing "the dancer from the dance." But there are occasions when, for the health of the art, clear distinctions must be drawn.

*New York Times*, 5 September 1982

# IDEALISTS, MATERIALISTS, AND THE THIRTY-TWO FOUETTÉS

*I*f in the Black Swan pas de deux the ballerina cannot adequately perform all thirty-two fouettés, may she replace them with other brilliant steps?"

Balletgoers occasionally ponder this question after performances and, for practical reasons, dancers must ponder it, too. Selma Jeanne Cohen once observed that more than practicality is involved here, for behind the question lies the whole problem of the identity of a dance.

Like a poem, a dance is something everyone can recognize, but no one can define. The definitions advanced often seem commonplace, even banal: thus, almost everyone would agree that a dance is an artwork involving movement through space and time. From the possible movements of which persons are capable, someone selects the limited number of movements which comprise a particular dance. But having summarized the obvious, difficulties still arise, since one can regard the movements in any dance in two distinct—and, at their extremes, nearly irreconcilable—ways. For convenience, I shall call these positions the "Idealist" and the "Materialist," and I use the terms solely in the sense I define here, without reference to other meanings they may possess in philosophy or theology.

Idealist dancegoers regard a dance as the incarnation in movement of ideas or effects; typically, Idealists may not mind that in different productions of what is ostensibly the same ballet, steps are changed, provided that the alterations express the same idea, produce the same effect, or illumine the work's central concept. The Materialist, in contrast, regards a dance as an assemblage of specific steps (or, in the case of improvisatory or indeterminate pieces, specific instructions for deliberately unforeseeable steps) from which ideas or effects may be derived. Therefore, the Materialist can maintain that it is possible for two productions of the same work to employ identical steps and yet be different in effect—a familiar example being the way in which some ballerinas offer a birdlike Odette, while others emphasize her humanity. To cite a more recent example, there is Emilia in José Limón's *The Moor's Pavane*. In conversation, Pauline Koner, the role's creator, said that she deplores those dancers who stress what one critic admiringly calls Emilia's "evil abandon," for both she and Limón wanted Emilia to be a warmhearted confidante. But a Materialist spectator might countenance such an interpretation, provided that the steps remain unaltered, for the interpretation would suggest that the steps are capable of many emotional colorations, just as in the theatre Hamlets have ranged from pale neurasthenics to stalwart men of action.

In the past, choreographers and ballet masters were frequently Idealists in practice, staging for local companies their own versions of ballets which other choreographers successfully mounted elsewhere. Necessity may have been partly responsible: before the age of air travel, choreographers could not whiz from city to city. Nor did there exist any compact record of a ballet comparable to a score or a playscript. So four years after Filippo Taglioni choreographed *La Sylphide* in Paris, August Bournonville staged his own *La Sylphide* in Copenhagen, while early *Giselle*s were produced in Italy and America which apparently did not employ the Paris choreography.

However, following the rise of the Diaghilev Ballet and modern dance came emphasis upon the Materialist position. A dance was increasingly regarded as a sequence of specific steps chosen by a specific choreographer. Fokine might tinker with his steps from season to season, modernist exponents of "self-expression" might alter their choreography nightly, but all would rage if they caught someone else trying to do an unauthorized version of "their" dances. Conscientious ballet masters started sorting out their memories with the result that, despite emendations, several older works came to be viewed in Materialist terms—among them the Bournonville *La Sylphide*, the Coralli-Perrot-Petipa *Giselle*, the Ivanov-Petipa *Swan Lake*, and the Petipa *The Sleeping Beauty*. Interest developed in notation—and in the copyright laws.

Nevertheless, Idealism again flourishes. As before, expediency may be partly responsible. There exist many fine companies and star performers. What we lack are fine choreographers. We do, though, possess adroit second-rank choreographers, while several top stars also interest themselves in stage production. Consequently, companies find it convenient to produce ballets derived from existing sources which may attract audiences because of the familiarity of their theme or score and which contain big leading roles which can be performed by the local stars and can also be learned by any guest stars who come to town. While the results may be pleasant, the practice may conceivably threaten the integrity of choreographic works.

Before indulging in dire speculations, it might be useful to examine how works exist in repertoires. Most contemporary ballets are regarded in Materialist terms. Who would think of doing "his own" version of, say, *Undertow* or *Ballet Imperial?* Antony Tudor and George Balanchine themselves may constantly fuss with their ballets: Tudor may assign one ballerina a double role in *Undertow,* while Balanchine may redo the mime and scrap the décor and even the very title of *Ballet Imperial.* But, as the authors of the works, their changes are comparable to a poet's revisions. No one else, though, would dream of touching these ballets.

In total contrast are works which exist not as carefully preserved choreography, but as scenarios or generalized production notions. The most familiar example of this sort of ballet is *La Fille Mal Gardée.* Jean Dauberval's choreography was forgotten long ago. What survives is the idea of a certain kind of ballet in which certain kinds of things happen and, in our time, the Ashton, Balachova, and Mordkin-Nijinska-Romanoff versions have fleshed out that idea in different ways. Yet even when the accompanying music varies, the results are identifiable as *Fille.*

More common are works which exist because of an idea which is coupled with a musical score, particularly when no single treatment of these ballets has managed to supersede previous versions (as the Ivanov-Petipa *Swan Lake* superseded Reisinger and Hansen) or to intimidate other choreographers from attempting their own versions. Examples include *Sylvia, Daphnis and Chloë, The Rite of Spring, Romeo and Juliet, Cinderella, The Miraculous Mandarin, Don Juan,* and *The Prince of the Pagodas.* Related to this type of production are hypothetical reconstructions of older ballets (such as anyone's *Pas de Quatre* and the Victor Gsovsky and Pierre Lacotte restorations of Filippo Taglioni's *La Sylphide*), as well as *Coppélia* and *The Nutcracker,* for which, in effect, no standard choreography now exists, although it should be theoretically possible to find people who could produce older versions of both.

Significantly, most examples of Idealist principles in dance are narrative or thematic, since these works can be summarized in verbal concepts which any choreographer can ponder. Yet, even though abstract dance is almost inevitably the product of Materialist thinking, there have been instances of an Idealist approach to abstraction: after the success of Balanchine's *Agon*, several European choreographers did their own *Agon*s, using Stravinsky's music and the general concept of a contest, and certain basic categories of abstraction seem to be dominant from season to season. Presently, the ballet of dreamy-lovers-and-Romantic-music has largely replaced the neat-geometrics-to-Baroque-concerti which flourished a few seasons back.

Judging from European critics and the few works shown here, it would seem that among current choreographers John Neumeier is emphatically Idealist. His ballets often employ existing scenarios, or he will take a familiar scenario and twist it to emphasize fresh, but thematically re-lated, ideas, as when (according to reports) in his *Daphnis and Chloë* schoolchildren visit the archaeological site where the events of the leg-end may have occurred and then become involved in a reenactment of the legend. Neumeier's speculations sometimes presuppose consider-able audience sophistication. His *Baiser de la Fée* virtually assumes fa-miliarity with the sensibilities of Tchaikovsky and H. C. Andersen, the scenario of Balanchine's *Baiser*, and the characteristics of Balanchine's choreographic style. It is refreshing when a choreographer assumes that an audience is intelligent. But works by Neumeier that we have seen are sometimes more interesting for their ideological superstructure than for their actual choreography.

Whatever one thinks of them, their existence poses no threat. But Idealist principles can menace works which have heretofore occupied an honored place in a repertoire. The classics—first *Swan Lake* and *The Sleeping Beauty*, and now *Giselle*—are gradually eroding. The influ-ence of Soviet ballet may be partly responsible, for the Russians since Alexander Gorsky have stressed ideas for dancing and remain fond of separating the functions of scenarist and choreographer. Such modern ballets as *Spartacus* and *The Stone Flower* have been repeatedly re-choreographed, each time by someone who tries to reveal more clearly than his predecessors the essence of the scenario and score. Similarly, the Soviets use the classics as though they were the dance equivalents of Greek myths, the stories of *Swan Lake* and *The Sleeping Beauty* serv-ing each new choreographer in the same way that the Electra myth has served playwrights from Aeschylus to O'Neill.

A few non-Soviet modern ballets have also been so regarded. Some years ago when Festival Ballet revived Fokine's *Schéhérazade* with moderate success, a critic wrote that he thought greater success might have been possible if the ballet had been rechoreographed, apparently considering *Schéhérazade* not as steps by Fokine, but as an idea for a ballet. For several years the Royal Danish Ballet tried to get Frederick Ashton to restage his *Romeo and Juliet*. When attempts failed, the company presented a totally new *Romeo* by Neumeier. My point has nothing to do with the strengths or weaknesses of Neumeier's ballet (several Danish critics admire it): what does fascinate me here is that the company seems to treat *Romeo and Juliet* not as a specific ballet by Ashton (or by Neumeier either, for that matter), but as an idea for a certain kind of ballet (by any appropriate choreographer) which the Danes ought to produce.

Idealists often accuse Materialists of pedantry for their concern with the establishment of a choreographic text. They like to remind Materialists that choreographers change their ballets and that many old ballets are works by several choreographers (or by a choreographer and his assistants), and they will argue that since certain variations were designed to feature the specialties of particular dancers, it should therefore be permissible for other dancers to introduce their own specialties into these passages.

Idealists are correct in claiming that in watching dance we do not always notice steps as detachable entities. As a dancegoer, I confess that I cannot supply the technical names for most of the steps I see, and I can describe few passages of choreography from memory in elaborate detail. Nor can I recall many passages from Shakespeare by memory. But if substantial changes were made during a performance of Shakespeare's language or someone's choreography, I might feel uneasy. For the changes would suggest that, for whatever reason, a particular work was being remade.

Several Idealist arguments appear less weighty when one examines how the other arts deal with comparable issues. Certain poets have constantly rewritten poems, and their revisions are often included by publishers in variorum editions. Choreographers have likewise changed their dances; frequently, these changes are small, but they can also be extensive. Which version is the "true" version? Since all are by the same choreographer, they might all be called "true." A greater problem is that of determining which is "best," especially since dance companies (and theatrical troupes) cannot publish alternate readings in a variorum. If the choreographer is also the company director, he will probably declare that, despite possible protests to the contrary, his latest version is best. But if the choreographer is not in charge of the company—or, more drastically, happens to be dead—then the artistic director, like a scholar studying quartos and folios, must pick and choose among alternates.

That some variations were designed to display their original performers should not deter anyone else from preserving their steps. Artists are inevitably inspired, or limited, by the interpreters they have at hand and tailor their works accordingly. Some passages in Shakespeare are probably phrased as they are because of Burbage's abilities, while the operatic repertoire contains several roles for decidedly odd voices: in *The Magic Flute* alone are such curiosities as the Queen of the Night and Sarastro. But if the creative artist happens to be talented, he does more than devise stunts; from the idiosyncrasies of his performers he invents steps which are both appropriate and beautiful. It is, after all, Odile, not Odette, who does the fouettés. Therefore, the choreography's very peculiarities may constitute a genuine artistic challenge to succeeding interpreters.

As for multiple authorship, only obdurate upholders of the purist view that an artwork is necessarily the product of a single genius should find it troublesome that ballets may have passages by several choreographers. Many old master paintings contain the brushstrokes of both the master and his students, and successful theatrical collaborations extend from Beaumont and Fletcher to Kaufman and Hart.

However, the performing arts must resolve problems related to a particular kind of multiple authorship. During some, but by no means all, past periods, performers could add ornaments to the music they played or the choreography they danced. Should performers today add comparable ornaments? If so, how many? And of what kind? In dealing with these questions, one should remember that the personal touches were only ornaments: decorations added to an existing structure, not a substitution for that structure—an extra trill in the music or turn in the choreography, but no wholesale rewriting. The story is told of the soprano who auditioned for Rossini by singing a heavily ornamented version of one of his own arias. "Very nice," the composer remarked. "Who wrote it?" Rossini later explained that, while he expected his music to be embroidered, he did not want it distorted out of recognition.

At least, since that soprano was Rossini's contemporary, her ornamentations probably contained no gross anachronisms. Adding ornaments becomes more difficult today when one has to make sure that they harmonize with the original. Among the peculiarities of John Cranko's *Swan Lake* was the fact that the new choreography did not always blend with the bits retained from Ivanov-Petipa. To avoid comparable discrepancies, musicians study tables of ornamentation and sometimes, instead of inventing their own ornaments or cadenzas, play the conjectural ones suggested by scholars. Therefore, perhaps dancers today ought to be chary about embroidering steps, even where dancers of an earlier generation might have embroidered freely.

A related problem of authorship is peculiar to dance. Since dances are passed down by memory and memories are faulty, gaps exist in some ballets which have to be filled. Thus, parts of our Bournonville stagings derive from Hans Beck and Harald Lander. If Beck and Lander, why not Rudolf Nureyev or Kenneth MacMillan? The question admits of no conclusive reply, but several factors may be taken into account. Obviously, if gaps exist, they must be filled—preferably with style and taste. In some circumstances, totally new dances may be added to expand a ballet, but they should not displace old choreography. The Royal Ballet was reprehensible when it supplanted Marius Petipa's *Swan Lake* pas de trois with an Ashton pas de quatre (attractive though it was); it is no longer reprehensible now that it dances both divertissements.

Yet even when old choreography is retained, too many interpolations may destroy the character of a work; and the more time that elapses between the date of the original and the date of the interpolations, the greater danger there is of this occurring, since gaps in time also imply gaps in sensibility. Take Bournonville's *La Sylphide.* Modern producers wonder whether there should be a solo for Effie. Adding one probably does no mischief, since it can never take more than a few minutes. But what about a full-scale duet for James and the Sylph? A *Dance Magazine* critic writes that *La Sylphide* is "unsatisfactory" because it lacks "a proper pas de deux." But is what would be proper for Petipa or Balanchine also proper for Bournonville? The very lack—indeed, the impossibility— of physical contact between the principals is part of Bournonville's conception and contributes to the individuality of his ballet. To add a pas de deux might blunt that individuality. When Lander added such a duet for his Ballet Theatre production, some viewers thought the results, though tasteful, made the ballet ponderous. In the same way, despite the arguments that heroes in classical ballets should get chances to dance, the melancholy solos which recently have been devised for the princes in the Tchaikovsky classics not only look disquietingly alike, they usually look uninteresting. Curiously, cutting scenes entirely often produces less artistic trouble than replacing old choreography with new or adding extra choreography to an existing scene: almost nobody pines for the restoration of *Giselle*'s happy ending in which Albrecht and Bathilde are reunited at Giselle's tomb, while the supposedly complete Russian *La Bayadère* lacks the fifth act which Petipa originally choreographed. Natalia Makarova restored this act—but with choreography by herself— in her production for American Ballet Theatre.

Staging ballets might be less vexing if dance possessed a universally accepted system of notation. Yet there are dancegoers who may secretly rejoice that such a system does not exist. These fans insist that, rather than consisting of steps which may produce effects, a dance consists primarily of effects embodied in steps. Therefore, steps may be altered if comparable effects are gained. According to this theory, one might contend that while Marie Camargo, in her time, astounded audiences with entrechat quatre, any revival of a Camargo ballet (granting, for purposes of argument, the possibility of such a thing) should contain not entrechat quatre, which no longer astounds, but some other flashy step. This would then be called preserving the ballet's spirit, if not its letter.

But would it be? For who today can view the eighteenth century so unaffected by the artistic and social upheavals which have transpired since then that he can create choreography which would in all ways be equivalent to genuine choreography of the period? And just what shall our modern Camargo do, if not entrechat quatre? Thirty-two fouettés, perhaps? An obvious anachronism! Yet what step would not be? However, in our Camargo revival, if all the steps were preserved as they existed in her time, then the entrechat quatre—simply for being unlike the others—might still possess theatrical potency of a kind.

It is dangerous to believe that we know for sure what the "real" effects of a dance are supposed to be, for the kinds of effects we treasure may be partially determined by the taste of our age. Not long ago, sincere commentators argued that because Bach was hampered by the provincial musical forces he had at hand, the best way to achieve the true effects of the Bach cantatas was to utilize symphony orchestras and huge mixed choirs. Today, the vogue is for chamber orchestras, ancient instruments, and small all-male choirs, as we now consider sweet radiance more important than massive solemnity. Who knows what we shall feel a decade hence?

Similarly, in dance we have at different times prized different effects. At one time Odette's mimed account of her tribulations was dropped from the second act of *Swan Lake*, perhaps because producers considered it stilted. Now it is back, possibly because the sheer multiplicity of Odette's gestures (even if one cannot literally "read" them all) conveys a sense of dramatic urgency. To achieve another effect, Benno no longer participates in the *Swan Lake* adagio. This traditional bit was changed only recently—but the change is well-nigh universal. Presumably the reason for dropping Benno is that it seems odd for a third person to intrude upon a love scene; besides, Benno was only put there in the first place to assist the aging Pavel Gerdt in handling the ballerina. Yet

Ivanov, being a genius, made Benno's presence part of the beauty of that scene, for Odette was then able to swoon in a more ecstatic manner than she has been able to do now that a single man must hold her, let her go, and then also catch her.

Perhaps, someday, someone will want to rehabilitate Benno. (He has already turned up in the Ballets Trockadero de Monte Carlo travesty production.) But will people remember the choreography? At least, despite vagaries of taste and textual corruptions, scores exist for Bach. Still, some Idealists would regret the development of dance notation, since they fear that notation might stunt the organic growth of dance by making dance become cut and dried and, finally, mummified.

Arid choreography is always deplorable, but notation need not bring it about. Notation might even encourage individuality. After all, though musical scores are notated, conductors or instrumentalists often interpret them in very different ways. With the standard balletic repertoire notated, producers could feel free to stage that traditional choreography as they pleased—setting *Swan Lake*, for instance, in any historical period or in outer space—for the Materialist approach to production implies that at various times the same choreography can be used to produce quite different effects, just as Shakespeare's words have been subjected to Christian, Freudian, Marxist, and existentialist interpretations. Moreover, with standard choreography notated, a choreographer might be emboldened to create a totally new and different ballet based upon a classic story, just as a playwright might reinterpret a classic myth. One trouble with even our most radical revisions of the classics is that they seldom are radical enough. Thus, every *Swan Lake* contains a semblance of Ivanov's second act as an obeisance to tradition. But with Ivanov notated, an innovator could choreograph a *Swan Lake* which in no way resembled Ivanov stylistically, just as O'Neill's conception of Electra is stylistically different from that of Sophocles.

Our present willingness to tolerate extensive changes in extant works may be a hangover from the old attitude that dance is not really an important art—that, finally, it does not matter what is danced, provided the results are diverting. Yet in our century dance has gained enormous artistic significance, and so what is danced surely matters as much as how it is danced. If no two performances of any work in the theatrical arts can ever be exactly the same, the work itself should possess some sort of solid identity and integrity.

Until the time when dance acquires a sense of its own identity, we are left with our original question about the Black Swan: to fouetté or not to fouetté?

Idealists will not hesitate to permit the ballerina to substitute steps, while Materialists would caution against the substitution. Conceivably, the ballerina, reluctant to look less than dazzling, might go ahead and change the steps anyway. Even so, her artistic conscience ought to be reminding her that she still remains at least thirty-two fouettés short of perfection.

*Ballet Review* 5/1 (1975–76): 13–21

# WHY DOESN'T THE PRINCE STAY TO WATCH AURORA DANCE?

Newcomers to ballet who attended this summer's performances by American Ballet Theatre, the Royal Ballet of England, and Milan's La Scala Ballet and who saw the nineteenth-century classics for the first time could easily have been puzzled by the carryings-on of characters in them who kept entering and leaving the stage for no clear reason.

After seeing dancers forever rushing off into the wings, the balletic innocent might well ask, "Where are they going?" This question is particularly apt to be raised by works which were originally choreographed by Marius Petipa, the greatest creative force in nineteenth-century Russian ballet, or which, like *Giselle*, come down to us in revised versions by Petipa.

For instance, take the second act of *The Sleeping Beauty*, in which the Lilac Fairy arranges for the Prince to behold a vision of Aurora. At one

point, both Prince and Aurora suddenly run out. Where are they going?
(No smirking answers, please. This is a serious question.) Later, Aurora
returns for a lyrical solo, then vanishes, then returns for another solo.
But the Prince is not there to see her. Where has he gone? If Aurora is a
vision conjured up especially for him, why isn't he around to watch her? *

Or take the second act of *Swan Lake*. Odette and Siegfried fall in love,
and Siegfried saves her swan maidens from the hunters. Just after he
does so, she moves alluringly offstage and he follows her. Where are they
going? Since Odette is under a magic spell, where can they go? Soon
Siegfried returns alone. But what's happened to Odette? Where has she
gone, and why was Siegfried so careless as to lose her along the way?
And having gone out with her, why should he now expect to find her back
at the lake?

Similarly, in the second act of *Giselle*, Albrecht and Giselle move on
and off the stage with surprising freedom, even though Albrecht is supposedly being pursued by the Wilis and Giselle is in their power. Other
nineteenth-century classics are also peculiar in this manner, and their
peculiarities do not simply arise from careless staging. Rather, all traditional productions of these works contain such moments when characters
leave the stage in apparent defiance of dramatic logic. No wonder, then,
that the question can be asked: where do they go?

There's an answer to that question. Where do they go? They go nowhere. When they leave the stage, they, in effect, cease to exist.

At this point, it might be helpful to quote a statement by the late
James Waring, the experimental choreographer and dance theorist. In
one of his essays, Waring wrote that "all of dancing happens on the
stage."

Waring is not simply belaboring the obvious. He is reminding us that
dance exists in an eternal present. For some choreographers, then, what
can be shown is all there is. Unlike playwrights, choreographers cannot
easily provide biographical backgrounds for their characters. What these

---

* In Kenneth MacMillan's 1987 staging of *The Sleeping Beauty* the Prince stands at the
side of the stage while Aurora dances.

people have done in the past must be implicit in what we see them do now in the present. If background material had to be presented, nineteenth-century choreographers often introduced it in mimed narratives, and some, like August Bournonville, prepared elaborate written scenarios of their ballets.

In contrast, the dance sequences of many nineteenth-century ballets consist of a succession of kinetic images—or moving pictures, if you will—which can be enjoyed for their own beauty and which also heighten the emotional content of a given episode. An image is presented. Then it may be followed by several related images, and we may find ourselves reacting emotionally to the cumulative effect of all those images. When characters leave the stage for no given reason, they may not necessarily be going anywhere to accomplish anything. Instead, they leave only so that they may return and, by the movements and poses of their return, create a new image or reinforce an old.

The way that Siegfried and Odette keep vanishing and returning in *Swan Lake* may defy common sense. But their vanishings and reappearances make one aware that Siegfried has encountered a magical being. Similarly, Giselle's meltings away are signs that she is no longer a village girl but a specter. If the vision of Aurora dances without a Prince to behold her, that is because, in choreographing these images, Petipa wants the focus to be entirely on the beauty of the ballerina so that we, too, may regard her as a lovely vision. And as we watch and admire her, we in the audience have collectively become the Prince.

If one regards the dance sequences in Petipa's ballets as a succession of kinetic images, one can see how they can be considered forerunners of today's abstract ballets, particularly those of George Balanchine, who has been called Petipa's heir. The contemporary abstractionist has jettisoned even the slightest dramatic motivation for sequences and has retained only formal design and, possibly, emotional implication. When dancers leave the stage in an abstract ballet, one never thinks of asking where they are going or what they will do when they get there. One knows that they exit so that the dancers who remain can form a new stage picture. And since we respond empathically to the degrees of tension or calm in their entrances and exits, we may be possessed by strong feelings as we contemplate images of visual beauty.

Yet there are choreographers who do believe that the world of a ballet can extend into the wings and that information about this world can be conveyed to an audience. Such choreographers seek to make every entrance and exit dramatically meaningful and will have nothing to do with entrances and exits that exist solely to create stage pictures. Michel Fokine was the pioneer of this sort of dance-drama and, when sensitively produced, his works still possess impact, as New Yorkers discovered when his *Schéhérazade* of 1910 was revived by both Dance Theatre of Harlem and the Oakland Ballet.

When the Shah exits in *Schéhérazade*, it is clear by his actions that he wishes to suggest that he is going hunting. When he returns and discovers that his wives have been unfaithful, it is equally clear that he has not gone hunting at all. The hunting trip was merely a ruse. For Fokine, the harem room that we see onstage is not the only room that exists; there is a whole palace beyond that room in which the Shah can lurk as he spies on his wives.

Similarly, in the works of Antony Tudor, our greatest choreographer of dramatic ballet, there is also a world beyond the stage action. Thus, in *Pillar of Fire* when the rejected Hagar exits into the house of her puritanical sister, one can almost guess, from the sister's stiff, prim behavior, how that house will be furnished.

Choreographers, then, can treat the stage in at least two ways. For some, it is the only place that exists. For others, though it is the only place we see, it can also imply the existence of other places. Therefore, when characters exit in a ballet it might be both fun and aesthetically instructive to speculate, "Where are they going?" The answer is likely to be either "nowhere really" or "somewhere else," and that answer alone will help define just what sort of a ballet that particular ballet is.

*New York Times*, 20 September 1981

# TWO
## Out of the Past

*Summer Lee Rhatigan as the Bride and ensemble in Bronislava
Nijinska's* Les Noces *as revived by the Oakland Ballet
(Ronn Guidi, artistic director). Photo: Marty Sohl.*

*or purposes of convenience, dance history teachers often cite* Le Ballet Comique de la Reine, *a court spectacle of 1581, as the most important forerunner of the art today known as ballet. Yet its chore-ography has been lost. Indeed, although in recent years several scholarly attempts have been made to reconstruct choreography from the sixteenth to the early nineteenth centuries, it is not until we come to Vincenzo Galeotti's* The Whims of Cupid and the Ballet Master *of 1786 that we have a ballet that has had any tradition of continuous performances over the centuries; and we possess it in a version containing technical embellishments that would have been unknown to dancers of 1786. The next ballet to have survived in repertoire is August Bournonville's* La Sylphide *of 1836. Com-pared with the wealth of plays upon which theatrical troupes can draw, dance is an impoverished art.*

*This has created problems for dance historians, dancers, and audiences alike. Few guidelines of scholarship or even of custom exist to aid produ-cers who seek to stage old works. And there are dancers and dancegoers who scorn all revivals as foolishness. Some of these skeptics argue that because dance is a physical art, works created for the bodies and stage personalities of an earlier era are bound to have little impact when per-formed by today's dancers. Others, because they discover that many works of the past dealt with gods and goddesses or with elves and fairies, auto-matically assume that they must have been trivial or escapist.*

*But dancers who take revivals seriously also have problems. Actors cast in productions of such rarely performed plays as, say,* Alcestis *or* The Spanish Tragedy *may well have had no previous experience with those works, but they probably have some general idea of what Greek or Eliza-bethan drama is like because they have seen, or acted in, other plays of the period. However, the small number of dances that have come down to us from the past makes it difficult for dancers to acquire a comparable breadth of stylistic knowledge.*

*Nevertheless, sensitively mounted revivals can be revelations. Works may indeed seem to be very much of their time. Yet far from being merely quaint, they may provide insight into their time, and the best of them may possess unexpected relevance for our own time. As recent reconstructions have demonstrated, more than specific works may be revived. There may also be revivals of older dance forms: thus, tap and ballroom dance are both enjoying a newfound popularity among scholars and ordinary dance-goers alike. Revivals of all kinds may make us ponder the changes of both history and artistic taste that can cause certain works, or certain aspects of works, to date, while others appear eternally fresh. Dances of the past can be—and deserve to be—taken very seriously.*

# THE WORLD OF EIGHTEENTH-CENTURY DANCE COMES BACK TO LIFE

What's new in dance? The eighteenth century, for one thing. Dancers and historians are attempting to restore both the letter and the spirit of eighteenth-century productions. And certain aspects of those works seem surprisingly in tune with contemporary sensibilities.

In the autumn of 1986, two exhibitions—"Four Hundred Years of Dance Notation" at the Grolier Club and "Transformations in the Arts in 18th-Century France" at the New York Public Library at Lincoln Center—touched upon aspects of eighteenth-century dance. Also at the Grolier Club, Régine Astier, a French-born dancer and scholar who now lives in California, offered a lecture-demonstration during which she performed a chaconne by Louis Pécour, one of the greatest of eighteenth-century choreographers. Ann Jacoby, another dancer and researcher, included choreography by Pécour in a lecture-demonstration at the Lincoln Center library. All these reconstructions were of dances recorded in an eighteenth-century notation system known as Feuillet notation.

Two unusually elaborate productions were offered at Hunter College Playhouse by Concert Royal, an early-music ensemble conducted by James Richman, and the New York Baroque Dance Company, directed by Catherine Turocy and Ann Jacoby. What made these endeavors remarkable was their adherence to eighteenth-century practice in music, staging, and dancing. *Les Fêtes d'Hébé*, a spectacle by Rameau dating from 1739, was staged by Roland Jullien, a French director, and choreographed by Turocy and Jacoby, while Handel's *Ariodante* of 1735 was staged and choreographed by Turocy. As if wishing themselves into the past, they used only eighteenth-century steps.

A series of dramatically independent episodes united by the thread of a common theme and making use of both singing and dancing, *Les Fêtes d'Hébé* exemplified the eighteenth-century theatrical form known as opéra-ballet. To twentieth-century eyes, it looked wondrously strange— yet curiously familiar, too, for its three acts, each telling a separate story about love and the power of art, constituted an evening not unlike the mixed bills of one-act works ballet companies offer today. And the way drama, dancing, singing, and spectacle were combined could be said to prefigure both nineteenth-century grand opera and our own era's mixed-media experiments. Like mixed media, opéra-ballet brought the arts together; and because an opéra-ballet involved many arts, the resultant theatrical variety prevented a production from seeming monotonous.

Vocal scenes constantly gave way to dancing in *Les Fêtes*, and the choreographic sequences included brisk dances for mariners, an allegorical dance about a battle, and some pastoral gambols. *Les Fêtes* was set in ancient Greece. But, following the custom of Rameau's time, the singers and dancers wore eighteenth-century plumes, wigs, heeled shoes, and white gloves.

The singers' dramatic gestures were as carefully choreographed as the dances. In fact, what one first noticed about *Les Fêtes* was its artifice. Gestures were broad and stately. Often, the arms were held outward from the body, then slowly brought closer to the body, only to unfold gravely again. Yet, for all their calculation, these gestures did not falsify the characters' feelings. Rather, they could be termed crystallizations of feelings, and their slowness and broadness helped make their import' legible. So did the visual effect of the white gloves. Indeed, in eighteenth-century candle-lit theatres, the gestural clarity that white gloves helped create may have been welcomed for practical as well as aesthetic reasons. And when performers struck poses in *Les Fêtes*, those poses seemed punctuation for the work's musical and dramatic sentences.

*Ariodante* more closely resembled what we today recognize as opera. It told only one story, and though Handel included many dances, he did not mix singing and dancing as Rameau did. Lasting three and a half hours, *Ariodante* never hurried. Some directors might have attempted to conceal this deliberation with jazzed-up stage business. Instead, Turocy trusted Handel and the way he structured his opera. Arias followed recitatives throughout its three acts until, in the finale of each act, Handel inserted a suite of dances.

The steady succession of arias had the effect of slowing time down and allowing characters to linger over thoughts and emotions. But the dances in the finales served to speed time up and to refresh the eye with brilliance of movement. By refusing to rush her dramatic movement and by making her dances spirited, Turocy permitted each act to build to a vivid close.

In one sequence, where the dancers represented benign and malevolent spirits, Turocy put everyone into masks. Despite her fondness for eighteenth-century conventions, she otherwise avoided masks, even though all dancers would have been masked in the theatre of Rameau and Handel. One can sympathize with her reluctance. We are so unaccustomed to masks in our theatre that the mere sight of them can make us uneasy.

In her lecture-demonstrations, Jacoby has been known to perform the same dance with and without a mask so that audiences may understand how the presence of a mask affects one's perception of choreography. And Astier wore a mask in her Grolier Club program. Moving masked through the room in a plumed headdress and a resplendent gown, she seemed otherworldly.

Audiences today may think of masks only as a means of concealment. But masks may transform as well as hide. They can change a person's image and make one look larger than life. No wonder they were popular in an age of ostentation.

But, of course, this justification for masks is the work of a twentieth-century mind mulling over what seems to be a curious eighteenth-century phenomenon. To eighteenth-century theatregoers, masks were not peculiar objects that had to be accounted for, they were simply part of the way the theatre was until tastes changed and dancers discarded them.

One wonders whether modern audiences will ever totally accept masks. But musicologists once wondered whether concertgoers would accept harpsichords. Whatever balance may eventually be established between historical authenticity and contemporary theatrical effectiveness, the fact that researchers are willing to experiment with masks in revivals is a sign that they are taking scholarship seriously. And what was exciting in the fall of 1986 was the way Turocy, Jacoby, and Astier used scholarship not to add footnotes to dance history, but to restore dance history to life.

Their revivals were not the only recent rejuvenations of old theatrical practices. As an entertainer at the 1986 "Bessie" Awards ceremonies at the Brooklyn Academy of Music, a young performance artist named John Kelly stepped forward in twentieth-century male attire and sang, in an attractive falsetto, "Mon coeur s'ouvre à ta voix," Dalila's aria from Saint-Saëns's *Samson et Dalila*. He made no attempt to impersonate a woman. Nor, though his gestures were totally artificial, did he mock operatic style.

Anyone who had seen the productions at Hunter College Playhouse would have had an inkling of what Kelly was up to. Like an eighteenth-century singer or dancer, he wore a costume of his own period, even

though he portrayed a biblical character. And his gestures both crys-
tallized the feelings expressed in the aria and served as gestural marks of
punctuation. His neo-Baroque performance was a reminder that the
eighteenth century was not the last age of ostentation.

*New York Times*, 16 November 1986

# STAGING THE CLASSICS
# IS NOT SO SIMPLE AS IT SEEMS

*V*irtually everyone who saw it agreed that American Ballet Theatre's production of *Swan Lake* this spring needs refurbishing. Not
only did the décor look shabby, so did some of the choreography.
However, before Ballet Theatre commissions a new *Swan Lake*, it had
better ponder what sort of a production it wants. Similarly, all other companies that seek to revive familiar nineteenth-century classics ought to
think long and hard before hiring someone to stage them.

Surprisingly often, dancers and company directors profess to respect
choreography, yet countenance stagings that treat choreography in a cavalier fashion. In fact, it is only recently that the whole problem of determining what is the choreographic text of a ballet has received serious
discussion. But, judging from the policies of companies everywhere,
ballet directors have given the issue little consideration.

Directors must be concerned with practicalities, as well as with aesthetic theories. Nevertheless, the ways in which productions are staged
do derive from aesthetic attitudes, of which company directors may or
may not be consciously aware. And since classical productions are
costly undertakings, it is advisable for those people responsible for them
to be cognizant of the principles that are guiding their efforts.

There exist at least three approaches to staging classics, which, for
convenience, can be called the traditionalist, the eclectic, and the delib-

erately innovative. The traditionalist producer tries to reproduce the choreography danced at a ballet's premiere or, occasionally, at some important later date. For instance, most producers of *La Sylphide* seek to reproduce August Bournonville's choreography of 1836, rather than Filippo Taglioni's version of 1832. And no one in his right mind would want to copy *Swan Lake*'s original production of 1877, when it had a clumsily arranged scenario and mediocre choreography by Wenzel Reisinger. Instead, our versions of *Swan Lake* derive from the staging of 1895 by Marius Petipa and Lev Ivanov.

A traditionalist production tries both to preserve old choreography and to invest it with dramatic life. Yet that does not mean that all traditionalist versions of the same ballet will look alike for, provided they do not tinker with the choreography, the ballet's producer and designer remain free to create whatever settings they wish for it. Thus, Dance Theatre of Harlem's *Giselle* is set in the Louisiana bayous. Nevertheless, this scenically unusual production contains much traditional choreography.

In traditionalist productions, there ought to be few departures from familiar choreography, although, of course, if passages have been forgotten or are only hazily remembered, then new choreography must be invented. A fine example of a traditionalist production that effectively combines authentic old choreography with period pastiche is the *Giselle* staged by Mary Skeaping that London Festival Ballet danced here several years ago.

For the most part, choreographic tinkering should be subject to debate. For instance, if there exist several versions of certain sequences—perhaps one by the original choreographer and others by later ballet masters—every decision that a later version is better ought to be based upon serious thought, rather than caprice. It is also conceivable that a producer might argue that because a step done in a small-scaled fashion in the nineteenth century can be done in a larger-scaled manner by today's dancers, the contemporary version is preferable. Yet another producer might counter that argument by saying that just because the smaller-scaled step is no longer in general use, its inclusion will give the production a period charm. Arguments such as these are comparable to those regarding the use of a harpsichord or fortepiano rather than a modern concert grand for the playing of eighteenth-century keyboard sonatas.

Thoughtful traditionalist stagings are rare. Instead, most classical productions are eclectic. Such stagings are the creations of ballet masters or star dancers who may combine bits of what they remember of traditional choreography with choreography by themselves when they cannot remember or do not like the old choreography. Ballet Theatre, which used to have a reasonably traditionalist *Swan Lake* (but with some emendations of the old choreography), now has a quite eclectic *Swan Lake*, thanks to the further emendations of Mikhail Baryshnikov.

The trouble with many eclectic productions is that they are hodgepodges that appear to have been thrown together for no apparent reason. And even when producers of eclectic versions have interesting dramatic ideas, they do not always have the choreographic skill to make those ideas convincing. In fact, one may seriously question the advisability of regularly commissioning classical productions from certain famous stars, as many companies do, for some of those stars, though great dancers, may be mediocre producers.

Over the years, such stars as Baryshnikov, Rudolf Nureyev, Natalia Makarova, Alicia Alonso, and Erik Bruhn have all attempted versions of the classics, and their productions have ranged from the admirable to the annoying and from the fairly traditionalist to the wildly eclectic. And when they are eclectic, they can also seem insufferably presumptuous. Although star dancers occasionally choreograph ballets of their own, few if any of today's stars are considered major choreographers. Yet when Petipa created *Swan Lake* in 1895, he was 76 years old (the same age at which George Balanchine choreographed *Robert Schumann's "Davidsbündlertänze"*), had been choreographing ballets since the 1830s, and had established himself as the most important figure in Russian ballet. Given this, it is hard to understand why comparatively inexperienced choreographers, however wonderful they may be as performers, feel that they are capable of improving upon an old master.

Poorly conceived eclectic productions are often countenanced simply because they have famous names attached to them and look more or less the way classics are expected to look. However, there is one type of classical production that may look in no way familiar. This is the deliberately innovative production. Creators of such productions take a familiar balletic plot or piece of ballet music and choreograph a totally new work to it that may bear little relation to the original choreography. Music and story here serve as source materials for fresh flights of fancy, just as Greek myths have long served as source materials for playwrights.

As an example of a deliberately innovative—and provocative—treatment of a classic ballet subject, one could cite Mats Ek's modern-dress *Giselle*, staged for Sweden's Cullberg Ballet, in which, to new choreography by Ek, Giselle is sent to a psychiatric hospital. However, the many charming one-act ballets that Balanchine devised to Glazunov's music for Petipa's three-act *Raymonda* can also be considered deliberately innovative, for in those works Balanchine scrapped the original story of *Raymonda* to create dance suites in which he combined fleeting references to Petipa's choreography with new choreography of his own.

Since, presumably, it is choreography—and not just plot or music—that gives a ballet the status of a classic, I usually champion the traditionalist approach to staging old ballets. Yet other approaches are possible. What is important is that company directors know exactly what they want—and how to obtain what they want—when they decide to stage a classic. Many productions may be called *Swan Lake*, but not all of them will be the same. Any company that hopes for one sort of production and, through lack of knowledge, gets another instead may find its *Swan Lake* a dead duck.

*New York Times*, 29 July 1984

# THE GREAT WORLD
# AND THE SMALL: REFLECTIONS
# ON THE BOURNONVILLE FESTIVAL

*O*ne thing that students of dance history are often unable to study is choreography itself. Although research can reveal much about the music, decor, and dramatic significance of a choreographic work, the evanescence of dance may make it impossible for us to know how that work lived and moved upon a stage.

Therefore, the Royal Danish Ballet's Bournonville Centenary Festival in Copenhagen (24–30 November 1979) was one of the most important dance events of recent years. Honoring the great Danish choreographer August Bournonville, who died in 1879, it offered, on the "Old Stage" of the Royal Theatre, nine works that are considered authentically Bournonville in their choreography. Except for the *William Tell Variations* and a few miscellaneous bits and pieces (for instance, such trifles as the *Polka Militaire* and the *Jockey Dance*, presented in America by the touring ensemble of Royal Danish Ballet soloists), that is just about all the Bournonville that has survived, and one of those nine items is merely a pas de deux. But Bournonville choreographed more than fifty works, so one can only wonder what treasures have been lost. However, since we have no ballets at all by Jean-Georges Noverre or Salvatore Viganò, and since *Giselle*, our sole surviving ballet by Jules Perrot, is a collaboration with another choreographer, we should feel lucky to possess nine works. Come to think of it, how many more ballets have survived by Marius Petipa? And, surely, only a few more ballets by Michel Fokine are now revivable—even though Fokine was a choreographer of our own century. Bournonville's nine ballets are therefore quite a lot.

As most dance lovers know, they survived simply because Denmark in the late nineteenth and early twentieth century was isolated from the rest of Europe. Choreographic fads may have swept through London, Paris, and St. Petersburg. But Copenhagen went on preserving much of its

Bournonville repertoire, thanks to such guardians of tradition as Hans Beck and Valborg Borchsenius. The Bournonville ballets that have been preserved may not be entirely representative of his output (we have none of his ambitious works based upon Scandinavian history), but seeing them one after another at the festival revealed not only that they are excellent as individual compositions, but that they also share certain attitudes toward life and art.

That realization, too, was something of a surprise. Ordinarily, we do not expect to find philosophies of life or reflections upon human nature in ballets in the same way that we might find them in poems, plays, or novels. On the basis of his surviving choreography, one cannot really say what philosophical views Petipa might have held. Nor can we say much more about Fokine's attitudes. To be sure, some critics do maintain that the personal values of Balanchine, Ashton, Graham, and Cunningham are implicit in their creations. Yet, for the most part, choreographers seldom philosophize. In a curious way, however, Bournonville does, although he is one of the world's least pompous choreographers. Repeatedly, his ballets extol balance, proportion, and harmony—even snugness and coziness—and he is always concerned with human happiness and humane behavior.

Except for the evening of 26 November, when the three-act *Napoli* occupied the entire bill, each festival program featured one long dramatic ballet accompanied by one or two short works in the nature of divertissements. These short pieces included *La Ventana* (conceived by Bournonville himself as a divertissement) and the dancing-school scene of *Konservatoriet* and the *Flower Festival at Genzano* pas de deux, both of which must now be considered divertissements because the dramatic ballets from which they derive have been lost. The closing performance paired *La Sylphide* with the third act of *Napoli*—and when this act is presented out of context, it also can be considered something of a divertissement, especially since, under such circumstances, it begins with the pas de six and not with the dramatic scene that precedes it when all three acts are performed.

Bournonville's sparkling divertissements are well known outside Denmark. Indeed, *La Ventana, Konservatoriet,* the *Napoli* variations, and the *Flower Festival* pas de deux have all been produced by American companies. These delicious pieces abound with intricate choreography that attests to Bournonville's fondness for light, airy, nimble dancing that never seems to pause and that always surprises one with its changes of direction.

But such divertissements typify only one aspect of Bournonville. And the very fact that they may be particularly appealing to contemporary balletomanes fond of obviously "dancey" choreography may actually make it difficult for us to come to terms with the dramatic ballets. Of them, only *La Sylphide* and, to a lesser degree, *Napoli* have entered the international repertoire. As for the rest, it is hard to recommend what company other than the Royal Danish Ballet itself ought to perform them. Yet they deserve to be performed—and with a minimum of modern "improvements," for, judged choreographically and historically, they reveal Bournonville's own personal solutions to some of the artistic and philosophical problems of Romanticism.

Nevertheless, Bournonville's dramatic ballets sometimes puzzle audiences. People who do not like them complain that they are "all mime and no dancing," and these skeptics are not likely to be convinced when one points out that each, in fact, contains quite a lot of dancing. What bothers modern audiences is Bournonville's attitude toward mime and dancing. Today, we often tend to consider mime to be inherently inferior to dance. Our century has seen the rise of the abstract ballet—the ballet that is "all dance"—and some choreographers have even tried to eliminate mimetic gesture from dramatic ballets. Bournonville, however, does not appear to place such value judgments upon mime and dance. For him, they are both equally important, equally valid forms of movement, and his willingness to draw upon either form as he chooses increases the choreographic richness of his ballets.

Bournonville constantly seeks the most expressive and appropriate movement for each specific occasion or situation—be that movement conventionally categorizable as mime or dance. Mime and dance intermingle in his works. Mime is not something that one endures until the dancing begins. And only rarely can the dancing be totally separated from the mime. Bournonville was clearly influenced by Noverre and the theorists of the ballet d'action, and he anticipates Fokine (another choreographer whose ballets have been accused of containing "not enough dancing"). One could almost go so far as to say that Bournonville is experimentally daring in his attitude toward movement, for he always uses the movement he needs, whatever that movement may happen to be.

The dramatic ballet for the first night of the Bournonville celebration was *Far from Denmark*. Initially, that seemed an odd choice with which to open an international festival, for *Far from Denmark* has the reputation of being a ballet that can be fully understood only by Danes. Its score is full of references to old Danish songs that even serve as commentaries upon the stage action. But if many of its allusions go unrecognized by visitors from abroad, *Far from Denmark* is still a cheerful comedy, and seeing it plunges one directly into Bournonville's theatrical—and moral—universe. Through miming it tells of how Vilhelm, lieutenant of a Danish frigate anchored in an Argentine harbor, momentarily forgets his fiancée back home to pay court to the coquettish Rosita, going so far as to give her his engagement ring.

The ballet also includes what purport to be dances of peoples from around the world—dances which, to modern eyes, are filled with ethnic stereotypes. Eskimos rub noses, American Indians pound tom-toms and brandish tomahawks, a Chinese variation is filled with pointy finger gestures, and black servants cavort when they are entranced by a tune on a piano. Yet these dances, though naive, are not really offensive. Instead, they seem to be the responses of people from a little, cozy, enclosed place like Denmark gazing in wonderment upon the great world outside their borders. Significantly, though they are glad to have seen the great world, the ballet's Danes ultimately prefer their secure little world, and there are several patriotic tributes to Denmark, including one in which a child kneels reverently before a Danish flag.

Again and again, Bournonville acknowledges the allure of some sort of great world, be it the great world of nations or of human emotions, yet decides that "east, west, home's best," particularly if home is a place where one may live peacefully and harmoniously. At the climactic moment of *Far from Denmark*, Rosita tosses overboard her fan, to which she has tied Vilhelm's ring. Vilhelm dives after it and returns chastened, his passions dampened in more ways than one, for he now realizes that this fiery femme fatale is not for him. Bournonville's depiction of the incident is typical of how he mingles dance with mime: Rosita makes her impulsive gesture during the course of a fandango. Most choreographers would probably first bring the fandango to an end—thereby making it a Spanish divertissement that could even be excerpted and performed as an independent item on gala programs—and only then would Rosita toss her fan. Bournonville's Rosita, however, tosses the fan *during* the fandango, an act that so startles the others that they abruptly stop dancing. Thus, dance steps and dramatic gestures are inextricably bound together.

Rosita goes too far in her enticement of Vilhelm. Besotted by her, Vilhelm momentarily forgets his Danish fiancée; therefore, Rosita must be rejected. Living in an age when some Romantic artists allowed themselves to be entranced by excess, Bournonville chooses to ponder the problems of how far is far enough and how far is too far.

He deals again with a straying lover in danger of going too far in *The King's Volunteers on Amager*, which concerns a wife who discovers that her husband has been flirting with other women while serving on National Guard duty. Most of *The King's Volunteers* is pure mimodrama. A born storyteller, Bournonville lets the mime rush ahead at a merry pace, the gestures establishing character and developing dramatic situations. Mime, for Bournonville's characters, is no mere convention; rather, it seems the natural way in which these people express themselves. Performed clearly, deftly, and with conviction, mime contributes specificity and immediacy to Bournonville's ballets, and good miming can be as exciting as virtuoso dancing. Through mime, Bournonville in *The King's Volunteers* creates an entire early-nineteenth-century village. In it live the young and the old, the fat and the thin, the wise and the foolish. It is so complete and so believable a community that watching *The King's Volunteers* is like eavesdropping on another century.

Finally, in the party scene that concludes the ballet, there is dancing—lots of dancing: folk dances, polkas, reels, quadrilles, and much more. Dance follows upon dance so rapidly that one feels exhilarated, even slightly intoxicated. But Bournonville views intoxication with suspicion, for intoxication may cause one to take leave of one's senses. It is during all this intoxicating revelry that the wife, to play a trick upon her errant spouse, disguises herself and lets him flirt with her, only to reveal her true identity afterward. Startled and abashed, he promises to be faithful. A marriage has been saved. Yet the masquerading also implies that if marriage is not to grow stale, it must retain some measure of surprise and adventure.

Once one has attained a state of harmony or balance, one can be thoroughly ebullient. The dances that conclude the third act of *Napoli* are ebullient indeed. But they celebrate a marriage—a joining together of people in what it is hoped will be a harmonious relationship. Lasciviousness is alien to Bournonville. Yet *Napoli*'s tarantella does contain a faintly lascivious moment when Teresina, the bride, allows another lad to flirt with her. Gennaro, her husband, is momentarily jealous, but things soon right themselves and there is no row. Teresina and Gennaro have achieved a harmonious relationship.

In the previous act, however, all was disharmony. Teresina, captured by sea demons and naiads in the Blue Grotto, lost her memory of earthly life and seemed fascinated by the demonic existence of the grotto spirits. What she was experiencing at that point was the intoxicating lure of excess. Gennaro saved her from capitulating to temptation by holding up a religious medal, before which the sea spirits quailed. With that gesture, morality triumphed over the demonic. But Bournonville is no dour puritan. Right living, *Napoli*'s third act implies, is also joyful living. And the joy of right living, being a joy that comes from something other than intoxication, is a joy that produces no eventual hangover. This joy refreshes without befuddling. *Napoli*'s third act, always a delight when presented by itself, acquires fresh meaning when seen after the other two acts.

For many balletgoers unfamiliar with the body of Bournonville's work, the festival's great revelations were *The Kermesse in Bruges* and *A Folk Tale*. The former is a rollicking comedy that recounts the misadventures that occur when three brothers receive three magic gifts: a sword that always brings victory, a ring that causes everyone to fall in love with its wearer, and a viol that causes everyone to dance joyfully when it is played. At present, only the young lovers' pas de deux from the first act of *The Kermesse* is widely known in America. It is one of Bournonville's finest duets. But how different it looks when it is performed in its proper place in the ballet! One tiny fragment of a vast choreographic mural, it comes amid lusty boot and clog dances, on a stage filled with robust Flemish merrymakers. Consequently, the choreography seems unusually delicate; the lovers, unusually tender.

Because it bustles so jauntily along, *The Kermesse* can be enjoyed as pure entertainment. Yet it is possible to relate it to some of Bournonville's favorite themes, for in its own way it is a ballet about excess and the power of the irrational. Since it is a comedy, Bournonville wisely minimizes the potentially gruesome capabilities of the magic sword. But he lets us see a lot of what the ring and the viol can do to people. Wear the ring, and everyone will fall in love with you, whoever you happen to be. No rational explanation can be given for this: that's simply how things happen. The ring, then, may symbolize irrational passion or infatuation.

Strike the viol, and anyone who hears it will start dancing. Again, reason and logic cannot account for this. At one point, the limbs of some young women twitch happily in response to the viol, although these girls have just been pining over their absent boyfriends. And in the ballet's great final scene, the whole town dances wildly, madly, and deliriously about. Even the condemned tied to the stake cannot refrain from tapping their feet. This is totally irrational behavior, and in such scenes Bournonville may be reminding us that we do not always know the sources of our feelings or why feelings may suddenly come and go without warning.

Yet feelings should not be allowed to run amok. Eventually the sword of war and the ring of infatuation are destroyed. The viol of happiness is preserved, however, but in a special, carefully controlled manner. The viol is put away, to be taken out only on proper festive occasions. *The Kermesse in Bruges*, then, is a ballet about the safekeeping of the emotions.

One of Bournonville's most complex creations, *A Folk Tale* is unusually rich in dance: there are folk dances, court dances, classical dances, grotesque dances, and dances that reveal psychological states. However, except for the gypsy pas de sept in the last scene, none of this dancing can be excerpted, for it is closely bound to the dramatic action, arising out of the mime at moments of emotional intensity and then sinking back into the mime again. As a narrative, *A Folk Tale* is just that: it is indeed a folk tale, a fairy story about Birthe, who seems to be a noblewoman but is really a troll; Hilda, who lives with trolls but is really a human being; and Junker Ove, who is betrothed to Birthe but comes to love Hilda. Like many fairy tales, it is often funny—the trolls squabble and fuss most amusingly, and their number includes nagging wives, prattling gossips, bratty children, and quarrelsome parents. At the same time, *A Folk Tale* is mysterious and faintly disturbing.

Again, there is a preoccupation with the irrational. When Junker Ove first beholds Hilda, he loves her; but the trolls deny her to him. He is then plagued by beautiful elf maidens who swirl around him. Reminiscent of the Wilis in *Giselle*, these elf maidens represent the power of lust and they drive Ove mad. Later there is an astonishing solo variation for Birthe. Standing before a mirror in her bedchamber, she tries to dance elegantly, but her graceful phrases are constantly marred by grotesque hops. These hops reveal her essential troll nature. But since she is unaware of her true nature, her tendency to hop terrifies her, and the solo becomes a portrait of what we today would call a split personality.

Much of *A Folk Tale* concerns finding one's own level and understanding one's nature. Birthe, despite her airs and graces, cannot stop bursting into temper tantrums and hopping like a troll. Hilda's delicacy—the way she jumps lightly and skims across the ground—indicates that she is not a troll. Whereas church bells make trolls' ears ache, when Hilda hears church bells she instinctively bows her head in reverence. A kind troll helps her to escape from the troll hill. But kind as he is, he can never be fully human; he must remain a troll. One is what one is.

Preached by someone other than Bournonville, that message could be a terrifying example of Calvinist predestination or behaviorist determinism. But in the ultimately benign realm of *A Folk Tale*, although there is salvation—Hilda becomes aware of her human nature, Junker Ove recovers from his madness—there is no real damnation. Even Birthe, though driven from her manor house, manages to find herself wealth and a husband. And with the possible exception of the woebegone helpful troll, the trolls do not suffer. There are no pangs of hell. If anything, the trolls seem positively happy to be misshapen in both their physical appearance and their behavior. Bournonville, however, idealizes a more harmonious state of existence and so brings *A Folk Tale* to an end with a serene wedding waltz for his human lovers.

Therefore, it may seem odd that, just before the waltz, the wedding party should be entertained by the rousing gypsy pas de sept. But this gypsy dance, like *Napoli*'s tarantella, may indicate that Bournonville believed that high spirits and marriage are not irreconcilable. At the same time, by making the waltz essentially dignified, he also reminds us that marriage must be taken seriously.

In *La Sylphide*, Bournonville's most famous balletic fantasy, harmony is not to be achieved, and conflicting supernatural and psychic powers eventually destroy its protagonist, James. A prime example of a melancholy Romantic hero, James is trapped between two irrational forces: on the one hand, he is infatuated with the Sylphide, an infinitely changeable creature who is all whim and impulse and as insubstantial as the air; on the other hand, he is cursed by the Witch, a creature hard as the winter earth who bears grudges everlastingly. When James breaks the pattern of the reel in the first act, deserting his partner and fiancée to pursue the Sylphide, he separates himself from the human community and from communally held values. His rejection of the human world and his inability to be part of the spirit world condemn him to a hell of isolation. The events of *A Folk Tale* lead to salvation and a wedding party; those of *La Sylphide* to damnation and a man weeping alone in a cold forest.

But Bournonville did not invent the story of *La Sylphide*; he borrowed it from another choreographer and never treated another fantastic theme in quite the same way again. No blind optimist, Bournonville was well aware of the dark powers of the psyche. One can observe their workings in his ballets. But he always sought to make light out of darkness. He was a Romantic idealist who refused to wallow in Romantic excess or agony.

Thus, when the festival's final performance paired *La Sylphide* with the third act of *Napoli*, one could see disruption followed by harmony and joy. If when confronted by the prospect of some great world—including the great world of unruly passions—Bournonville, after taking a close look, chose the familiar world of friends and family, he did so not out of smugness but because he sought some place where human happiness was possible, where mutual affection could cause the spirit to soar. And because Bournonville let dancers' bodies express spiritual states, his ballets are filled with soaring.

It was harmony, not complacency, that Bournonville idealized. No wonder, then, that his ballets can seem both poignant and heartwarming in troubled times; and no wonder, too, that when the great world came to little Denmark in November 1979, the great world gazed with wonder and admiration upon the choreography of August Bournonville.

*Dance Chronicle* 3/3 (1979–80): 275–284

# FOKINE — THE UNDERVALUED
# REVOLUTIONARY

*H*ere we are, more than halfway through 1980 and there is still no sign of the festival that ought to occur this year. What festival? Why, the festival honoring the 100th birthday of one of the world's most important choreographers, Michel Fokine.

As the first choreographer for Serge Diaghilev's Ballets Russes, Fokine brought modern ballet into being. Yet he has fallen somewhat out of favor, and attempts by American Ballet Theatre and the Joffrey Ballet to revive his works have met with a mixed response.

Fokine's career was a strange one. Although he lived until 1942, most of his significant work was done before 1914. Then, following a break with Diaghilev, came a long period in which he continued to choreograph, but without equaling his previous triumphs. For many years, he taught in New York. Yet, despite the fact that his pupils included Patricia Bowman, Nora Kaye, Pauline Koner, and Paul Haakon, he did not play quite the same active part in the development of American ballet as did his colleague from the Diaghilev Ballet, Adolph Bolm, who founded companies in Chicago and San Francisco. Finally, in the late 1930s for René Blum's Les Ballets de Monte Carlo and in the early 1940s for Ballet Theatre, Fokine entered upon a new creative period.

Fokine may have been a reformer, but he was no iconoclast. Inspired by Isadora Duncan as a young man, he nevertheless could not see the reason for any school of dancing outside the classical tradition, and he once had a bitter argument with Martha Graham about their differing concepts of "beautiful" movement during a lecture-demonstration at the New School. He could also be a nagging literalist who criticized George Balanchine's *Apollo* and Bronislava Nijinska's *Les Noces* on the grounds that neither ancient Greeks nor Russian peasants ever wore pointe shoes.

Today, Fokine's ballets are occasionally found wanting both by members of the general public and by certain members of the balletic intelligentsia. For the intelligentsia, Fokine's choreography can be stodgy. Devotées of abstract dance have difficulty summoning up interest in his narratives. The very subjects of those works can seem silly: *Petrushka*, a ballet about dolls; *Schéhérazade*, a harem orgy; *Carnaval*, a commedia dell'arte frolic. And that rose (or, more accurately, that spirit of a rose) jumping about in *Spectre de la Rose!* How quaint! As for fans who are impressed only by obvious virtuosity, they complain that Fokine's productions, even with stellar casts, do not contain enough "real dancing." One also suspects that some dancers who are infatuated with technical display may agree with the fans. Therefore, Fokine revivals are often insensitively performed, and audiences may approach them with inappropriate aesthetic preconceptions.

Nevertheless, a case can be made for Fokine, provided one remembers that, although Fokine may be the father of modern ballet, his ballets no longer look modern. They are as much the product of a particular historical period as the ballets of August Bournonville or Marius Petipa. But once this is recognized, one can go on to appreciate Fokine's achievements.

First of all, he established the one-act ballet as the choreographic norm. Considering the full-evening ballet to be a hodgepodge, lacking unity and sometimes even coherence, Fokine advocated the short, unified, and stylistically consistent ballet. Moreover, his concern for unity and coherence led him to develop the two major forms of ballet that still dominate contemporary choreography: the dance-drama and the abstraction. Fokine devoted most of his attention to the dance-drama, yet with his *Les Sylphides* of 1908 and his lesser-known *Les Elfes* of 1924 he demonstrated that movement could exist apart from narrative structure.

Fokine believed that there is no such thing as an all-purpose balletic form; rather, each specific work must be choreographed in the form or style that is uniquely appropriate to it. Thus, both *Petrushka* and *Firebird* involve Russian themes, but the realistic crowds and Expressionistically tormented dolls of the former do not at all resemble the storybook figures of the latter. And neither has the abandon of *Prince Igor* or the Arabian Nights exoticism of *Schéhérazade*.

Many of Fokine's ballets concern passion—adult passion. The way in which the passion is expressed may strike us as coming from another era. Yet when those ballets were new, audiences recognized their passions as genuine, which is one reason why some of them touched off scandals. The fact that the dolls in *Petrushka* have human feelings helps make that work more than a diversion for a children's matinee. *Schéhérazade* is not merely an exotic spectacle. It is a ballet that proclaims that adults have sexual drives.

Fokine may have wished his ballets to be unified around some central theme, but to reinforce that theme he was willing to use many different kinds of movement, and this helps make his works fascinating. *Les Sylphides* may derive from academic technique, yet in other works he utilized folk dance steps. His dramatic ballets often contain expressive gesture and, as in *Petrushka*, dramatic action may be linked with both classical dance and folk dance.

The choreography for the character of the Firebird is filled with rapid dartings of the head and quiverings of the arms. But the finale of *Firebird* is a powerful image because it contains almost no movement at all. Everything in *Prince Igor* is big and bold; everything in *Carnaval*, as dainty as porcelain. And in *Spectre de la Rose* Fokine dared to create a male role containing virtuoso steps that must be performed in such a soft manner that, since its premiere in 1911, *Spectre* has worried some balletgoers who complain that the choreography is not properly "masculine."

Fokine's willingness to incorporate many kinds of movement into a ballet, provided they are appropriate, makes him a distant ancestor of all the choreographers who have experimented with movement in our century. Fokine set a precedent, and both he and the modern dancers helped widen the range of choreographic expression.

Provided they are properly mounted, and provided one views them with historical perspective, Fokine's ballets might still be absorbing. It is also at least theoretically possible to stage quite a few of them. Within the past quarter century, America has seen, at one time or another, productions of *Les Sylphides, Prince Igor, Carnaval, Schéhérazade, Firebird, Spectre de la Rose, Petrushka, Igrushki, Adventures of Harlequin,*

*Les Elfes, Bluebeard,* and excerpts from *Le Pavillon d'Armide.* London Festival Ballet has revived *Le Coq d'Or.* Old rehearsal films exist of *Don Juan* and *L'Epreuve d'Amour.* One could assemble quite a festival, a festival that could be as revealing as the Bournonville Festival of 1979 was. Fokine certainly deserves the honor.

*New York Times,* 7 September 1980

## LEGENDS IN THE FLESH

*I* am fortunate enough to be too young to have been a dancegoer when Léonide Massine was the single most important figure in all ballet—when his adulators wrote panegyrics while his detractors hissed in the gallery, convinced that Massine's eminence was artistic despotism. To the proponents of native American or native British ballet, Massine—the personification of Ballet Russe—must have seemed a menace. These old controversies, with their hardened ideological positions, still echo through critical writings. I escaped all this acrimony and invective.

But being fortunate enough to have missed the debates over Massine has also meant—unfortunately—that I have missed Massine's ballets. Until American Ballet Theatre revived *Aleko* in 1968, I had seen only *Gaîté Parisienne* and *Beau Danube* by the Ballet Russe de Monte Carlo and the negligible *Ballade* by the Anna Galina company—scarcely a fair sampling. And now, right before my very eyes, City Center Joffrey Ballet has revived *The Three-Cornered Hat.*

*The Three-Cornered Hat (Le Tricorne),* the work historians call the perfect dance-drama, the perfect artistic collaboration . . . Here at last it was, a legend in the flesh. I was ready for it (I thought): I tend to wax sentimental over the Diaghilev era in general, I had no aesthetic prejudices against Massine, and, unlike some balletgoers, I had enjoyed *Aleko.*

Oh yes, there were stretches in *Aleko* where the choreographic phrases and the musical phrases seemed about to get disastrously out of kilter.

But the rhapsodic sweep of the thing! The way Massine divided the stage into planes of movement and pitted groups in one against groups in another, or passed a phrase along from one plane to another—this struck me as genuinely interesting. As for the alleged foolishness of the plot, I was not convinced it was foolish. The gypsies Aleko runs off with are not real gypsies, they are not the slightly untidy women who peer from storefronts in midtown Manhattan—no, Massine depicts gypsies as idealized by a disillusioned Romantic for whom the conventions of society are cruelly repressive. Aleko's fantasies, as George Jackson has pointed out in *Ballet Today*, are not unlike those of the hippies. If no masterwork, *Aleko* at least impressed me as the work of a master.

So I was ready for *Tricorne*. The curtain rose and I reveled in the ballet's extravagance: the symphonic score, the offstage vocalist (dispensable in terms of dollars-and-cents practicality, yet so indispensably atmospheric), the painting to watch before the action began—what grand theatrical gestures! Then the ballet itself got underway. Picasso's décor and costumes were as beautiful as I had been told they would be. And Massine's choreography? Well . . .

I left the theatre feeling very sad. That first night was, for me, a fizzle.

I have been back three more times. *Tricorne* now seems honest, thoughtfully conceived, thoughtfully developed, an admirable addition to the repertoire. But where was the special glamour, the magic, the thrill I had hoped for?

Having seen *Tricorne* and with my ticket for the American Ballet Company's *Carnaval* in my pocket, I started to wonder about what we can legitimately expect of a revival. Some purists, particularly in modern dance, claim that choreography is so tied to the personal qualities of the bodies on which it is created that dances cannot really be revived. Granted that there is a truth here, this view strikes me as too severe. Provided a well-regarded work is not simply a star vehicle, it ought to have elements of form, musicality, characterization, pattern, flow, or architecture which remain interesting after the original performers are gone.

One trouble is that our ideas of satisfying form, musicality, characterization, and so forth, shift with time. We can never safely predict whether any revival will be successful. It has to be seen to be believed. Revivals of Graham's *Primitive Mysteries* and Nijinska's *Les Noces* were great successes. Some observers say this was because they coincided with our current liking of the abstract and nonliteral. Yet Kurt Jooss's doggedly literal *Green Table* is also successful—not simply for reasons having to do with the war in Vietnam. And, for all our alleged fondness for abstraction, revivals of Doris Humphrey's *Passacaglia* and *Water Study* have never caught on.

The passage of time has other effects. The first time *anything* is done in art, provided it is done with a certain flair, the event automatically has impact because of its novelty. This impact has no guaranteed staying power. Moreover, if a ballet is important, it may influence subsequent choreography, directly or indirectly, and so, when revived, its style may no longer look fresh: it has already made history. Much as we might like to have experienced the premiere of *The Rite of Spring*, we should not expect that the revival of every once-notorious piece will occasion fistfights in the orchestra and orgasms in the balcony.

"Astonish me"? To be sure, *cher maître*. But one form of astonishment is the joy of perceiving a continuing beauty. And that is what we have a right to expect of revivals. If the joy is intermittent or nonexistent, then, perhaps, tastes have so changed that the work should be returned to the dust of the warehouse and the glory of memory.

But there is also the problem of determining whether a revival's virtues and deficiencies are the results of the choreography or the casting. (The first time I saw Balanchine's *Apollo*, I thought it—at least as danced by the Royal Danish Ballet—dated chichi. I have since modified *that* opinion!) To hazard some comments about the Joffrey *Tricorne*, Basil Thompson's Governor is acceptably creaky, but little more (or is that all there is to the role?); both Alaine Haubert and Barbara Remington seem too spiritually Nordic for the Miller's Wife: both are conscientious, Haubert excelling in the high-spirited passages, Remington in the serious, but neither having the vibrancy which can project emotions across a big theatre. Luis Fuente is charmless as the Miller: totally self-preoccupied, with no rapport with his partner. In contrast to Fuente's pouting, Edward Verso, while possibly less authentically Spanish, communicates a genuine ebullience and an interest in the people around him. As a result, there is an overall gaiety about the Verso-Haubert cast which makes me realize that the choreography is a tribute to the free spirit and the joy of life.

Massine's Spanish style cannot seem as novel to us as it was to its first audiences. It has virtually become the norm for Spanish-inspired ballets. Clearly, Massine possessed uncommon skill in blending Spanish steps with ballet. For all this, especially on first sight, the ballet appears distinctly odd; the action, busy; the plot, tangled. Yet the plot is not really complicated. Granted, there are moments when Massine and Picasso do make things unnecessarily difficult, as when the bedraggled Governor, changing into the Miller's clothes, chooses not some garment previously associated with the Miller, but an outlandish outfit resembling a clown suit. On the whole, though, the action is straightforward.

Nevertheless, *Tricorne* seems crowded and full of bustle—all fits and starts, starts and stops. This impression of hubbub derives, I think, from Massine's fondness for short phrases and scenes. Even one of the longest dances, the Miller's *farruca*, is but a succession of flickering swings and swivels, stamps and finger snaps, kneebends, bounds, and nervous hands. There is no reason why ballets must necessarily be composed of long, sustained phrases, no reason why phrases cannot be short and fragmentary—yet to get used to Massine's phrases takes effort. Thus, one of the passages I liked best occurred after the Miller's arrest when the Wife moves slowly downstage on a diagonal, arms stretched wide, fingers fluttering like a bird vainly beating its wings against the bars of a cage. The Wife, who has previously taught a caged bird to sing, now feels herself to be caged. When the Governor tumbles into the river, she again moves diagonally downstage, but this time in little spurts of energy like a bird, freed from its cage, joyfully testing its wings. This whole section is a sustained unit; there is time for it to have an effect.

I suspect that, with such a bits-and-pieces style, scenes either have instant effectiveness or none at all, dancers either communicate immediately or never. If someone blurs details in *Tricorne*, a point may be totally lost. Take the scene in which the Miller follows workmen carrying sacks of grain: he is distracted by a girl with a jug, flirts with her, is discovered by his Wife; they quarrel and are reconciled—and it all goes by like lightning. This vignette must be sharply etched; otherwise, it is nothing. Or take the bit just before the *farruca*. The Wife appears with a shawl for an extremely short sequence of poses. If the dancer is not vividly intense, the poses are nothing. Since, pose by pose, they are photogenic, it occurs to me that our expectations of a work may be misleadingly influenced by photographs we have seen of it; the purely pictorial—and static—highpoints which can be isolated from a ballet need not coincide with its kinetic or dramatic highpoints. All ballet fans have seen pictures of poses from old ballets. When the poses come to life, they may move in ways we had not imagined.

I expected much less of the American Ballet Company revival of Michel Fokine's *Carnaval* than I did of *Tricorne*. I had seen *Carnaval* once before, ten years ago, danced by the National Ballet of Canada. It had bored me then. Looking at it now, I saw a ballet of great, but faded, charm. Some of that fading, in the present version, may have been unnecessary. The restoration of Bakst's patterned borders would reduce the funereal impression created by the black curtains. Konstantinov's orchestration is coarse; Fokine himself deplored it in his memoirs. Since *Intermezzo*, *Liebeslieder Walzer*, and *Dances at a Gathering* have accustomed us to the sound of a piano at ballet performances, might it not be possible to play Schumann's score in its original form?

Choreographically, in *Carnaval* Fokine balances sweetness and irony in a way Eliot Feld may have been striving for, but which he only intermittently attained, in *Meadowlark*. The sentiments are unforced and easy, so the work never grows saccharine or cute. Nor does Fokine succumb to the temptation of using his commedia dell'arte figures to gain easy laughs. The opening, with its partygoers dashing impetuously across the stage, conveys a nice sense of anticipation. I particularly relished the images of Pierrot flopped despondently over the edge of the stage while the waltzers approached, and of Papillon fluttering about while Pierrot peeped shyly at her from behind a sofa. And there was a lovely little variation for three women whose arm weavings heralded those of Balanchine.

But, as with *Tricorne*, some of the characterizations were pallid. The waltzers were reasonably convincing while in motion, less convincing when they were required to stand in quaint nineteenth-century party-going attitudes. The Philistines looked flustered rather than menacing. Harlequin failed to dazzle with either technique or personal projection, and Pierrot never made the most of the delightful bit of business in which he tries to net Papillon with his tall white hat. The fact that Fokine's original Pierrot was not a dancer but the actor (and future stage director) Vsevolod Meyerhold makes me wonder what sort of dramatic training is necessary to perform these old ballets well.

In recent interviews, several dancers with Russian backgrounds, from Alexandra Baldina of early Diaghilev days to Nicholas Beriozoff of the René Blum company, have said, in effect, that whereas "you dancers today may be the better technicians, we were the better actors." This cannot be completely true, for if dancers of the past were not fine technicians, they could not have performed the variations of Petipa or Bournonville, while today's dancers are extraordinarily convincing in the dramatic ballets of Tudor and Graham. Where our dancers are deficient may be in character dancing, using that term broadly to include both balletic stylizations of national dances and—the balletic equivalent of character acting—the depiction of odd or distinctive character traits. This way of acting, with its almost Jonsonian humours, is more obviously artificial than the "psychological" style in which our dancers, like our actors, excel and requires a mastery of well-timed, quirky gestures.

Arnold L. Haskell, reviewing a revival of *The Rake's Progress* with members of the original cast, speaks with admiration of the expressive eyes of the old Sadler's Wells dancers. Now it is conceivable that some of these dancers may have cultivated certain traits (such as "expressive eyes") to compensate for technical faults, hoping to make up in personality what they lacked in bravura: if so, they had a gimmick. Nevertheless, to ignore totally such elements of performing is to hamper our dancers' expressiveness in a whole genre of ballet.

Whether our dancers will master this genre finally depends upon how many character ballets we revive and whether, having revived them, we consider them worth the effort. But to decide whether character ballets or any other types of ballets are worth the effort, we must first revive them and take a look. Even when unsuccessful, revivals are useful, for they indicate how much ballet taste changes over the years—which we may forget, since choreography exists in no universally comprehensible notation which can be easily consulted for reference. Sometimes revivals show us glories we were foolish to let fade. Sometimes it seems incomprehensible that revived ballets were ever taken seriously. But, good or bad, they cast light upon where we are by showing us where we have been.

So now, please, let us have revivals of *Petrushka, Prince Igor, Schéhérazade, L'Epreuve d'Amour, L'Après-midi d'un Faune, The Good-Humoured Ladies, Boutique Fantasque, Parade, Choreartium, Symphonie Fantastique, St. Francis, Le Train Bleu, Concerto de Chopin, Letter to the World, Deaths and Entrances, New Dance, Apparitions, Nocturne, Scenes de Ballet, Horoscope*, the Tudor *Romeo and Juliet, Judgment of Paris, Three Virgins and a Devil, La Chatte, Cotillon, Baiser de la Fée, Balustrade, Danses Concertantes*, the Haieff *Divertimento, Orpheus, Symphonie Concertante, Opus 34, Figure in the Carpet, Bourrée Fantasque, A Folk Tale, The Kermesse in Bruges, Bayadère* (all of it), *Raymonda* (also all), and *Daughter of the Pharaoh* (to mention only a few titles, as a start).*

*Ballet Review* 3/2 (1969): 33–38

*Many of these works have since been revived—but not enough! Nor have many of them remained in the repertoire.

# JOFFREY BRINGS BACK
# ITS *FAUNE*

Vaslav Nijinsky's *L'Après-midi d'un Faune*, one of the most strangely beautiful ballets of our century, returned to the Joffrey Ballet's repertory on 29 January 1982 at the City Center. As in 1979, when the Joffrey first performed the piece, Léon Bakst's original décor and costumes were lovingly restored by Ralph Holmes and the choreography was reconstructed by Elizabeth Schooling and William Chappell.

The ballet caused a stir at its premiere in 1912 because of its depiction of a faun's shyly amorous pursuit of some nymphs. The way the Faun presses his body against a nymph's scarf at the ballet's conclusion remains a surprising erotic image because of its hints of fetishism and masturbation. Yet what makes *Faune* interesting is not its faintly spicy scenario, but its peculiar combination of sights and sounds.

Debussy's music is lush, almost perfumed, and Bakst's set is a shimmering landscape. Music and décor thus join to give an impression of endless idyllic summer afternoons. However, Nijinsky's choreography features angular movements and, in terms of phrasing, proceeds by fits and starts.

The angularity derives, in part, from Nijinsky's love of Greek friezes and vase paintings. Yet the choreography is more than a reflection of an interest in art history, for the gestural abruptness symbolizes the forces that have disrupted the afternoon's sunlit calm. The Faun's occasionally almost awkward movements express his lack of confidence and the intensification of emotional powers that he does not know how to control. In contrast, the women's movements show the nymphs' desire to maintain their self-possession and their distress when the Faun tries to blurt out his feelings for them.

By creating movement that is unlike the music and décor, Nijinsky demonstrates that the arts that are allied in a ballet production need not simply echo or reinforce one another's effects, but can exist in juxtaposition, as well. Nijinsky here took a step toward the formulation of an aesthetic view that holds that choreography need not be a simple visualization of the music to which a ballet is set. And by using the tensions he set up among dance, music, and design to indicate states of feeling, Nijinsky added psychological truth to what might otherwise have been only a quaintly exotic sketch.

*New York Times*, 31 July 1982

## MASSINE'S *PARADE*

When the Joffrey Ballet announced a revival of Léonide Massine's *Parade*, many balletgoers feared it might look flimsy. Yet Lydia Sokolova in *Dancing for Diaghilev* (Macmillan Company, 1961) maintains, "*Parade* was so delightful that I am sure it would be a favourite if it could be done today. . . . *Parade* has been represented by people who have written about it as a mere stunt. This was not the case at all. The public always seemed to be most enthusiastic, and so was our company."

The revival proves Sokolova to be right—mostly right, anyway. On one small point, she is wrong. Otherwise, just as she predicted, *Parade* is delighting a new generation—but on its own special terms.

Let no one harbor illusions about *Parade*. It may have scandalized audiences in 1917 because of its jazzy score, Cubist décor, and choreographic references to circuses and music-halls, but it does not seem scandalous now. It possesses neither the eroticism of *Schéhérazade* nor the monumentality of *Les Noces*. Indeed, in terms of scale, it is very small, requiring only eight dancers. A clue to its nature is the choreography for the Horse. Though it gallops and kicks most nimbly, this Horse is clearly two costumed men: the dance is a stunt. Sokolova to the contrary, *Parade* is one big stunt, a collection of tricks and pranks. But the pranks are carried off with such insouciance that they never fail to entertain.

Satie's score is ravishing, Picasso's décor remains ingenious, yet the principal reason for *Parade*'s vitality is Massine's choreography. Some Diaghilev experiments have been accused of subordinating movement to painting. *Parade* does not. Even the Managers, encased in huge Cubist constructions, exhibit distinct ways of moving. The First Manager's choreography is particularly effective, for the staccato, almost dainty, steps for the feet contrast amusingly with the bulk of his upper body. The Conjurer (well danced by Gary Chryst) first cleaves the air with exuberant leaps to attract attention, then pulls in space tightly around him, miming the magical appearances and disappearances of an egg by focusing upon one separate part of his body after another. The Acrobats combine balletic virtuosity with steps derived from wire-walking. The American Girl's variation, all jerks and fidgets, flickers like a silent film, the movements suggesting such things as typing a letter, driving an automobile, shooting a gangster, and the lurchings of a storm-tossed vessel. Gestural changes occur so abruptly that (at least as performed by Donna Cowen) the solo becomes the ballet's most problematical element, for it forever seems ready to shatter into smithereens.

Massine's dances and Picasso's décor complement each other. Both utilize Cubist principles. Just as a Cubist still-life distorts ordinary objects, so Massine distorts ordinary gestures. Part of the fun of looking at Cubist paintings comes from the chance to solve the visual riddles by identifying the objects the artist has arranged in his composition. Similarly, in watching Massine's ballet it is fun to track down the whimsical movements to their commonplace origins. However, deriving choreography from gesture has potential dangers as well as delights, for if a spectator cannot discern an episode's realistic basis, befuddlement may ensue. And I must confess I was perplexed by moments in the variations for the Conjurer and the American Girl. But I suspect they may grow clear once I have seen *Parade* several more times.

"New York Newsletter," *Dancing Times* (May 1973): 428

## NIJINSKA'S *LES NOCES*

*Q*f all choreographers, it was probably Bronislava Nijinska, who died in 1972, who showed the greatest concern for making choreography a kind of architecture. And in none of her works is her architectural sense more amazing than it is in *Les Noces*, her ballet of 1923 about a Russian peasant wedding that the Oakland Ballet revived at the 1982 Spoleto Festival in Charleston, South Carolina.

*Les Noces* is almost without precedent, for whereas many choreographers have been noted for visually pleasing ensembles or groupings, no one has ever used human beings as bricks and mortar to build monumental structures in quite the way that Nijinska did.

Yet *Les Noces* directly initiated no trend, fad, or artistic "school." Although Nijinska went on to create dramatic ballets, topical satires, and abstractions to symphonic music, she seldom returned to the grandly austere manner of *Les Noces*. In fact, one of her few later efforts in this genre came two whole decades after *Les Noces*, in 1944, when she choreographed Moussorgsky's *Pictures at an Exhibition* for the short-lived Ballet International. (Does anyone still remember *Pictures?* Is it worth reviving?)

Nevertheless, though unique, *Les Noces* does hint at trends to come. Thus, its ritualism allies it to the efforts of the early modern dancers. There is even a startling moment when men leap fiercely in circles around the motionless Bridegroom that anticipates a similar moment in Martha Graham's *Primitive Mysteries*, a work from 1931. But in the Graham, the motionless figure is a symbol of the Virgin Mary, and the ensemble consists of women leaping in adoration.

The way Nijinska constantly repeats choreographic figurations to make one perceive their patterning also points the way to some of the pattern experiments of Laura Dean. And, by a happy aesthetic coincidence, Dean's company was dancing in Charleston at the same time as the Oakland Ballet.

But the ballets that most resemble Nijinska's *Les Noces* are other choreographers' versions of *Les Noces*. These versions may vary in quality—in the case of Jerome Robbins's production for American Ballet Theatre, the quality is very high.

Yet, thanks to the comments of dance historians and the photographs that exist of the first version, even choreographers who never saw Nijinska's ballet apparently cannot conceive of setting Stravinsky's score for chorus, percussion, and four pianos without thinking in architectural terms. By making the first *Les Noces* so remarkable, Nijinska has provided us with archetypal images of what we expect all succeeding productions to look like.

"Critic's Notebook," *New York Times*, 10 June 1982

## ANNABELLE GAMSON AS ISADORA

*M*ore than half a century after her death, Isadora Duncan continues to fascinate choreographers, dancers, and dancegoers. Thus, in 1981, the Royal Ballet offered the American premiere of *Isadora*, Kenneth MacMillan's controversial evening-long ballet about Duncan's life and art, and solo choreography by Duncan was featured at the Carnegie Hall recital that Annabelle Gamson shared with pianist Garrick Ohlsson.

Although *Isadora* managed to give a lurid account of Duncan's life, for many viewers it failed to give any sense of Duncan's greatness as an artist. However, Gamson's recitals—including this one at Carnegie Hall, where Duncan herself performed—have abundantly demonstrated that Duncan was not merely a flamboyant personality and a tremendous influence, but also a choreographer of genuine consequence.

Of course, Gamson is not our only specialist in Duncan revivals. In recent seasons, such dancers and teachers as Maria-Theresa (one of Duncan's own pupils), Julia Levien, and Kay Bardsley have valiantly served the cause of Duncan dancing and have reconstructed some of

Duncan's group works, as well as her solos. Nevertheless, Gamson's concerts remain very special events that reveal much about Duncan's merits as a choreographer.

For one thing, Gamson makes no attempt to impersonate Duncan. She performs Duncan's choreography, but does not try to look like her. This alone is significant. No contemporary ballerina would try to look like Carlotta Grisi, the first Giselle, or Pierina Legnani, the first Swan Queen, for we assume that the choreography of *Giselle* and *Swan Lake* is so strong and valid in itself that it need not be associated with the physique or stage presence of any single dancer.

Because modern dancers have always regarded their art as an art of personal expression, it is easy to fear that once the person who created a dance is gone, the dance's power will also vanish. Intellectual balletomanes have even argued that modern dance's reluctance to separate the artist from the art makes it inferior to ballet, an art in which style and technique are treated as objective considerations that transcend the strengths or limitations of any individual. But Gamson demonstrates that Duncan dancing can exist and be effective without Duncan.

Gamson is also a strong performer who can make a case for Duncan's dances. Whereas some Duncan revivals are performed by dedicated, but relatively inexperienced, women with little projection, Gamson, in contrast, both shows the structure of a dance and lets that dance come emotionally alive. Conceivably, if other talented dancers ever thought of taking Duncan solos into their repertories, one might then during the course of a single season be able to see X, Y, or Z, as well as Gamson, do the same work, and their interpretations could be compared in much the same way that ballet fans compare the Giselles of various ballerinas. Gamson's success in the Duncan repertory raises the intriguing possibility that a form of dance deriving from one individual's personal expression can also be open to another individual's personal interpretation.

That possibility might not even arise if Duncan's dances—at least, the ones Gamson performs—were not carefully shaped entities. Too often, we tend to accept the notion that Duncan simply pranced about in mystic rapture as the spirit moved her, that she was essentially an improviser.

Judging from accounts, she could improvise brilliantly, her stage behavior could be unpredictable, and she had her mystical moments. Yet, whereas mystics meditate or prophesy, artists construct—and Duncan could construct works that are as capable of being analyzed and taught to other sensitive dancers as works of the classical ballet repertory. If Duncan could waft beautifully, her dances suggest that she was capable of other things than wafting.

Her dances can seem deceptively simple, for they often consist of nothing more than skips, gallops, and runs and the height of virtuosity is a small leap. Yet these dances are not boring, for although the steps may not be acrobatically complicated, their gradations of intensity are very precisely calculated and Duncan's use of dynamics makes some of them kinetic crescendos and diminuendos. Thus, in the *Valse Brillante* (Chopin) the rhythms of the waltz constantly propel the dancer forward or drive her back. In contrast to these liltings, the solo dating from 1905 to Chopin's Prelude No. 7—the same prelude Fokine later used in *Les Sylphides*—is a dance that comes close to being motionless. Evoking a moment of magical stillness, it makes the dancer pose as if hearing elfin music and slowly lift her arms in a gesture of aspiration.

One of the most striking things about Duncan's choreography as performed by Gamson is its ebb and flow of movement. For every bound, there is a rebound. In the *Brahms Waltzes* the dancer often appears to be propelled to and fro by gentle breezes. But this same ebb and flow can also take on a starkly dramatic character. Thus, in the *Revolutionary Etude* (Scriabin) plummetings to the floor beneath the implied weight of bondage are followed by triumphant risings toward liberation.

This ebb and flow—this balancing of action with counteraction, of incoming with outgoing movement—helps give Duncan's choreography its own special look. Duncan liked to say that she was inspired by the rhythms of ocean tides or by the movement of wind in grass. One can see such rhythms in her dances. Indeed, the ebb and flow often appears to be that of breathing itself. Curiously, there was almost no such ebb and flow in the Duncan dances that MacMillan devised in *Isadora*. Though the poses and steps recalled those that Duncan did use, the dances remained unconvincing: they never "breathed."

The modern dance pioneers who followed Duncan also derived technical principles from the act of breathing. Martha Graham's famous concepts of "contraction and release" are specifically based upon breathing. So, to a great extent, are Doris Humphrey's related principles of "fall and recovery." Therefore, it is misleading to say—as some critics have said—that Duncan had no technical system. She may never have drawn up a graded syllabus of instruction, but she did initiate a salutary "back to basics" trend that encouraged dancers and dance teachers to analyze the human body and its capacities for movement.

Duncan's dances, then, though often mystical or ecstatic in character, are carefully composed, and anyone who wishes to perform them well must possess the proper technique and style. Indeed, it is only after mastering Duncan's technique and style that a dancer can enter into Duncan's rapture, for that rapture is the end product of technique and style: it is the moment of spiritual illumination that follows hours of meditation. In Gamson's reconstructions of Duncan one can study and admire the technique and style. And one can sense the rapture.

*New York Times*, 30 August 1981

# WHEN BALLROOM DANCES
# TAKE TO THE STAGE

*S*ome dance forms exist primarily for the fun of doing them, and the people who do them don't particularly care whether or not they're being watched. Other dances are meant to be watched. Into this category belong all examples of theatrical dancing from hoofing to ballet.

Yet rigid distinctions cannot be drawn between these types of dances.

In ballrooms, dancers may pause just to watch a particularly graceful couple. Waltzes and tangos are often transformed into nightclub acts. Societies of exhibition ballroom dancers hold competitions which their fans find as exciting as balletomanes find the international ballet competitions. And, on occasion, social or ballroom dances may be presented in a format akin to that of a ballet program or modern dance concert. At least three notable examples of such theatricalization were seen during the 1984–85 season.

*Tango Argentino*, a program of tango music and dancing devised by Claudio Segovia and Héctor Orezzoli, delighted audiences at the City Center. At Marymount Manhattan Theatre, the Court Dance Company of New York offered Elizabeth Aldrich's *Fleeting Pleasures*, a survey of nineteenth-century American social dancing. And American Ballroom Theatre's *Sheer Romance*, at the Bessie Schönberg Theatre, was a potpourri of ballroom dances, choreographed by John Roudis. All three events were in theatres where one usually sees ballet or modern dance and were presented with the artistic seriousness associated with ballet and modern dance. Therefore, these attractions might be termed "ballroom-ballet," especially since, today, "ballet" is often used to mean not only traditional classical dancing, but virtually any type of dance that has attained a theatrical form.

The Argentines were so exciting that two hours of tangos did not seem too much, even though the musicians were badly amplified. With its insinuating rhythms, the tango proved to be a dance of passion, and during the course of a single tango there might be several passionate outbursts. Usually, the couples kept their upper bodies calm and let their feet do the talking. Yet a man might lean toward his partner, causing her to bend backward. It was as if he had just whispered something to her that threatened to sweep her off her feet. A man might also drop to one knee before his partner or unexpectedly lift her upside down. And, at times, the women would whirl away from the men, only to rejoin them moments later.

Nevertheless, it was the footwork that made the tango varied. The shifting choreographic patterns were like the flaring up and ebbing away of emotions. Occasionally, dancers simply walked or glided enticingly. But feet could also caress the floor and the air and stamp with petulance and exuberance. In some sequences, the feet hurried forward, then paused, but not for long; and when they started up again, they darted back and forth like adders' tongues. Little kicks to the side and constant changes of direction suggested the wiles of worldly people who were virtuosos in the art of flirting. And when the women entwined their legs around their partners, dancing became embracing.

*Tango Argentino* was something special. Yet the season's other manifestations of ballroom-ballet were also attractive. The members of the American Ballroom Theatre were smooth as silk in their dancing and could flow without effort from phrase to phrase.

Elizabeth Aldrich's presentation for the Court Dance Company was instructive, as well as diverting. It purported to show balls after three presidential inaugurations: one in Virginia after James Monroe's inauguration in 1817, another in Louisiana after Zachary Taylor's inauguration in 1849, and the third in New York City after Benjamin Harrison's inauguration in 1889.

The episode from 1817 was unusually interesting because it provided one with a peep into a time when ballroom dances and theatrical ballet employed some of the same steps. Thus, certain passages made use of turnout. There were intricate allegro steps, including a few that required the performer to rise upward on the ball of the foot. To our eyes, such steps looked balletic and the risings upward even seemed harbingers of pointe work. By 1849, ballet and ballroom dance had gone their separate ways. Although ballroom steps still contained some fancy footwork, the dances emphasized the sweepings of couples across the floor. Dancers swept around the room even more ostentatiously in 1889. Perhaps that was not surprising, for this was the so-called Gilded Age.

No one lectured at this concert. Yet it still preached a message, for it appeared to demonstrate that during the nineteenth century American social dancing steadily declined in complexity as it gradually gained in pretentiousness. By assigning her most intricate dances to Southerners, Aldrich may also have been implying that technically complex social dances can exist only if there is a leisured class able to take the necessary time to learn them—in this case, a leisured class made possible by the existence of slavery.

Only another researcher could say for certain whether or not Aldrich's theory is valid. Yet her presentation did raise fascinating questions. So did the other examples of ballroom-ballet. Some of the American Ballroom Theatre's least convincing items were in gypsy and Latin American styles. One wondered why: do these styles always threaten to turn corny? or are Roudis's stagings in these styles simply less imaginative than his treatments of other styles?

The fact that many members of the Argentine troupe looked middle-aged made me wonder if tango dancing is now out of favor among the young. Or is the tango an art that requires the wisdom of years, as well as physical dexterity? I also wondered how much of the dancing we saw at City Center can now be seen in Buenos Aires and how often it can be seen there. On my own visit to that beautiful and invigorating, but politically troubled, city in 1974, Argentine friends told me that tango palaces still existed, but that they were no longer interesting. Consequently, I never went to one. Were my friends right? Or had they just grown blasé about their local entertainments?

Through their very excellence, *Tango Argentino*, the Court Dance Company, and American Ballroom Theatre make us wonder just what it is we are seeing when we see ballroom-ballet. Is it an adaptation of something that does, or did at one time, actually exist? Or is it a choreographer's vision of what could exist, in the same way that George Balanchine's *Liebeslieder Walzer* idealizes the waltz? To take one small point: in Aldrich's ballroom dances, the performers tended to embellish the basic steps with the same ornaments at the same time. Was this a characteristic of nineteenth-century dancing? Or was it a theatrical effect devised by Aldrich to insure that patterns were always clear?

To some extent, such niggling is irrelevant. If a production boasts imaginative choreography danced with genuine skill, it may not seem to matter much whether or not the good folk of Graustark really danced the schottisch like that back in 1847. Yet members of the audience who realize that there are pleasures in dance scholarship as well as in dance-watching will continue to ask questions in order to determine how much a ballroom-ballet program has preserved its source materials, how much it has stylized them, how much it has modified them for polemical purposes, and how much it has leaped into flights of pure fancy.

No doubt about it, *Tango Argentino*, the Court Dance Company, and American Ballroom Theatre offer great entertainment. Yet the fact that we can take these groups so seriously is one sign that their entertainment may also be genuine art.

*New York Times*, 7 July 1985

# THREE

# Some Contemporary Masters

*Members of the New York City Ballet in George Balanchine's* Agon.
*Photo* © *Steven Caras.*

*M*ost dancegoers of the mid-twentieth century have surely had to come to terms with six great choreographers: George Balanchine, Antony Tudor, Frederick Ashton, Jerome Robbins, Martha Graham, and Merce Cunningham. One cannot escape them. Both when their creations inspire and when they exasperate, one feels forced to mull over them. One has to take them seriously.

It was Balanchine who explored the possibilities of the plotless, or abstract, ballet. Tudor became known for the "psychological ballet." Ashton's works exemplify a lyrical manner that some viewers have pronounced "typically" British. Robbins first attracted attention for his balletic adaptations of jazz. Graham developed her own form of psychological dance-dramas on mythological or literary themes. Cunningham ignores traditional concepts of theatrical unity by creating dances in which he treats movement, music, and décor as independent entities that simply coexist in the same time and place.

For viewers inordinately fond of tidy categories—and for those young choreographers who do little more in their own works than imitate their elders—such summaries may suffice. But what helps make these choreographers so fascinating is their creative restlessness. Balanchine choreographed more than abstractions: he produced comedies, dramas, and symbolical mood pieces, and even some of his abstractions seem to possess a secret dramatic life of their own. Tudor engaged in social commentary as well as in psychological introspection. Ashton and Robbins have been astonishingly versatile. Graham, the solemn dance-dramatist, has also choreographed abstractions and giddy comedies. Cunningham may claim that all the theatrical components of his works are autonomous, yet, though they may have no direct connection with one another, they nevertheless often appear to fit together in such a way as to provide each of his works with its own special climate or atmosphere.

*In their plotless as well as their dramatic choreography, these six masters show worlds of behavior that can be pondered for their moral, as well as their purely aesthetic, meaning. They have all significantly shaped the dance of our time. And, as influences to learn from or rebel against, they may affect the development of choreography for generations to come.*

# THE GLORIOUS
# UNPREDICTABILITY OF
# GEORGE BALANCHINE

*I*t finally made sense. For years I'd been seeing George Balanchine's *A Midsummer Night's Dream*, liking parts of it, but finding other parts bothersome, parts which seemed to violate the most sensible rules for constructing dramatic ballets. It particularly annoyed me that the first act was mostly story, while the second was all divertissement. It annoyed me, too, that Balanchine had no pas de deux for Oberon and Titania. How could he miss so obvious an opportunity?

Now, after having seen the New York City Ballet perform *A Midsummer Night's Dream* during its 3 May–3 July 1977 season at New York State Theater, I think I understand. The ballet is peculiar not because Balanchine has fumbled, it's peculiar for a purpose. Balanchine wishes to show how passion deranges people, how passion is no respecter of persons, and how lovers in the throes of passion may appear ridiculous to detached outsiders. Typifying Balanchine's thematic concerns is the idiotic, yet curiously touching, scene where, to some of Mendelssohn's most ravishing music, Bottom transformed into an ass prefers to nibble grass, though the smitten Titania employs a whole arsenal of feminine wiles to entice him.

The most important beings love deranges are Oberon and Titania. They are beautiful people in both the literal and the slightly disparaging slang sense of that term. They lord it over elfin high society and, used to living in the lap of luxury, are capable of collecting people in the way other socialites collect *objets d'art*. Titania's pas de deux with an anonymous, compliant Cavalier is no structural fault, it says something about the extravagance of the leisure class. So does the fact that Titania has her own private limousine: petals on which she reclines like Botticelli's Venus on her seashell. What a great lady she is! Then she falls in love with an ass—a social blunder of the worst sort.

Eventually, she realizes her foolishness and patches up her differences with Oberon. But their reconciliation seems not an instance of newfound devotion, but an attempt to maintain proper social appearances. They like each other, to be sure, but their marriage is essentially a matter of social and political expediency.

There can be no grand pas de deux for such a couple. (Balanchine's attitude toward them is far tougher than that of Ashton in his equally admirable, but dissimilar, *The Dream*.) Nevertheless, Balanchine does wish to remind us of love's grandeur. The foolish mortals and sprites cannot do that. Therefore, to borrow Shakespeare's own terminology, Balanchine turns from the lunatic and the lover to the poet, making the second act divertissement not merely a graceful suite, but a lyric vision of untroubled love. A dance for several affectionate couples is followed by a duet for one very loving couple. The ballet's scale turns intimate during the duet, an effect intensified by the moments when the lovers come to rest facing upstage, as though the presence of an audience were unimportant. However, instead of concluding with the expected coda for the divertissement dancers, Balanchine brings back the plot's human lovers, as though to suggest that this divertissement is their fantasy and to remind us that fallible humans remain capable of imagining a love beyond themselves.

The company performed this Shakespearean adaptation very well, Jean-Pierre Frohlich's ability to disguise his transitions making him a nimble Puck, while Karin von Aroldingen's combination of beauty and acidity was just right for Titania. The company also danced well throughout the entire season, illuminating the repertoire and making one newly aware of how gloriously unpredictable, even irrational, Balanchine's choreography can be. In fact, it may be most unpredictable when Balanchine is working in supposedly familiar forms.

Take the so-called abstract ballet. Balanchine didn't invent the form, but he certainly developed it to its full, thereby inspiring countless emulators and imitators. We all know what an abstract ballet looks like. We could even concoct one here and now. Let's try. We'll employ some classic concerto and have the corps represent the orchestra and the ballerina and danseur represent the solo instrument. The first movement will be stately, the second movement will be a pas de deux (what else?), and the last will be a splashy ensemble. There we have it: the ready-made Balanchine abstraction.

The funny thing is, few of Balanchine's own abstractions look like that. Not even *Concerto Barocco*—which may superficially fit the formula. Yes, Bach's two solo violins are "represented" by two ballerinas. But not always. Not in the slow movement. Though the same two violins play away in the pit, one ballerina is replaced by a man. This is his only appearance, and his purpose is to partner the remaining ballerina. Yet he is no negligible porteur. His presence signifies a real change of focus. Especially when an artist like Peter Martins appears in the role, this man seems the quiet center around which the vinelike patterns of the other dancers unfold.

Frequently, Balanchine transcends ordinary compositional logic. In the "Ricercata" from *Episodes* he—logically enough—has a six-voiced fugal composition interpreted by six groups of dancers. However, though conservatory rules insist that fugal voices be of equal value, Balanchine makes four of his groups consist of two women, while one consists of a man and a woman, and one consists of a small ensemble—an ensemble, symbolically enough, of six. Balanchine's approach is, at once, rational and irrational. Instead of simply imitating the music, he builds his own personal choreographic structure upon it, yet in harmony with it. Look at *Stravinsky Violin Concerto*. There appears to be no logical reason why in the first movement the cast of twenty appears only in changing groups of five. Next, where convention prescribes a pas de deux, there are two—each very different. Finally, the cast of twenty returns, this time divided up into two groups of ten. This structuring—simultaneously strict and arbitrary—turns Stravinsky's score into a double concerto: a concerto for dancers, as well as a concerto for violin.

Balanchine's supposed abstractions often unfold secret emotional dramas. The ancestor of this type of ballet is *Serenade*, in which ambiguous situations inexplicably crystallize, and then, just as inexplicably, dissolve. The second movement of *Scotch Symphony* is similarly tantalizing, particularly when solemn guardians first hinder, then apparently aid the romantic Scotsman in his pursuit of a Sylphide. Moreover, the incident occurs twice, once on either side of the stage. The repetitions of Mendelssohn's music demand that it happen that way. And that makes the scene, though musically rational, visually irrational—and unforgettably mysterious.

Recently, Balanchine has added peculiar new choreography to two works. *Divertimento from "Le Baiser de la Fée"*, which once ended happily, now ends unhappily as, separated from each other, two lovers wander through a forest of dancers, then across the open stage, never to meet again. Considering that the ballet begins daintily, this seems a surprising reversal. Yet one can find premonitory hints of this from the beginning: when the lovers first enter in their pas de deux, the woman continually reaches outward, then backward, but always toward something which is beyond her and beyond her partner. Here the ballet already implies an eventual departure.

New choreography has also altered "Emeralds" in *Jewels*. The gentlest section of that ballet, "Emeralds" flows serenely along until the choreographic alterations darken its landscape. After what could be a finale, the ensemble steps backward offstage while the seven soloists assume stately groupings. Then the female soloists also move solemnly offstage. The men, left alone, sink to their knees, arms outstretched, their gaze questioning the distance. If the new choreography makes *Baiser* a leave-taking, "Emeralds" has become a summoning in which the dancers are called by powerful forces which, if not literally definable, are nonetheless genuinely sensed.

Because Balanchine often deals with love's pangs in a tender fashion, he may delude the naive into believing that the course of love, if seldom smooth, is at least bittersweet. But Balanchine knows better. And so he periodically shocks audiences with such a harsh work as *Variations pour une Porte et un Soupir* (currently danced by Karin von Aroldingen and Victor Castelli), a Strindbergian duet concerning the pain of forever-unslaked passion. Von Aroldingen's beckonings are automatonlike; her suitor is a dodderer. These characters are in agony. Yet von Aroldingen's come-hither mimings and the way Castelli beats his head upon the floor often elicit titters. And it's not surprising that they do for here, as in *A Midsummer Night's Dream*, Balanchine reminds us that, whereas one's own erotic predicaments may seem terribly serious, those of others may seem preposterous. Similar titters greet the "Five Pieces" section of *Episodes*, which shows a man and a woman desperately trying to get together, but managing to do so only awkwardly, at best—a pas de deux "absurd" in both the comic and the philosophical sense.

Equally peculiar, though far more elegant, is the andante of *Divertimento No. 15*. A hack would make this a pas de deux. Balanchine does something stranger and more memorable. Instead of choreographing for a single couple, he devises a communal pas de deux during which five women are variously partnered by three men, each new permutation succeeding the previous coupling without break. These shifting adagios invite surprising interpretations for, at times, they seem an orgy for angels, a glorification of the Don Juan temperament (which, ever restless, continually seeks the same experience of love, but through different bodies), or, more simply, an eloquent reminder that, though individuals may pass away, love remains an eternal power.

In many ballets Balanchine glorifies social occasions, yet also contrasts them with idiosyncratic personal behavior. The finale of *Chaconne* shows people taking pleasure in public display, as does the pas de deux from the "Diamonds" section of *Jewels*, where ballerina and danseur do much parading about before each other. Confident without conceit, each is pleased to be a show-off, and each is pleased to watch the other showing off.

*Monumentum Pro Gesualdo* suggests actual social dancing. Just as

Stravinsky's score adapts Renaissance madrigals, so Balanchine's choreography suggests court dancing through the way the couples who comprise the cast tread a stately measure as though traversing a great hall. As in actual Renaissance dances, the emphasis is upon floor patterns, so that the few uses of the air come as exclamation points, as when a cavalier raises the ballerina, then drops her into the arms of male attendants. Come to think of it, that may be not only an embellishment of social dance, it may be part of a formal courtship between heads of state, the sort of courtship so important that, for all its intimate nature, it must have some visible public manifestation: remember how, in the most traditional stagings of *Swan Lake*, Prince Siegfried would drop Odette, Queen of the Swans, into Benno's arms?

*Square Dance* finds room for privacy within a public festivity. Most of *Square Dance* is happily gregarious. But there is also a solo for Bart Cook which seems to concern solitude. Part of the time, Cook dances with one hand on his hip while with the other he sketches designs in the air. Leaping forward, he may double up—as though unwilling to commit himself to anything full-out—then restore himself to balanced calm. This drawing inward implies that Cook's attention is upon something interior, while his quiet assurance makes one feel that his private meditations may help strengthen him for public occasions.

Its contrasts between public and private make *Square Dance* unexpectedly akin to *Bugaku*. This pseudo-Japanese wedding ceremony allows Balanchine to hold up an image of a culture marked by extreme distinctions between public convention and private reality, a culture which prescribes that men stride martially and women tiptoe demurely, heads glancing humbly downward, as though forbidden to look anyone directly in the face. But once the bride and groom are alone, they dance a pas de deux so fierce it resembles a combat in which both man and woman possess equal strength. When performed by the admirable Allegra Kent (in one of her all too rare appearances with the company these days), the leading female role acquires an extra dimension. For Kent, in the supposedly submissive dances for the women, indicates that this woman has so mastered official etiquette and has such a capacity for cunning that she can use the very role-playing which society has forced her into as a weapon for gaining her own way.

Balanchine's two new ballets this season also concerned public and private matters. The Scriabin *Etude for Piano* (commissioned by the American Spoleto Festival in Charleston and given its first New York performance on 17 June) was entirely private: a moment of passion as purple as the costumes by Christina Giannini. In this tiny pas de deux for Patricia McBride and Jean-Pierre Bonnefous, Balanchine suggests rapture by means of repeated backbends, the ballet beginning with McBride leaning backward, facing outward, supported by Bonnefous's outstretched arm. Away from Bonnefous, at one moment she moves in an almost dazed fashion on pointe as though staggering beneath the weight of her own feelings. The ballet ends with McBride back on Bonnefous's arm, this time with her head turned to the side and her hair loosened, as though a consummation or resolution had been reached.

The season's hit was *Wiener Walzer* (*Vienna Waltzes*), premiered on 23 June after a preview showing at a 15 June gala. Lavishly designed by Rouben Ter-Arutunian and Karinska and set to light music by three Viennese composers, this is a forty-five-minute extravaganza for a cast of seventy-four which, like *Stars and Stripes* and *Union Jack*, celebrates a national image. Though not a masterpiece, I think it the nicest of the three, for while *Stars and Stripes* and *Union Jack* derive in part from military drill (an activity I find dull at best and distasteful at worst), *Wiener Walzer* glorifies social dancing, a public activity which permits the expression of personal sentiments.

The first three episodes, all to the younger Johann Strauss, are set in the Wienerwald. Women in long gowns and men in uniforms (led by Karin von Aroldingen and Sean Lavery) stroll amongst the trees, then start waltzing to "Tales from the Vienna Woods." Although patterns grow complex, the choreography remains rooted in ballroom conventions. "Voices of Spring," which follows, has the look of Romantic ballet. Patricia McBride, Helgi Tomasson, and a small female ensemble (with all the women in Romantic tutus) leap and whirl like forest sprites or elves. "Explosion Polka" returns to the realm of social dance, and the ballet thereafter never leaves that realm. In the ballet's only piece which is not a waltz, the men (headed by Bart Cook) wear striped trousers and high-collared coats, while the women (headed by Sara Leland) are in powderpuff tutus. As the title suggests, the polka is an explosion of bodies bobbing down and popping back up.

The scene changes to a ballroom with a reflecting surface for a back wall. As couples waltz to Lehár's "Gold and Silver," Peter Martins meets Kay Mazzo. In her long black gown, she seems the Merry Widow with whom he may once have had an affair. Waltzing together, their gestures and expressions almost speak operetta dialogue: "Heavens, it's you again." "Yes, it is I." "And after so many years." "It has been a long time, hasn't it?" "I never dreamed I would find you here." "No. Nor did I." "Tell me, in all that time, did you ever think of me?" "Ah, you know the answer without my saying." On they waltz until Mazzo runs off, leaving Martins alone once more.

The ballroom grows larger, the mirror shines brighter, and Suzanne Farrell starts dancing alone to waltzes from Richard Strauss's *Der Rosenkavalier.* She is joined by Jorge Donn, then by the principals of the previous scenes and a corps of twenty couples—the men in black, the women in white. Repeatedly, the stage is invaded by surges of dancers until the spectacle is as dizzying as one too many glasses of champagne. In sober retrospect, one must admit that in *Wiener Walzer* Balanchine does not invest waltzing with either the drama or the emotional resonance of *La Valse* or *Liebeslieder Walzer.* He remains content to whip up a confection. But it is the confection of a master pastry cook.

*Dance Magazine* (October 1977): 75–78

# BY ANY NAME, IT'S STILL
# AN IMPERIAL BALLET

*Q*n 12 January 1973, George Balanchine's *Ballet Imperial* was re-named *Tchaikovsky Piano Concerto No. 2*, thereby becoming yet another work in the New York City Ballet's repertory known only by the title of its musical score. Nevertheless, it can be argued that it still remains "imperial" in manner.

Balanchine has long avoided decorative titles—his *Le Palais de Cristal* became *Symphony in C* in 1948 and *Caracole* became *Divertimento No. 15* in 1956—and his choreographic colleagues at the New York City Ballet have tended to follow his example in naming works. Thus, the company's repertory listings, filled with references to suites, symphonies, and concertos, have come to resemble symphony orchestra programs.

*Ballet Imperial*'s scenery was discarded along with its title. Since 1973, *Tchaikovsky Piano Concerto No. 2* has been performed against a plain cyclorama, as if to demonstrate that movement can be expressive in itself apart from any clues as to mood or theme that titles or décor may provide. However, the choreographic concerto's new look startled people at first, for *Ballet Imperial* had long been one of Balanchine's most celebrated works.

It received its premiere by the American Ballet in 1941 in New York, the same city in which sixty years earlier—in 1881—the New York Philharmonic, conducted by Theodore Thomas, offered the concerto's world premiere with Madeline Schiller as pianist. Balanchine created *Ballet Imperial* as a vehicle for Marie-Jeanne, who was celebrated for her speed and prowess, and other soloists in the first production included Gisella Caccialanza and William Dollar.

In 1942 *Ballet Imperial* was danced by the ballet corps of the New Opera Company as a curtain-raiser to short operas. Caccialanza and Dollar were again on hand, but Mary Ellen Moylan took the leading role. She did so again, and with enormous success, in 1945 with the Ballet

Russe de Monte Carlo, heading a cast that also included Maria Tallchief and Nicholas Magallanes.

Featuring Suzanne Farrell, Patricia Neary, and Jacques d'Amboise, *Ballet Imperial* entered the New York City Ballet's repertory in 1964. When reincarnated as *Tchaikovsky Piano Concerto No. 2* in 1973, it starred Patricia McBride, Colleen Neary, and Peter Martins. Abroad, the work has figured in the repertories of such companies as the Royal Ballet and the Ballet of La Scala, Milan.

All American stagings before 1964 utilized décor by Mstislav Doboujinsky that showed ermine-trimmed blue draperies framing a glimpse of the spires of St. Petersburg. For the first New York City Ballet version, Rouben Ter-Arutunian designed a similiar view of the St. Petersburg skyline.

Although such décor has led some observers to call the ballet a nostalgic tribute to prerevolutionary St. Petersburg, the present stripped-down production reveals that, however fond Balanchine may be of the city in which he received his ballet training, this work is not primarily a tribute to the imperial czarist regime. Rather, it pays homage to the metaphorically imperial attributes of classical ballet itself, which, though fostered at St. Petersburg's Maryinsky Theatre, can be preserved under many different political systems.

Despite the modified title and décor, nothing has really changed about this ballet. Actually, to be scrupulously correct, it should be noted that, as is his wont, Balanchine has tinkered with his choreography over the years. For instance, he has removed some miming in the second movement. Yet nothing essential has been altered. *Ballet Imperial* or *Tchaikovsky Piano Concerto No. 2*—call it what you will—remains a ballet of grandeur, dignity, opulence, and extravagance. And all of these qualities are inherent in the choreography.

Balanchine's first extravagance comes right at the start. He keeps the curtain down for the entirety of Tchaikovsky's spacious presentation of the first movement's principal theme. Thus, Balanchine has given his ballet an overture—a long one, too. In these nervous times, most choreographers don't like to keep audiences sitting in the dark listening to music—and, considering how some ballet orchestras sound, that may be just as well. Today, curtains are apt to go up after only a measure or two. But, in more leisurely times, overtures were commonplace, and by providing this ballet with an overture Balanchine flatters us by assuming that we all know how to make an art of our leisure.

At last, with the tremolo that announces the second theme, the curtain rises upon eight couples and the men step forward and bow like courtiers or graduates of a fine ballet school. This in itself is a grand sight. But, suddenly, it becomes even grander as eight more women appear. Such intensifications of effect occur throughout the ballet.

To cascades of piano music, the secondary female soloist rushes in. Since this is a plotless ballet, nobody in it has a name. But let's, for convenience, nickname its two leading women Prima and Secunda, whereas its cavalier will be called—what else?—Cavalier.

Now Prima enters—and what an entrance it is, for without any preparation she must greet the audience with a taxing solo to one of the concerto's several cadenzas. Can Balanchine equal this? He does indeed, for Prima is replaced by Secunda, accompanied by two other women. A brilliant solo female variation has given way to another female variation. But this one, in a sense, is in triplicate.

The entrance of Cavalier leads into a stately duet with Prima during which each dancer performs brief variations that make the sequence resemble a traditional pas de deux in miniature. But, just as he did after Prima's cadenza, Balanchine proceeds to magnify what is already an impressive effect. He brings Secunda back, this time partnered by two men. Having seen a woman adored by one man, we now see a woman adored by two men and, perhaps, recall Balanchine's theory that "ballet is woman." But Prima is still Prima in this hierarchy, so it is only fitting that she should lead the ensemble at the movement's conclusion.

The meditative second movement begins with a pensively posed Cavalier and, linked together by holding hands, five women to his right and five to his left. He swings them dreamily from side to side as if they were passing fancies in his mind. Then the women form a line that breaks open as Prima enters for a duet that epitomizes all the vision scenes that were so popular in nineteenth-century ballet. As many of those did, this one ends sadly, as Prima exits through the space between two parallel lines of women, an image that has the visual effect of a disappearance into a tunnel.

The last movement returns to a realm of pomp; here, Balanchine makes daring use of multiple focus by placing the entire corps stage right while Prima whirls alone stage left and, by so doing, demonstrates that one dazzling presence can hold the attention as easily as a large ensemble. Soon afterward, the corps parades back and forth, momentarily swallowing up Prima in their ranks, only to let her shine forth again as they pass her by. The finale introduces one formation after another of small groups and large until a glorious unison is reached and the concerto comes to an end.

It is a work of great choreographic richness. Therefore, under any title, Balanchine's interpretation of Tchaikovsky would still be an imperial ballet. And its particular imperialism is one that champions glory without tyrannizing anyone.

*New York Times*, 30 January 1983

## BALANCHINE'S *SCHUMANN*

The New York City Ballet offered the preview of a new work by George Balanchine at a gala on 12 June 1980 and its official premiere on 19 June. Two remarks heard about it in the lobby afterward are worth quoting here.

One balletomane declared: "That title's got to be changed! People don't go to ballets they can't pronounce." And another fan said: "It's the most morbid thing I've ever seen." Both balletomanes have a point.

Balanchine called his latest creation *Robert Schumann's "Davidsbündlertänze"* (yes, that is exactly how the ballet is billed in the program), and even balletgoers who can pronounce that long German word must agree that this is surely the most awkward title we have had to contend with since Balanchine's *Metastaseis and Pithoprakta* of 1968. As for its emotional atmosphere, this piece to piano music by Schumann is grandly morbid. It is also a major work.

The piano is onstage, and the eight dancers, dressed for a fancy ball, usually appear as couples (Suzanne Farrell and Jacques d'Amboise, Karin von Aroldingen and Adam Lüders, Heather Watts and Peter Martins, and Kay Mazzo and Ib Andersen). All the women except Watts enter wearing heeled shoes, then change into pointe shoes.* So described, *Schumann* (as I propose to call the ballet for short) may sound like *Liebeslieder Walzer.* But the two works could not be more dissimilar.

Rouben Ter-Arutunian's setting alone suggests that this is no ordinary ballroom. True, the sides of the stage are hung with filmy curtains and there are two chandeliers. But there the resemblance to a ballroom ends, for the stage is also decorated with wintry branches and the backdrop is a view of a shoreless ocean from which (or into which) a ghostly cathedral is rising (or sinking). Whatever this setting may represent, it is no place for *Liebeslieder Walzer.*† And although *Schumann* concerns love, its dances do not resemble the tender love songs of the Brahms ballet. *Schumann*'s dancers may be at a party, but they are also on the edge of heartbreak, the choreographic contrasts between desperate mirth and unrestrained melancholy paralleling comparable contrasts in Schumann's music and life.

Most of the ballet consists of duets. Some are delicate and pensive. Others are restless, agitated, impulsive. But when the dancers become intense, they look fevered, rather than happy. The episodes that are not duets are equally peculiar. In one, two couples enter performing the same steps. Then they have a danced dialogue, one couple doing a series of steps to which the other couple responds, each phrase being sadder than the one before.

---

*Changes are often made in ballets, and what is presented at first performances of a work is not necessarily what dancegoers will see in later performances of the same work. Currently, every woman enters wearing heeled shoes.

†Ter-Arutunian later said in interviews that it was inspired by a painting by the German Romantic artist Caspar David Friedrich.

Farrell appears in a coquettish solo, yet its gaiety looks artificial. After all the men but Lüders dance together, their partners solemnly return. However, when they pair off, the men are initially not paired with their usual partners, the incident suggesting the irrationality of love. Von Aroldingen, in a solo, could be searching for a vanished lover. Lüders, her partner, has a stormy solo of his own during which figures in funereal black materialize like personifications of destiny.

At one point, all the couples try to be sociable. But when they discover that they cannot keep up appearances, they drift away. Finally, there is a duet for von Aroldingen and Lüders. Throughout *Schumann,* Lüders has been the most pale and consumptive-looking of the men, and this duet is a leave-taking during which he shrivels up and goes off into darkness.

Passion inevitably brings pain, *Schumann* implies. And because its cast includes both some of the company's youngest principals and some of its veterans, the ballet may also imply that this is true of passions at any time of life. Yet the dancers' fervor hints that Balanchine believes that it is better to be passionate and in pain than to have no emotional life at all.

"New York Newsletter," *Dancing Times* (August 1980): 739–740

# THE VIEW FROM THE HOUSE OPPOSITE: SOME ASPECTS OF TUDOR

The usual generalization made about Antony Tudor is that he developed something called the psychological ballet. The curious thing about this claim is that so few dancegoers question its implicit assumption that the psychological ballet is worth developing.

Distressed or demented individuals—Giselle, Dr. Coppelius, Petrushka—have long been common in dance, but not until comparatively recently have choreographers attempted to depict mental processes in all their intricacy. These attempts are generally encouraged. Yet one may argue that dance is ill suited to psychology, that the analysis of motivation—being reflective, rather than kinetic—is best attempted through verbalization in poetry and fiction. What passes for psychology in most ballets is preposterously oversimplified. Typically, Agnes de Mille's book about Lizzie Borden contains more interesting insights than her more famous ballet on the subject, *Fall River Legend*. Choreographers tend to offer psychological platitudes in an overwrought manner which, by its turbulence, initially holds one's attention. After a work grows familiar, however, it is possible to see that, say, Richard Kuch's *The Brood*, inspired by Bertolt Brecht, is a farrago of violent images providing little serious commentary upon either Mother Courage or the psychology of war, and that even Martha Graham's *Clytemnestra* hammers monotonously at a limited number of notions. Moreover, fashions in psychology change, and when they do, certain once-admired ballets—Rudi van Dantzig's *Monument for a Dead Boy*, for example, or Herbert Ross's *The Maids*—are apt to look antiquated.

Action, rather than motivation, could be called the stuff of dance, and one can point to such phenomena as the abstractions of Balanchine and Merce Cunningham as significant examples of pure choreographic action. To those who fear that avoidance of psychology limits dance, one might reply that if the twentieth century has witnessed a rise of psychological art, it has equally witnessed a rise of resolutely antipsychological art, and dance reflects this development. Similarly, the absence of psychology need not deprive dance of moral significance, for there is a theory of ethics which holds that we reveal and make ourselves through behavior and that, therefore, actions are more important than intentions.

Still, all theories can be deflated by concrete realities. Though I sympathize with the viewpoint that the realm of dance is action, not psychology, factors which prevent me from dismissing the psychological ballet include, on the one hand, the hack abstractions now commonplace everywhere and, on the other, the creations of such fine choreographers as Tudor.

Yet perhaps one reason why Tudor's best ballets work is that, despite the convenient label attached to them, they are seldom totally psychological. They deal with more than mental states. At least one of Tudor's major dance-dramas is not primarily psychological; and some of his most extreme psychological ballets present their data in a special way (one, in fact, ultimately refusing to psychologize). Usually, Tudor's ballets simultaneously concern themselves with social and psychological realities, with the outer as well as the inner world. Even those which are most strongly outer or most strongly inner contain polarities of some sort. Not only in *Pillar of Fire* but in Tudor's work as a whole, there is always a House Opposite.

Possibly the least psychological of serious Tudor ballets is *Romeo and Juliet*. It discloses little about the psychology of either Romeo or Juliet. To be sure, the characters are not ciphers. The very first scene is quite telling: in contrast to Rosaline's unruffled poise, Romeo droops and sags, yet makes an impatient brushing step with his foot, a gesture suggesting both lovelorn weariness and lovelorn impetuosity. But the treatment of Rosaline is more typical of how Tudor presents his characters: she is a facade, and the ballet is a series of facades. Essentially, it is all exterior, and Tudor's steps and groupings and Eugene Berman's designs are taken from the grandeur of Renaissance painting.

Yet the ballet is chilling—partially because of its beauty. Romeo and Juliet, despite the sumptuousness of their world, are caught up by grim forces they cannot control. Tudor ignores their psychology because their psychology is irrelevant. They are already trapped. There are no intimate revelations: there is nothing intimate to reveal. Part of the tragedy of Romeo and Juliet is that intimacy is impossible for them. Their meeting in the ballroom is interrupted by other guests, the walls of the Capulet mansion keep them apart in the balcony scene, their one night together is broken by Romeo's flight, and when they meet again in the tomb it is a meeting before death. The ballet's action constantly separates them and rushes them along toward death with the implacability of fate.

The implacability gives the ballet a horrible beauty. The ballet is also, despite its gowns and palaces, physically horrible at times, for it is filled with the halt and the lame. Its low-life characters, unlike the whores in Kenneth MacMillan's *Romeo and Juliet*, are not romanticized to add local color, they are simply there, always around, an accepted part of the Renaissance world.

Some prettier, but equally disturbing, characters in the ballet are the female attendants present in many episodes. In theatrical terms, they are functional: they facilitate scene changes by drawing curtains or otherwise rearranging the stage. But their constant presence, even at supposedly private moments, is a reminder that in Renaissance times many confidences must have been witnessed by servants who saw all, knew all, and were expected to say nothing. These particular servants could conceivably alter the tragedy by telling their secrets to their employer. But they know their place and they keep their place in an opulent world which, nonetheless, contains physical ugliness and in which calamity wears beautiful guises.

Just as *Romeo and Juliet* uncovers a blight in the Renaissance rose, so *Jardin aux Lilas* also shows pain behind splendid trappings. Unlike *Romeo*, which concentrates upon contradictions in society's external appearance, *Jardin* opposes the inner and the outer world, offering both psychological revelation and social comment. Rightfully, the psychological revelation is much admired. Tudor suggests depth of feeling by such small details as the placement of a hand in a social gesture and by such large-scale devices as the way the Mistess literally and figuratively throws herself at the man she loves, and by the lack of movement, in the most dramatic pause in all ballet, in which time momentarily stands still for Caroline.

But the ballet's social implications are equally important. One of *Jardin*'s ironies is that its people—so charming, gracious, and used to affluence—are also so bound by their social station that they cannot act freely. Affluence restricts, rather than liberates, them. Denying affection, Caroline must enter upon a marriage of convenience, probably so that she will have enough money to keep up social appearances. Propriety forbids her from going to the extreme of earning money as a shopgirl or waitress, and she probably lacks the skills necessary for such jobs, even should she decide to assert herself. Similarly, she is probably ill equipped to become a teacher or librarian, even though these are at least genteel occupations. Consequently, she marries a man she does not love.

The necessity of keeping up appearances is important to *Jardin*. The characters maintain an erect, almost stiff, stance in public; it is only fleetingly, in private, that they can unburden themselves. Truth and honesty thus become furtive things. The tone is set by the opening. Caroline and her Fiancé are seen posed decorously. Suddenly, her Lover enters and is about to greet her, but she raises her hand in warning. *Jardin* becomes a succession of stealthy approaches, hurried partings, and eventual blockages. The swirlings and interruptions make the ballet as heady as the scent of summer flowers or the taste of the wine the party guests must be drinking. Everyone in this garden hides secrets, even while trying to discover the secret of everyone else. In one episode, a slightly malicious young woman appears on the verge of discovering Caroline's secret, but Caroline is protected by a more sympathetic woman, while still a third remains mystified by the incident. I occasionally fantasize that the kindly woman is Caroline's sister, and that she may even be the party's hostess. (Determining just who is giving that party is a game dancegoers like to play. Many make Caroline the hostess, but it seems unlikely that she would leave her own party with the guests still present. Anatole Chujoy identifies the Mistress as the hostess, but, given her desperation, it is hard to believe that she would have the emotional stability to hold such a party.)

With its misalliance of external prosperity and internal misery, *Jardin* might not inappropriately serve as a socialist tract. Interpreted more broadly, it may be seen as a protest against all purely arbitrary considerations which prevent people from attaining happiness. So viewed, it remains of potential interest to everyone living under any social system this side of utopia.

In *Jardin* the threat to happiness arises from social pressures. In *Dim Lustre* the characters themselves are their own worst enemies. The ballet's premise—a love affair breaking up because both participants are preoccupied with memories of past affairs—hints it will be worldly and scintillating. Instead, it never quite succeeds in performance. The characters are superficial, and their memories, like most people's, are banal. Tudor's realistic honesty here produces drab art. *Dim Lustre* almost demands dialogue, bittersweet reflections or glittering repartee to make the characters' triviality amusing. But all Tudor's choreographic people can do is waltz. Of Tudor works which contrast inner and outer worlds, *Dim Lustre* is the one which distinguishes most carefully between these opposites. This is necessary to show unambiguously what is reality and what is memory. Unfortunately, the distinctions require cumbersome theatrical machinery, and the very separateness of the two kinds of experience weakens the ballet by making it stilted. In our own lives we pass back and forth instantaneously between perception and reflection, and in his best works Tudor also makes instantaneous progressions. For example, they occur constantly in *Pillar of Fire*.

On the surface, *Pillar of Fire* seems a straightforward presentation of events arising from Hagar's fear that the man she loves does not love her. In an impulsive moment, she shames herself, but is finally forgiven by her Friend. That much is certain. But when one examines the ballet in detail, one finds that many points are ambiguous and it becomes surprisingly difficult to determine what literally happens. Sometimes I am even tempted to say that it may all largely occur in Hagar's head. The work's peculiarities become apparent as soon as one tries to figure out just what the House Opposite is and what goes on there. It appears to be a place where studs and floozies slink, swagger, and embrace—and, in so doing, they verge upon caricature. They are not individuals, they are types. Actually, the House Opposite may be nothing more than one of those cheap rooming houses which can often appear among still respectable dwellings in old neighborhoods undergoing social upheaval. What makes it especially lurid is that we see it, not necessarily as it is, but as Hagar sees it. For Hagar, it is a shocking place.

Although *Pillar* seemingly portrays a whole community, everyone in that community is presented solely through Hagar's eyes and we have no way of knowing whether we can trust Hagar to see things truly. She is the ballet's only multidimensional character. The persons closest to her—her sisters, the two young men—are less complex, although still individualized, while everyone else is a stock, almost stereotyped, figure corresponding to some idea in Hagar's head. These characters appear at moments of despair or yearning when Hagar is troubled about love or guilt. Hagar fills the streets with her own passing fancies. When she fears spinsterhood, prim maiden ladies go out for a stroll. When she thinks about romantic love, Lovers-in-Innocence skim lightly by. And when she bursts with desire, Lovers-in-Experience flaunt themselves. That they look like characters from trashy movies or novels may be because that is the only way Hagar can imagine such people; lacking actual experience, she imagines them in terms of movies and novels, or whatever their equivalents were in her day. Significantly, they look swarthier than Hagar's own family. This, too, may be a product of Hagar's imagination, reflecting the old superstition that the lower classes or certain racial or ethnic groups (blacks, Sicilians, Puerto Ricans) possess unusual sexual powers. For someone as repressed as Hagar, the people of the House Opposite are simultaneously fearsome and enviable.

If at least some of the townspeople may be Hagar's fantasies, then the entire action becomes tantalizingly ambiguous. Without question, Hagar feels shame. But what exactly has she done? A nagging literalist might observe that, even within the terms of stage conventions, so little time elapses between her entrance into the House Opposite and her exit from it that she has not had an opportunity to indulge in much carousing. But what Hagar has or has not actually done is finally unimportant. She feels that she has crossed a forbidden threshold and degraded herself. Likewise, it is unimportant whether or not, after her shame, the townspeople really regard her with contempt. Hagar believes this is so—and psychosomatic ailments hurt as much as purely physical ones.

Because one cannot always tell what is external reality and what is fantasy for Hagar, *Pillar*'s time scheme becomes fluid and encourages speculation. Just how much time is supposed to elapse during the ballet? A year? A week? A day? One could argue a case for almost any length of time, provided that in that time there are moments of despair, shame, and forgiveness. The title supplies the final hint that *Pillar of Fire* deals with fantasy inextricably mingled with actuality. Agnes de Mille recalls that when American Ballet Theatre toured Russia, audiences asked about the title, but were satisfied to learn that it derived from the Bible. Perhaps they were too easily satisfied. For the title remains puzzling. Apparently, it comes from Exodus XIII:21, which states that during the Israelites' march out of Egypt, "the Lord went before them by day in a pillar of a cloud to lead them the way; and by night in a pillar of fire, to give them light. . . ." Just as the Bible's pillar is an extraordinary phenomenon which never vanishes, so the pillar of the ballet is an omnipresent eroticism which burns forever. It is perhaps just as well that this image is not dwelt upon explicitly in the ballet: should Hagar have recognized its phallic significance, she would surely have trembled, aghast at both her blasphemy and the ferocity of her passion.

*Pillar of Fire* makes psychological fantasy from an anecdote about a neighborhood scandal; a ballet about seemingly outer circumstances becomes essentially inner in nature. *Undertow*—with its allegorical birth scene, its mythological names for its characters, and its intention of tracing the process which causes someone to commit a sex crime—seems as though it should be predominately inward. But the ballet's inwardness is its dullest feature. The mythological names seem like the attempts of a self-educated man to demonstrate that he is as learned as any academically trained scholar, while the ballet's official psychology is simpleminded pseudo-Freudianism: maternal rejection leads to thumbsucking and then to murder.

After the prologue, *Undertow* focuses almost entirely outward upon the physical realities of slum life. Unlike the symbolic subordinate cast of *Pillar of Fire*, the subordinate cast of *Undertow*, despite the mythological names, consists of individualized people. They even get variations according to a tradition of robust character ballet. Tudor's tipsy Bacchantes mouth their song in a manner recalling the Ballad Singer in Ninette de Valois's *Rake's Progress*, and the slum dwellers mill about in a grim parallel to *Petrushka*'s fairground. *Undertow* is crammed with incessant nervous movement suggesting urban restlessness. Everyone constantly rushes to and fro, creating the effect of a low fever which in the sex scenes mounts toward hysteria. But this is not merely the Transgressor's hysteria in the sense that *Pillar of Fire* is Hagar's hysteria. This is an objective hysteria which can be noted in many cities. One can feel it as one walks down certain streets, or as one observes the fidgetiness of slum children. Things are always buzzing. Danger may lurk anywhere. No wonder the Transgressor's habitual stance is a wary half-crouch.

Tudor's slum is a place where indifference and sordidness comprise the natural state of affairs. Worse yet, these conditions are infectious. Badness corrupts the good: an older man tries to pick up little girls, a sanctimonious Salvation Army lassie makes a fumbling pass at a boy precisely when he seeks an image of unimpeachable virtue, a nasty girl beckons teasingly to boys and invites her own rape. Tudor tries to balance this tawdriness by presenting some happy working-class newlyweds. But he gives no indication that if they have come thus far through life unscathed their luck will continue indefinitely.

Except for this pair, Tudor's streets are peopled with rejects. *Undertow*'s prologue thus becomes symbolic, not merely of the protagonist's case history, but of the ballet's total social realities. Just as the mother rejects her child, so society rejects members of the human family. The mother at the end of the prologue turns slowly in a downstage corner, and when the lights come up again she has been replaced by a slowly turning prostitute, both figures suggesting degradation of affection. Later, by killing Medusa, the Transgressor hopes he has killed the evil mother who rejects her young (a point underscored by having both characters played by the same dancer.) Society then rejects him once again by passing legal judgment upon him. In the epilogue, however, he seems to accept the judgment that he is guilty. But that acceptance makes *Undertow* unnerving, for though it shows someone committing a monstrous deed for which he must be punished, it also hints that monstrousness was the condition in which he was raised and hence he cannot avoid being monstrous. The moral dilemma this poses continues to haunt psychology and penology.

*Undertow* and *Pillar of Fire* combine the inner and outer in various degrees, while *Romeo and Juliet* almost totally concerns the outer world. Two other important works, *Dark Elegies* and *Shadowplay*, look constantly inward. In writing that *Dark Elegies* is "all grieving and no corpse," Paul Gellen summarizes the usual complaints of people who dislike it. The ballet's disasters are unspecified, its tone verges upon stuffy piety, and its title, though imposing, contains a redundancy (what, after all, are "bright" elegies?). No wonder its detractors place it among those annoying ballets which try to browbeat audiences with their solemnity, but remain essentially hollow. Nor does it help that the characters are costumed like stereotypes of the noble Peasant. But neither would it be any better if, following George Jackson's suggestion, the characters looked middle-class. Those who found the peasants smug would surely loathe the burghers.

What impresses me about *Dark Elegies* is its treatment of the psychological process of mourning, the way it shows how an individual comes to terms with grief. There is no single leading individual and the ballet suggests a communal ritual. Nevertheless, through communal patterns, Tudor shows what happens within an individual in a situation of loss. The movement throughout is compulsive, repetitive. There is a much-used halting gait with arms reaching outward, then sinking weakly down. There are repeated images of cradling a child. People turn and turn, and never break free. A woman flagellates herself, then stops: no essential change appears to have occurred. A woman keeps running away, a man keeps catching her; that, too, seems to happen eternally. The ballet is like some dreaded midnight telegram read over and over again. It does not matter that we never learn what the telegram says, that we never see a corpse. This is any loss, any grief, any dislodgeable feeling of emptiness. Events recur, and before the blackout in the final scene the entire cast is running in circles.

When the lights brighten, all is as before. Only not quite. The movement remains repetitive, but there is a hint of solace in it now, and the dancers walk or crawl on their knees with quiet dignity. They seem to have realized that what is lost can never return, that loss cannot be canceled, but that mourning itself brings comfort, for through mourning they face up to their loss and accept grief, absence, and death as a part of life.

*Shadowplay*, like *Dark Elegies*, concerns a psychological process. But, maddeningly, *Shadowplay* never announces just what process it depicts. Nor does it place a value judgment upon this process. Presumably, the process relates to maturation and enlightenment, since the Boy with Matted Hair encounters, then detaches himself from, some foolish chattering monkeys, some birdlike figures, a male guru, and a woman who seems part-human, part-goddess, each encounter apparently leading to a higher state of awareness.

But *Shadowplay* is no testimonial for yoga lessons. Just what the Boy gains remains shadowy, and the ballet has faintly scandalous undertones. The scenes with the woman and the guru possess sexual implications, the guru seeming both a homosexual lover and a master (in either the pedagogical or the sadomasochist sense). After the Boy extricates himself from these situations, he does no more than pick at fleas along with the monkeys, so that the question remains whether this is liberation or another form of bondage, whether he has found true enlightenment or has only exchanged personal entanglements for emotional sterility. Like Graham in her enigmatic *Dark Meadow*, Tudor here uses psychology to explore, but not to explain. But whereas Graham has explored with passion and compassion, one cannot even be sure of Tudor's tone.

Elucidation must come from some other source than Tudor. Here, then, is the most extreme example of Opposite Houses found throughout Tudor's ballets. Usually, these "houses" are the polarities visible in the stage action. *Shadowplay* contains no visible House Opposite. Instead, its House Opposite is each individual viewer's mind. Each viewer thereby becomes a Hagar, for one can never be certain that each is seeing exactly the same ballet. *Shadowplay*'s images flicker upon the walls of our minds, and in interpreting them we may illumine our own characters, rather than Tudor's choreography. This is do-it-yourself psychoanalysis, and I suspect Tudor would smile wryly to see that, in trying to explain his ballet, we ultimately confront ourselves.

*Ballet Review* 4/6 (1974): 14–23

# PARTY MANNERS
# AND FREDERICK ASHTON

Watching the Royal Ballet perform Frederick Ashton's *Birthday Offering* in the spring of 1970, I was puzzled by its mildness. Though designed for the company's birthday festivities, it does not scintillate. With its well-tailored solos and its gracious opening and closing ensembles, it resembles one of those parties which, despite charming guests, are somehow slightly dull, since all the controversial and really interesting topics—sex, politics, religion—are studiously avoided. One longs for at least a good spicy story.

Ashton is frequently a choreographer with party manners. Many of his works are elegant or whimsical dress-up affairs; the figures in them seldom behave in ways unworthy of their station (except for comic effect), and they would never think of stripping naked in public. These characteristics give some of his ballets a genteel air which irritates me, just as I am irritated when I hear an Englishman in conversation make trivia seem profound by means of an impeccable accent.

But Ashton's ballets also contain qualities which are rare and beautiful. There is a sweetness, a vernal tenderness to his lyricism. The patterns of *Monotones* interlock with total serenity. The untroubled figures in *Symphonic Variations* have all the time in the world to move, including time to stand still. Ashton favors the curve, the arch, the flowing line which completes its course with grace, rather than abrupt impact. When bodies touch, they touch delicately and with care. Ashton's ballets suggest a love of fine behavior and a respect for the human body. These choreographic virtues are civilized virtues of a sort which is rare, on or off the stage.

Ashton's treatment of fairy tale and legend reflects his fondness for dressing-up and polished manners. He does not employ legend in the debunking, muckraking fashion of modern dancers; nor is it for him, as it is for choreographic hacks, merely an excuse to create a plushy spectacle with fat roles for all the principals. Ashton apparently likes the wonderful and extraordinary events of legends for their own fanciful sake. Thus, he tends to choose charming stories (*Cinderella, Ondine*), rather than stories fraught with menace. Here, again, is evidence of a gentle artistic temperament.

Too gentle, perhaps, I occasionally think. Some of Ashton's ballets could benefit from more iron. Even his abstractions have curious moments of insubstantiality. What prevents the lightness of *Symphonic Variations* from seeming unduly wispy are the reminders of weight which exist throughout the choreography: the way at least one couple is almost always standing still while the others move, or such suggestions of tension as those created by the women's repeated gesture of bringing their arms across their bodies. These devices are very slight—but they suffice to prevent the ballet from flying off into airy nothingness.

Several of the narrative works of Ashton with which I am familiar do not consistently have a dramatic equivalent of this weight. They lack a sense of the dark powers of the spirit—the powers of evil or of extreme passion. I do not know what philosophical convictions Ashton holds in private. His ballets suggest that man is essentially good; although susceptible to temptation, he can be restored to goodness. The hero of *The Two Pigeons* wanders but returns. Love's arrows in *Sylvia* do not produce fatal romantic infections. Neither Daphnis nor Chloë does anything really wrong; wrong is done to them, yet they emerge unscathed. Of course, these peculiarities are not Ashton's inventions; they exist in the traditional scenarios he chose—but the fact that he *chose* them suggests something about his outlook. Conceivably, such pieces I have not seen as *Dante Sonata* or *Tiresias* may refute my conclusion, but on the basis of the ballets I know, I would say that Ashton evinces little concern for the powers of darkness. (*Persephone*, a deliberate attempt to evoke primordial mysteries, looked merely crabbed the one time I saw it.)

Although I am glad that he has not dabbled in angst just for the fun of it, as dance's minor Freudians have done, Ashton's minimization of human imperfection mars, for me, several ballets, including a few that I know British dancegoers value highly. Possessing a blandness, which can become almost too smugly comfortable, they resemble certain types of British plays (*A Man for All Seasons, The Royal Hunt of the Sun*— make your own list) which are undeniably literate, yet also lacking in depth. *Marguerite and Armand* is "preposterously virginal," to borrow Edwin Denby's description of another *Camille* ballet. *Romeo and Juliet*, for the Royal Danish Ballet, captures the poignancy of young love, but is deficient in magnitude of social scale, never quite establishing that these young people are victims of a cruel dynastic war. *Illuminations* has an air of decadent elegance appropriate to its source in Rimbaud, but the action proceeds much too calmly, without Rimbaud's feverish roil of images. When the hero runs off with the gypsies in *The Two Pigeons*, I expect some contrast to be made between innocence and experience. Instead, the gypsies turn out to be merely mischievous operetta gypsies.

Equally unsatisfactory in this respect is another ballet about innocence and experience, *Daphnis and Chloë*. It has never worked for me. Its contrasts always appear tepid. Presenting the myth in modern dress is an intriguing idea, but little is done with it. The steps might just as well be performed with the cast in tunics. The quarrel of the four rivals in the first scene is nothing but mugging and obvious gesticulations. The pirates are ludicrous—no threat whatsoever. At most, they leap about with Polovetsian glee. Therefore, the restoration of Chloë fails to touch my heart: experience has been as naive as innocence. This overall blandness makes some beautiful passages in the last scene less moving than they ought to be—for example, Daphnis's ecstatic swinging of Chloë after their reunion, Chloë's solo while Daphnis plays the flute, and the way the peasants tentatively brush one foot in front of the other or quietly tap the ground as though trying to recall some age-old folk dance (one of the ballet's few instances where the combining of ancient myth and modern dress has real point).

Ashton seems best at treating passions of middling intensity which manifest themselves in foibles and peccadilloes, rather than sins and manias. Significantly, he is a great comic choreographer. *La Fille Mal Gardée* is a perfect expression of his artistic benevolence. The dramatic complications are ingenious and of great concern to the characters involved. Yet the problems can be solved, the mistakes can be mended and the mistaken forgiven. As in Molière, all balance which can be attained is attained (the lovers marry) and any remaining sources of imbalance are neutralized (Molière's hypochondriac becomes a doctor himself, Ashton's Alain goes off with his umbrella).

Each set of characters has its distinct style. The young lovers dance in a now playful, now softly melting classicism. The farmers' choreography combines classicism with folk dance borrowings to suggest the union of man with nature and a love of meaningful work. Simone, Thomas, and Alain derive from farce, pantomime, and music-hall. The dancing chickens, which some balletgoers find annoyingly "unrealistic," may be there to be deliberately artificial, to emphasize right from the start that this ballet, however homely its subject, is not photographic naturalism, but instead uses the exaggerations of comedy to point to certain human truths.

For all his love of party manners, Ashton can be aware of the occasions—particularly the comic occasions—when they block, rather than facilitate, social intercourse. The Royal Ballet's version of *Facade* made an interesting distinction between two kinds of comic style not apparent in the Joffrey Ballet's production. First, there is purely frolicsome comedy: the Scottish dancers bumping into each other, the Mountaineers pretending to be the Milkmaid's cow. (The Royal's staging of this episode contained a really gross bit which I am glad the Joffrey cast passes over: the Mountaineers grimacing over the Milkmaid's smelly feet.)

*Facade* also contains, as the Royal made wonderfully apparent, social commentary condemning the alliance of affluence and tedium. The Foxtrot dancers have the strained gaiety of tourists splurging on a Cunard Line's New Year's cruise. The Royal Ballet's Waltz (which the Joffrey performs as a parody of Balanchine) was danced by four incredibly prune-faced debutantes, Medusas of the drawing-room. The Popular Song team was lackadaisical, as though bored with their routine, their audience, and each other.

Ashton does not use comedy as a scourge. While he indicates the sins, he avoids damning the sinners—a tactful gesture about which I have mixed feelings. On the one hand, since every line of thought, taken to the extreme, may lead to the stake or concentration camp, I am glad that Ashton is not making that trip. Yet his retreat into amused tolerance can defang his humor. *Jazz Calendar*, for instance, had little of interest to say about the "swinging" London styles from which it derived. Apparently, we were supposed to be amused by the fact that the director of a Royal Ballet had done a jazz ballet at all.

In *Facade*, fortunately, Ashton makes the follies eminently clear, and then consigns his characters to the trivia they deserve. The Debutante may be a gaga nit for having gotten mixed up with that Gigolo, but the situation is not tragic or even unduly deplorable: it is, instead, a subject for gossip, and gossip can be an amusing occupation like whist or flirting.

*A Wedding Bouquet* is delicious gossip. "My *dear*, did I tell you about that wedding I went to? It was so *ghastly*, it was *marvelous*. And you'd *never* guess *who* I saw. . . !" Just as the language of gossip heightens certain characteristics at the expense of others for piquant effect, so Ashton does the same in his choreography. He has a keen eye for a person's idiosyncratic gestures, mannerisms, and ways of moving which can serve as the basis for a danced interpretation of personality. In *A Wedding Bouquet* this results in cartoons of people which can be manipulated by the choreographer in the same way we manipulate people by means of gossip. The maid is total bossiness. Arthur is completely summed up by the phrase, "Very well I thank you." The tipsy Josephine climbs upon the table and exhibits her legs (excuse me, her limbs) to every passerby. The jilted Julia is so teary with grief that she has grown squishy; she moves with all the strength of a damp washcloth. The bride and groom look as manufactured as the little dolls on the tops of wedding cakes. The accompanying Gertrude Stein narration mixes pertinence with irrelevance, just as we do in daily conversation.

Although it ends in disarray, the ballet never hints at disaster. This is not *Jardin aux Lilas*, although with the slightest shift of tone it could be. The bride and groom will ignore their fundamental indifference to each other and settle down to a busy social life. Josephine and Julia will make a career of misfortune. We shall constantly meet them at parties and excuse their weaknesses, just as we do those of our other friends who are professionally dipsomaniac or lovelorn.

Comedy—at least in certain of its older forms—assumes that errors, provided they are not monstrous, are correctable because they can be related to social or psychological structures which remain reasonably sound. Our current black comedy, in contrast, is anxious laughter in the vertigo caused by the discovery that everything, absolutely everything, is out of joint. Ashton's comedies assume that sound structures may still be found—or at least imagined.

He has also choreographed a ballet version of a play which it is now fashionable to interpret as a precursor of black comedy—*A Midsummer Night's Dream*. But *The Dream* treats the play neither as black comedy nor as the saccharine anodyne it has usually been to middle-class theatre-goers. The romantic complications are made thoroughly ridiculous, an interpretation underscored by costuming the mortals like Dickensian caricatures. But once the snarls of mistaken identity are untangled and human affection is shown to be as changeable as the wind, Titania and Oberon dance a pas de deux which is one of Ashton's most radiant inventions. The lifts are simultaneously spectacular and tender. The ceaseless curves and circles suggest that love aspires to an eternal realm. The particular infatuations of foolish mortals may be preposterous; our vision of what love can be is not.

People are capable of being better: they can dream, they can work, they can try harder. Such assumptions may seem old-fashioned and un-duly optimistic. But they have not yet been proven totally wrong, and I can conceive of no satisfactory social relationships without them.

One of Ashton's most unusual ballets on these themes is *Enigma Variations*. Formally, *Enigma* is daring—much more so than many ballets which ostentatiously proclaim their originality. For one thing, it is filled with "nondance." Elgar studies a manuscript. Two eccentrics ride bicycles. Lady Elgar examines a score. Nevinson yawns. Elgar and Jaeger gesticulate as though actually conversing in the "Nimrod" variation, which concludes with the men and Lady Elgar walking, arms linked, backs to the audience. The telegraph boy is tipped and the ballet ends with the taking of a photograph. Amidst these gestures—distillations of character traits akin to those Ashton uses in his comedies—passages of heightened movement occur like surges of feeling, as in "Nimrod" where the weighted stride of "real" walking gives way to low lifts and the long, eloquent line of classical ballet, only to subside back into walking. A master of choreographic repose, Ashton knows when not to move a dancer. In the passages for Elgar and his wife, a movement is usually allowed to come to rest before a new movement begins, which makes these actions seem to arise from deep founts of emotion.

The ballet is a quiet ode to friendship, to people one loves. The characters are not necessarily Elgar's friends as they were historically, they are his friends as he might have remembered them—an altogether different matter, since we glorify their virtues and convert their failings into eccentricities. And we see all in the light of affection.

The hero is a successful artist. What an unlikely subject for a ballet! For, as Ashton shows, artistic creation is untheatrical—a matter of solitude, work, and worry, interspersed with conversations with neighbors and confidences shared with wife and friends. Elgar is often alone. But his work and solitude are not in vain. The telegram from Richter arrives. A party is held and friends take photographs. And tomorrow the new work begins.

Art. Friendship. Meaningful work. Graciousness. Tranquillity. These are some of the things Ashton's ballets celebrate. In this respect, they are attempts to refine and better our habits and manners. So though I may cluck with irritation over what I consider to be limitations, I remain deeply grateful that such works exist. The best of them are tributes to the pleasures of being civilized.

I hope Ashton will create many more.

*Ballet Review* 3/4 (1970): 8–13

## A  M O N T H  I N  T H E  C O U N T R Y

By and large, the so-called literary ballet (the quirky mythologizing of Graham excepted) is out of choreographic favor in America.* British ballet, however, has maintained close ties to literature, examples over the years including John Cranko's *Antigone* (after Sophocles), Robert Helpmann's *Comus* (after Milton), and Frederick Ashton's *Lady of Shalott* and *Lord of Burleigh* (both after Tennyson), *The Quest* (after Spenser), *A Wedding Bouquet* (after Gertrude Stein), and *Marguerite and Armand* (after Dumas), as well as such Shakespearian ballets as Ashton's *The Dream*, Helpmann's *Hamlet*, Antony Tudor's *Cross-Gartered* (*Twelfth Night*), and the *Romeo and Juliet*s of Ashton, Cranko, and Kenneth MacMillan.

If some of these ballets are essentially only footnotes to literature, others demonstrate dance's ability to transcend source materials and achieve something uniquely kinetic. One such ballet presented by the Royal Ballet during its New York season in the spring of 1976 was Ashton's *A Month in the Country*, set to a John Lanchbery arrangement of several Chopin pieces for piano and orchestra and based upon Turgenev's comedy-drama about how both an upper-middle-class wife and her young ward become enamored of the household's new tutor. To preserve domestic tranquillity, the tutor departs, as does a dapper family friend who has previously been accepted as the wife's "admirer."

Ashton's ballet is remarkable for its unbroken flow and for its use of

---

*With the rise in popularity of full-evening narrative ballets, this may no longer be quite as true as it was when this review was written.

movement. An inheritor of classic style, Ashton often chooses to ignore traditional classic structure. Instead of dividing his works into clearly demarcated units, he lets dance flow into dance without a halt. *The Dream*, for instance, contains several brilliant variations, but not one of them reaches a full stop. The ballet's only internal break follows the duet for Titania and Oberon, the pause serving as a respite after a steady rhapsodic outpouring.

Similarly, *A Month in the Country* contains instances of what initially seem conventional variations which never attain a conventional climax or exist solely for display. A vignette in which the husband (Alexander Grant) fumbles for some missing keys is not only an amusing pas d'action, it also indicates that he is a good-hearted bumbler who cannot be the romantic idol his wife desires. A whirling solo for their son (Wayne Sleep) is punctuated by moments in which the boy must bounce a ball, the solo thereby being a portrait of a very real child, rather than just a variation for Wayne Sleep in a straw-colored wig.

As he did in *Enigma Variations*, Ashton employs ordinary gesture and pure classicism in a manner uniquely his own. His fluid structure prevents the ballet from splitting into sections equivalent to the mime episodes and dance suites of nineteenth-century ballet. But neither does Ashton blur the distinction between these ways of moving to establish still a third style from the merger, as Tudor customarily does. Instead, Ashton keeps his distinctions distinct, using, depending upon what seems appropriate, classicism at some moments and everyday gesture at others.

When Ashton wants realism, he is very realistic. This is a ballet in which every object in Julia Trevelyan Oman's country-house setting looks not only real, but literally functional. It is a ballet in which people fan themselves in the heat, work at writing desks, and carry walking sticks. Ashton's realistic effects, though ingenious, are never merely effects, for they either illuminate character or further plot development. Thus, at the first entrance of the tutor (Anthony Dowell), the bodies of the wife (Lynn Seymour) and her ward (Denise Nunn) soften and their gazes turn moonstruck. Later, when the wife touches the tutor impulsively in greeting, she suddenly recoils, as though afraid she had committed an indiscretion. Alternations of ordinary and classical movement often make telling points. At the beginning, for example, the members of the family are seen posed in stiff gentility, but as soon as the husband leaves on an errand they dance vivaciously, as though his absence had granted them freedom.

In a uniformly excellent cast, Lynn Seymour ranks first among equals because of her ability to make the wife almost absurd yet heartbreakingly pathetic. When she dances with the tutor, the movements in their pas de deux both ascend with rapture and sink toward intimacy. When her husband demands an explanation of her apparent impropriety, her gestures turn brittle, as though she were trying to minimize the situation by laughing it off. But when she is left alone at the conclusion, her resignation suggests not simply the end of an affair which has scarcely begun, but the end of youth and of all future possibility of romance. *A Month in the Country* may be based upon literature, but because of Ashton's fresh use of movement the ballet does not suggest literature but life itself.

"Life, Literature, and the Royal Ballet," *Dance Magazine* (August 1976): 46–48

# ROBBINS'S NEW BALLET
# MAY MEAN MANY THINGS

alletgoers seem agreed that *In Memory of* . . . , Jerome Robbins's latest work for the New York City Ballet, is a choreographic meditation upon life, love, and loss and that Suzanne Farrell gives a memorable performance in its central role. But one matter about which there is no agreement is whether or not the eloquent new ballet to Alban Berg's Violin Concerto contains what could be called "hidden" or "secret" meanings. In fact, the whole issue of the ballet's possible meanings is well worth considering.

The work's action is clear enough. Farrell, who portrays a charming young woman, dances with a well-mannered young man (Joseph Duell and Alexandre Proia have both appeared in this role) and they are joined by other young and loving couples. Wearing costumes by Dain Marcus that are balletic stylizations of street clothes, they dance tenderly and playfully together. But, at times, they appear to experience mysterious feelings of unrest. During one such moment, they march stiffly, as if responding to urban anxiety or a threat of war, and Adam Lüders enters, as if he were yet another of the young men.

But he proves to be Death, and he has come to claim Farrell. She struggles with him until he subdues her, and she grows resigned to her fate. Members of the ensemble return, now wearing plain white costumes and moving slowly and serenely. Farrell enters their midst. At last, both Death and the young man she loves walk with her, as if toward paradise, and the work ends as the men raise her aloft.

The ballet emphasizes two themes often associated with Romantic art, themes that can be summed up by borrowing the titles of two famous pieces of music: "Death and the Maiden" (Schubert) and "Death and Transfiguration" (Richard Strauss). Through his emphasis upon Romantic imagery, Robbins may be wishing to point out that, in addition to being an explorer of serial-music techniques, Berg was also the inheritor of a whole tradition of Romantic music, and in such scores as the yearning, elegiac Violin Concerto he did not repudiate that tradition. Robbins's scenario even choreographically alludes to the circumstances that inspired the concerto, for Berg composed it after the death of a young friend, Manon Gropius (daughter of Alma Mahler and the architect Walter Gropius), who succumbed to polio at the age of 18 on Easter Sunday 1935. Berg himself died suddenly only seven months later, before the concerto could be performed.

Surely, few dancegoers would question this interpretation of the ballet. The controversies that surround it all involve speculations about secret meanings. Several factors have prompted the search for such meanings. First of all, the New York City Ballet's Playbill contains an excerpt from George Perle's *Operas of Alban Berg (Volume Two: "Lulu")*, in which that eminent composer and Berg scholar concludes—in part, on the basis of numerological symbolism in the score—that the Violin Concerto contains references to Berg's own life. Therefore, according to this argument, the concerto is not only a memorial to Manon Gropius, but also a work that could be regarded as Berg's monument to himself. Such auto-biographical touches are by no means uncommon in music: Bach incorporated the letters of his name into his music, Schumann referred to himself and his friends in several compositions, and the hero Richard Strauss celebrated in "Ein Heldenleben (A Hero's Life)" happens to be none other than Richard Strauss.

No one, to my knowledge, claims that Robbins's ballet is about Berg's life. Yet Perle's speculations have made balletgoers wonder just who *In Memory of . . .* may be in memory of. The most frequently advanced answer to that question is George Balanchine. Robbins has never concealed his admiration for Balanchine, and a tribute from Robbins to Balanchine is only fitting and proper. The theory that *In Memory of . . .* is indeed such a tribute is strengthened by the fact that it stars Farrell, a ballerina who created many roles for Balanchine, but who has not often worked with Robbins. Therefore, her mystical transfiguration in the finale can be seen as an affirmation that Balanchine's art will live on.

However, once one grants the validity of the notion that *In Memory of . . .* may contain levels of meaning, then one may find it as rich in significance as it is rich in choreographic invention. I made some interpretative flights of fancy of my own after one performance by the New York City Ballet when *In Memory of . . .* was preceded by Robbins's *Andantino*, a sweet pas de deux to the slow movement of Tchaikovsky's Piano Concerto No. 1. This duet in no way seemed alien to the one that opens *In Memory of . . . .*

The fact that lyrical movements to Tchaikovsky appeared to be similar in spirit to lyrical movements to Berg can be viewed as yet another example of Robbins's response to the Romantic elements in the Berg concerto. But I also started wondering if Robbins in his new ballet may be looking over his past choreography and finding that he, too, is something of a Romantic. He may have made his choreographic debut with a jazzy work about sailors on shore leave and he may have amazed audiences with ballet choreography about voracious insects and Broadway choreography about street-gang rumbles, yet he has also been a choreographer who at times has not been afraid to wear his heart on his sleeve.

Certain passages of *In Memory of . . .* may be compared with other ballets by Robbins. Just as the lyricism of the opening recalls *Andantino*, so the communal dances for the young people may recall Robbins's *Dances at a Gathering*, to Chopin piano music. The moments of unrest in the Berg ballet have a parallel in a scene of storm and stress near the end of *Dances at a Gathering*. Whereas the young people in *Dances* gain the courage to endure and continue, the unrest in the Berg ballet presages the coming of death. Yet the transfiguration scenes of *In Memory of . . .* suggest that Farrell has now joined the dances at some celestial gathering. The use of slow motion and walking steps in those scenes reminds one that both Robbins's *Afternoon of a Faun* and his *Watermill*, an allegorical depiction of the course of life, emphasize slow motion. And if the entire Berg ballet has the quality of a dream or a vision, it should not be forgotten that Robbins once titled a work *Opus 19 / The Dreamer*.

The melancholy life of Manon Gropius. Berg's affinities with Romanticism. The persistence of Romantic longings in life and art. Philosophical ruminations upon Robbins's own choreographic art. The inevitability of death, the death of a great choreographer, and the cherishing of his ballets. *In Memory of . . .* may be about all of these things. Then again, it may not. My speculations may be as insubstantial as passing clouds. When critics used to present Balanchine with elaborate explications of his ballets, he usually responded to these exegeses in the same way. "Too fancy!" he would declare. So these remarks may very well be too fancy.

Yet *In Memory of . . .* does invite musing and pondering, and not simply because it is a work by a distinguished choreographer created two years after the death of another distinguished choreographer. *In Memory of . . .* seems artfully constructed and rich in emotional depth. Like the Berg concerto to which it is set, it is more than an ingenious compositional exercise; it is a heartfelt creation. Robbins's ballet can speak for itself, and it will surely say many things to many people.

*New York Times*, 30 June 1985

# SOME PERSONAL GRUMBLES

# ABOUT MARTHA GRAHAM

At some point during Martha Graham's 1967 New York season, a disquieting thought entered my head: I realized that I did not like the choreography I was watching. At first, I refused to believe it. How could I not like these dances? Graham is a Major Choreographer who attempts Great Themes. She is a Vital Force, a Pioneer of American Dance. A season by her company is a Significant Cultural Event. Graham is no mere choreographer, she is the center of a mystique, a mystique far more intense than that which surrounds such phenomena as Balanchine, the Bolshoi, Nureyev, or the Judson Dance Theatre.

As a student of dance history, I am well aware of Graham's significance. As an American, I shall stoutly defend Graham against the sniping of any Briton still disturbed by the spectacle of "barefoot dancing." But as a member of the audience—furthermore, as a member of the audience who makes a distinction between going to the theatre and going to church—my feelings about Graham are very different. For a time, I had no clearly defined feelings about Graham. I was cowed by the Graham cult. Now, perhaps, as a reaction against the Graham cult I may regard her choreography more harshly than I shall at some future date. The fact remains: this spring I discovered I disliked it.

Disliked what? Not everything, surely. Although it was not in the repertoire last spring, I do not think that, if I saw it again, I would dislike *Primitive Mysteries*. Indeed, if I were asked to name what I considered the greatest single work by an American choreographer, I would probably answer *Primitive Mysteries*, a dance which miraculously balances restraint and rapture. And there are other works I like, too: *Diversion of Angels* and *Secular Games*, *Frontier* and *Appalachian Spring*, and a few more.

But what I do not like very much are the dances of the sort to which Graham has devoted most of her talents since the 1940s, the dances based upon mythology, literature, or history. These dances are the ones for which Graham is now best known (as a historian, I realize that Graham in the past choreographed several different kinds of dances—I wish I could have seen them!) These mythological dances are the ones which are taken most seriously by critics. And they are the ones which, with a few exceptions, bore me.

Formally, they do not bore me. Formally, I find them very interesting. The typical Graham mythological dance begins at a crucial moment in the protagonist's life, then proceeds both forward and backward in time, the protagonist remembering her past or jumbling it in some psychologically significant pattern as she goes toward her destiny. This dance form derives from the human ability to remember one thing while simultaneously doing other things. Onstage, it has potent theatricality. If she had contributed nothing else to dance, Graham would be considered important simply for developing this form of choreography. Unfortunately, I am seldom interested in how Graham uses this form.

Graham's sense of characterization is sometimes erratic. Her male characters are dully conceived, tending to be muscular dimwits, undeniably virile, but possessing little emotional or moral complexity. They are gymnasts, or satyrs, or stuffed shirts—or sometimes all three, but not much else. In contrast, Graham's women are so spirited and idiosyncratic that it is hard to understand why they bother with such fatuous men. However, these are minor matters.

Far more serious, for me, is the muddiness of some of Graham's narratives. If one does not already know the myths on which they are based, one may have trouble following the action of the dances. This is a peculiar state of affairs, for it is a refutation of an argument sometimes advanced in defence of the theatrical use of myth: the contention that myths, taken from a common storehouse of knowledge shared by literate theatregoers, contribute to clarity. Being more interested in the *how* and the *why* of an action than in its *what*, Graham may have seen in the use of myth a way to concentrate upon meaning and motivation without having to worry about the comprehensibility of the story. For the story would already be familiar. Thus, over the years Graham has utilized such familiar stories as those of Oedipus and Jocasta, Medea and Jason, Adam and Eve, Orestes and Electra, and Judith and Holofernes.

If myth rescued Graham from one set of difficulties, repeated use of myth has caught her in another trap. She has used up a good many of the familiar myths. But having once started upon systematically reinterpreting the myths of Western culture, it must be hard to stop ransacking *The Age of Fable* for source materials. The process can become a compulsion akin to doing crossword puzzles or nibbling potato chips. Graham's new *Cortege of Eagles* is based upon the murder of Polydorus, the blinding of Polymnestor, the sacrifice of Astyanax and Polyxena, and the grief of Hecuba. This is a very complicated plot, and the characters are not as familiar as Oedipus, Orestes, or Medea. The structure of the dance is the typically Graham one employing fragmented and telescoped time. The result is a grand muddle, not unlike a crotchety passage in Ezra Pound— but worse, since one can always interrupt reading to look up a reference in the *Cantos*, but cannot very well ask Graham to interrupt her dance while one mulls over who is supposed to be who in it. Graham's use of myth has come full circle. Originally adopted as a way to clarify action, myth in Graham's newest work has increased the action's opacity.

Little of this would matter, or matter much, if only Graham were able to invest the old myths with striking new meanings. Throughout the centuries, dramatists have employed myth and history to do just this. Shakespeare's chronicle plays are an analysis of the qualities requisite for a good monarch. Shaw retells the story of St. Joan to comment upon the origins of the Protestant spirit and to examine what fate is likely to befall a prophet or saint in any society. In such plays as *Tiger at the Gates* and *Electra*, Giraudoux uses Greek myths to reveal the destructive tendencies inherent in chauvinism and fanaticism.

Drama is not simply a visual art, it is also verbal, and intellectual concepts are most easily expressed by means of words. All the plays cited above are plays of notable linguistic power—it is through language that ideas crystallize and it is through their mastery of language that these playwrights have been able to crystallize their particular ideas. One reason why a work like *Mourning Becomes Electra* is, for all its virtues, not really a great play is that O'Neill's language is never quite equal to his obviously noble intentions. Dancers who treat comparable themes in a similar manner are in danger of producing dances akin to the plays of O'Neill—ambitious in intent, but flawed in execution. Worse still, they may choreograph dances which seem desperately in need of words, dances which seem not dances at all but crippled dramas.

Even when most seriously concerned with plot and characterization, a choreographer is not a dramatist. Despite the claims of Leroy Leatherman in his *Martha Graham* (Knopf, 1966), Graham is not a dramatist, her works are not plays. Therefore, any new meanings which Graham finds in old myths ought to be unlike the ideas a playwright would find; for if they do resemble a playwright's ideas, they will probably be inferior to them since they lack words. To me, Graham's meanings are not always very interesting. For example, in *Legend of Judith*, Judith mentally confuses the hated Holofernes with her adored dead husband; and in *Phaedra*, Hippolytus's sexual proclivities are ambiguous. But compared with the way history and mythology have been reinterpreted by the playwrights, such notions seem paltry.

Instead of investing myths with new meanings, Graham has adorned them with symbols. A symbol may easily seem profound. But it need not be. A symbol may be only a glorified cliché. Moreover, there is a certain type of symbolism which even tends to invalidate the claim that dance is worthy of being regarded as a major art form: the use of a symbol as a pictograph, as a substitute for a written or spoken word. If through gestures, stage action, or the use of props dancers seek to create what might be called unspoken words, then they come dangerously close to making dance subordinate to drama or poetry. If dance cannot express something other than words or beyond words, then it is only a poor relation of literature. Through her symbolism, Graham has probably unwittingly made a kind of literary dance. In *Cave of the Heart* the enraged Medea performs a solo while pulling a red string from the bosom of her dress. This string really symbolizes a snake which really symbolizes diabolical cunning. Later, Medea locks herself inside a spiky sculptural construction. This really symbolizes evil and Medea's isolation from common humanity. In *Night Journey* Oedipus and Jocasta on their marriage bed get entangled in some cords. These cords are really umbilical cords. And, for me, they are also faintly comic: is the palace housekeeping so bad that the servants leave ropes in the Royal Bed? (Graham's devotées will here accuse me of frivolity, yet it is my conviction that, before it can function as a symbol of a broader meaning, an object must first make sense simply as an object.)

Graham's symbolism can become as annoying as a dig in the ribs. A friend who agreed that parts of *Night Journey* were labored pointed out that the dances for the chorus called Daughters of the Night were beautifully suggestive of impending doom. They are. Then why not discard Oedipus, Jocasta, and the resounding symbols and just have a doom-ridden mood study called *Daughters of the Night?* But Graham would probably never think of doing such a thing. Oedipus, Jocasta, and the Symbols are undoubtedly what interest her most.

However, in at least two works Graham has splendidly managed to justify the use of historical or mythic materials: *Seraphic Dialogue* (concerning St. Joan) and the evening-long *Clytemnestra*. Superficially, they resemble *Cave of the Heart, Night Journey, Phaedra*, and others, yet each contains something special, something appropriate to movement theatre, rather than to verbal theatre. In contrast to those creations in which Graham tries to plaster layers of significance upon a story, *Seraphic Dialogue* is simplicity itself. At the moment of her exaltation, the spirit of Joan remembers herself as Maid, as Warrior, and as Martyr, then is led by angels into sainthood. Here, instead of symbolical meanings, Graham seeks bodily states of feeling, things which words can only describe but which dance can create directly and poignantly. *Seraphic Dialogue* becomes a beautiful depiction of religious ecstasy.

*Clytemnestra* achieves its power by means of insistent repetition. Clytemnestra, dishonored among the dead, relives the turbulent events of her life, at first in a confused, hysterical fashion, then with increasing clarity until, finally, she achieves spiritual rebirth. Possibly because in dance, as in other arts, vices tend to be more interesting than virtues, I find the rebirth unconvincing—although Clytemnestra strides about waving a laurel branch, dancers representing deities pose in benign attitudes, and vocal soloists carol, "Rebirth! Rebirth!" (Saying something is so does not necessarily mean that it is so.) What I do find impressive about *Clytemnestra* is not its conclusion, but its process of coming to its conclusion, the obsessive, nearly hypnotic way in which events recur again and again like memories which will not be dislodged. The sheer physicality of dance gives this recurrence a solidity and forcefulness a page of literature could duplicate only with extreme difficulty.

But even here, and to a much greater extent elsewhere, the preoccupation with myths and symbols makes much of Graham's work weighty in a manner I find weary. Despite her "modern" psychoanalytic references and chopped-up time schemes, Graham is surprisingly Victorian in the solemnity of her moral earnestness. Her compositions have the bulk and minuteness of detail of many nineteenth-century novels. This accumulation of information, whereby each gesture is dutifully invested with psychological or religious significance, robs much of Graham's choreography of the mystery and wonder it might otherwise possess. Like an earnest Victorian, Graham has an explanation for everything. It is perhaps this tendency to underscore her explanations which gives Graham's dances, for all their bloody plots and wild-eyed heroines, an aura of smugness.

Earlier in her career, such earnestness may have scared off a segment of the audience. For those people, Graham was too "highbrow." Today, in our era of monumental civic cultural centers, this same quality may attract another segment of the audience to her: eager pursuers of culture who have discarded the philistine notions that the performing arts are trivial or immoral, but who demand that art be unremittingly solemn, who almost seem to think, so far as dance is concerned, that if a dance is solemn it must automatically be Good, Edifying, and a Major Expression of Western Values. These are the dancegoers for whom Martha Graham is inseparable from all the fine words in capital letters. For them, Martha Graham is Culture; for them, she plays a role not unlike that played a few years ago by T. S. Eliot.

Everyone offered official obeisance to Eliot. But in the privacy of their pads and mimeographed magazines, the young poets proclaimed him a bad literary influence. So, too, with Graham. No important younger choreographer at present—not even any of those who danced devotedly and well for years in the Graham company—is creating mythic or literary dances inspired by Graham. The myths may still take the fancy of the critics, the audiences, the Jungian dabblers—but the choreographers, the creative artists, are all doing something else.

Yet here is an irony of sorts. I do not like Graham's mythological choreography. Still, it forces me to sit down and seriously try to think why. Most choreographers I do not like I can brush aside by citing blatant inadequacies. The works of Graham resist such brusque treatment. In this, too, Graham resembles Eliot. One may not like such an artist, one may be totally exasperated by such an artist, yet one knows that the artist is no fool. She cannot easily be dismissed. She cannot be ignored.

(And yet, dammit, and yet: I do not really like, I cannot get myself to like, the mythological dances of Martha Graham.)

*Ballet Review* 2/1 (1967): 25–30

## A  HEADY  SEASON

ivine Turbulence be ours . . ." begins one of the St. John Perse quotations Martha Graham utilized in a new work this season. The quotation is appropriate, not only to that particular work, but to Graham's choreography in general.

Graham is a choreographer of turbulence; her dances spring from turmoil. Much of her choreography consists of tense, broken patterns and gestures which withdraw inward just as they seem to be offering something outward. Lurches forward are often braked by sudden pulls backward, causing parts of the body to protrude while the rest of the body strives to move on. The first and last gestures of the Chorus in *Cave of the Heart*, Graham's version of *Medea*, offer striking examples of gestural turbulence. The Chorus, the sympathetic commentator upon this grisly myth, first raises one hand heavenward to request divine aid in telling her story, then covers her mouth in horror as she realizes the monstrousness of the story she has to tell. And once Medea has wreaked her terrible vengeance, the Chorus, after looking wonderingly toward the gods, buries her face in her robes, unable to behold any more pain.

Such turbulence is by no means found only in Graham's serious pieces. It occurs in lighter works as well, even in such a celebratory dance as *Diversion of Angels*. Although the movements are wide and open, there are surprising moments when the men in their leaps suddenly seem hunched-in because they have shifted their focus downward. And in a sequence of extensions—with the arms and raised leg pointing like arrows—there are times when, instead of tautening, the body unpredictably crumples up.

These passages were beautifully performed by Takako Asakawa during the 1973 season at the Alvin Theatre, a season which allowed audiences to see a sampling from the Graham repertoire for the first time in two years. Some of the members of the reorganized company—including such stalwarts as Mary Hinkson, Matt Turney, and Bertram Ross—have long been familiar to dancegoers. But there were also some promising younger dancers, and certain dancers who were rising into prominence in previous seasons (among them Takako Asakawa and Ross Parkes) have made remarkable progress. On the whole, the company lacks the polish of other Graham ensembles. Yet these are appealing dancers whose performances, though occasionally rough, are always fresh. And, thank heaven, they largely avoid the pontifical, self-congratulatory quality which occasionally made past Graham programs seem, not dance events, but gatherings of a sect of choreographic True Believers.

The ensemble appeared to good advantage in *Secular Games*, a whimsical piece which manages to express many characteristic Graham attitudes. The first movement, subtitled "Play with thought—on a Socratic island," starts in silence with six young men tossing a ball (symbolizing the progress of thought or conversation, perhaps). They look alert: indeed, they even look sexy—and Graham later shows why she wants them to look this way. Once Robert Starer's music begins, turmoil takes over: two men wrestle, one does a yoga shoulder stand, another juts sideways. But this turmoil is the invigorating turmoil of bright ideas or serious conversation. During the second movement, "Play with dream—

on a Utopian island," the women enter, and the choreographic contrasts between dreamy remoteness and contact with the ground—including a kittenish sequence involving a cloth which serves, in turn, as Denishawn veil, beach towel, and security blanket—act as reminders that utopian visions are simply projections of earthly forms. No wonder, then, that the finale, "Play—on any island," is an erotic romp: since human beings possess bodies as well as minds, they can play with both flesh and spirit. The play of ideas and sex play are charmingly joined.

Such unions do not come easily to Graham, who, as choreographer, is preoccupied with physicality, and yet is often revolted by it. This sort of dichotomy may derive from America's Puritan inheritance, and Graham's continued fascination with it accounts for the power of some of her works and the aggravations of others.

She tries to resolve the dichotomy in *Appalachian Spring*, in which the characters are products of a Calvinistic revivalist tradition. Much of *Appalachian* looks too insistently cute today: it served, after all, as a kind of morale booster for the home front during World War II. Moreover, the present cast accentuates its weaknesses. Phyllis Gutelius is coquettish, rather than artless, as the Wife, while William Carter, though basically appealing, could add still more sturdiness to his portrayal of the Husband. Traci Musgrove is almost totally devoid of the vein of iron which can make the Pioneering Woman an effective counterforce to Bertram Ross's effusive Revivalist.

But, even with its weaknesses, *Appalachian* is more than a folksy diversion: it meditates upon the dualism of flesh and spirit and the paradoxes of that dualism. With his own body, the preacher flings out stern warnings against the temptations of the body. However, his followers, who scamper about like little squirrels, are entirely female and are infatuated with him, not as a theologian, but as an attractive man. The folk wisdom of the Pioneering Woman tempers religious hysteria, and the ballet suggests that love, neighborliness, and meaningful work can triumph over guilt-ridden brooding upon man's fallen state.

Other religious tensions appear in *El Penitente*, Graham's depiction of a passion play staged by members of a flagellant cult in the Southwest.

Whereas *Appalachian Spring* seems to develop toward religious human-ism, the implications of *El Penitente* are far more unsettling—and fas-cinating. Flesh and spirit intermingle in unexpected ways. For one thing, the sect portrayed confuses all the Marys of the Bible, since the same dancer enacts each of them, turning at a moment's notice from Mary the Blessed Virgin to Mary the errant Magdalen. As Magdalen, she corrupts the Penitent (David Hatch Walker), and so the Penitent must be punished. But the punishment meted out by Christ (Tim Wengerd) is a mere slap on the cheek as though the Penitent were a naughty schoolboy. Sensuality leads to sin and must be punished; yet, though man is by na-ture a sinner, Christ's mercies are infinite. Appropriately, the Magdalen's dance of temptation is filled with hip thrusts (and Takako Asakawa does them most fetchingly). But the joyous dance after salvation has been granted is also based upon hip thrusts. Apparently, sensuality cannot be totally quenched; it only returns in a new guise. *El Penitente* is the oldest work in the present repertoire. Louis Horst's score possesses verve and snap, and the bluntness of Graham's choreography serves as an appeal-ing relief from the almost tropical lushness of her later efforts. It whets the appetite for further Graham revivals.

Reactions to Graham change with the changing times. Once—and not so long ago, either—her most admired works were those deriving from mythology and history. But some of these proved to be very weak this season. Wrenched with agony, boiling with turmoil, they nevertheless seemed peculiarly monotonous.

Takako Asakawa's Medea in *Cave of the Heart*—her face contorted with hatred, her hands clawing the air, her body shaking in spasms as though vomiting—was a creature of pure fury. As the perfidious Jason, Ross Parkes straddled two boulders like the Colossus of Rhodes and strutted with clenched fists in the athletically brutal fashion typical of many men in Graham's mythological ballets: part acrobat, part stud, he was irresistibly attractive and thoroughly loathsome.

Yet, despite its horrific action, *Cave of the Heart* soon loses my inter-est. It is much too schematic. Each of its personages is one thing and one thing only. They are not people but character types. Eventually, they

grow monochromatic. That this weakness may be fundamentally choreographic, rather than a quirk of casting, was demonstrated at a performance when Mary Hinkson portrayed Medea. Whereas Asakawa raged,
Hinkson was pained and aggrieved. It was a completely different interpretation, yet equally monochromatic. Conceivably, a performance which
began with Hinkson's tears and ended with Asakawa's venom could be
shattering, but the choreography may not permit such extreme internal
progressions.

In several Graham dance-dramas the figures have easily identifiable
character traits, but no personalities, if by personality is meant the specific ways in which all the different, and sometimes contradictory, character traits a person possesses manifest themselves in behavior. Graham
tends to label people, and even though the labels may be drawn from the
latest psychological theory, they remain labels. Since this is a practice
akin to allegorizing, it is not surprising that one of Graham's best dramatic works, *Seraphic Dialogue*, is a variant of a medieval morality play.

Graham's penchant for schematization became distressingly evident in
the much-awaited revival of *Clytemnestra*. Heretofore, I rated it, along
with Ashton's *Fille Mal Gardée* and the complete version of Merce Cunningham's *Canfield*, as one of the few successful modern evening-length
ballets. But at the Alvin it was tedious.

Dramatically, the ballet shows Clytemnestra in her private mental hell
reliving the events of her life. Choreographically, the ballet is organized
into blocklike, incessant, repetitive units. Guilt and grief have settled
permanently into Clytemnestra's mind as unbudgeable obsessions. The
entire ballet has a mechanized quality: significantly, Clytemnestra's first
dance involves a ceaseless drumming of her hands. The work is a huge
perpetual motion machine in which everything is locked into itself and
keeps on doing the same thing over and over. Conceivably, it could be
half its present length or three times as long and no one might know the
difference, for the same events and attitudes would always recur.

This is total determinism. Unfortunately—leaving aside the question
of determinism's validity as a scientific or philosophical concept—this
particular theatrical manifestation of it is unsatisfactory. To meet the

characters once or twice is to know almost all there is to know about them. Each consists of a limited number of attitudes and behavior patterns, and there are few surprises (the device of having the same dancer portray both Agamemnon and Orestes now seems elementary in its psychology). The resultant ballet proves enervating rather than liberating, and Graham's attempt at the end to break the determinism by granting Clytemnestra redemption appears unmotivated and arbitrary, a happy ending tacked onto a work which, given its basic premises, would otherwise be endless.

If *Clytemnestra* looked obvious, the season's two premieres were both terribly obscure. But one was so lovely that, even if it could not be intellectually explicated, it still could be emotionally experienced. The other, *Myth of a Voyage* (to an efficient, if unmemorable score by Alan Hovhaness), offered a muddled retelling of the *Odyssey* in which Graham suggested that she was playing with obfuscation for its own sake. Ming Cho Lee's setting, a rope construction with hints of looms, flowers, crossbows, and cat's cradles, was all too appropriately snarled and tangled.

The action consisted of Bertram Ross embarking upon adventures which could be traced back to Homeric sources. A mysterious unattainable woman (Takako Asakawa, identified in the program as the Goddess of Change) led him onward, while another woman (Matt Turney, dancing with the quiet dignity she brought to all her roles this season) acted as a comforting presence. The choreography was patchy. Character development and narration remained unclear, and no momentum existed to propel the action from episode to episode. The most striking moment, in fact, was largely static: Ross lay exhausted on the ground, while the rest of the cast passed slowly across the back of the stage like figures on a frieze.

Clearly enough, Matt Turney played Penelope to Ross's Odysseus. However, the program called her "The Gray-Eyed One," an epithet associated with Athena, goddess of wisdom. At the end of the ballet, the two principals joined hands, as though about to settle down together, the implication here being that wisdom equaled domesticity—a sentimental notion totally unworthy of Graham. But then, once again, Change appeared and Ross looked toward her. Apparently, this Odysseus can never fully settle down.

Neither, fortunately, can Graham. In *Mendicants of Evening*, the other premiere, she has created her most beautiful ballet in many a season, a ballet in which the choreography glows with a soft radiance amid Fangor's setting of colored panels and silky draperies. Like certain surrealist paintings or Graham's own *Dark Meadow*, the images of this work remain totally private, yet manage to be compelling. Let me hazard some guesses about them, being fully aware as I do so that this analysis may be far from what Graham herself intended.

Bertram Ross portrays a character that the program calls The Poet, while Matt Turney (identified as The Guide) is a muse. Above the solemn bell sounds and low murmurs of David Walker's electronic score, Marian Seldes (termed The Witness in the program) speaks lines by St. John Perse which, though cryptic, consist essentially of a hymn to the wonders of the universe: these are, presumably, the poems Ross's Poet has written, his testimony and testament. The three principals wrap and unwrap themselves in heavy draperies variously recalling robes, cocoons, swathes, and shrouds. The movements assigned to Marian Seldes, who is not a dancer but an actress, have such a fluid grace that they suggest that, should Graham ever decide to abandon choreography, she could enjoy a new career as a director of plays or operas.

Around the principals, and in contrast to their stateliness, the ensemble swoops and swirls like The Poet's flights of fancy or like the flux of existence itself. Dancers melt together, indulge in bits of rivalry or meet in erotic encounters, then break away and sweep rhapsodically off. Even when they occasionally are caught in the draperies of the others, they manage to regain their fleet independence. At the conclusion, The Poet removes his robes as though willing to bare himself to the possibilities of new experience, a gesture which, like the entire work, seems a declaration of faith.

"Divine Turbulence be ours," Marian Seldes recites, and I want to reply, "Yea, verily." Elsewhere, she says, if my ears heard rightly, "Those who are in the midst of things do not speak of dust and ashes." Still creative, still controversial, Martha Graham remains very much in the midst of things.

*Dance Magazine* (July 1973): 42A–42D

# DANCES ABOUT EVERYTHING AND
# DANCES ABOUT SOME THINGS

*M*erce Cunningham has often been a problem. His nonliteral choreography has been a problem. His treatment of music and décor has been a problem. His utilization of chance has been a problem.

The latest problem Cunningham has posed for dancegoers is that of the Theatre Event. Events, as Cunningham uses the term, consist of sections of previously choreographed dances (and, occasionally, of new dances still in rehearsal) performed not as a suite of detachable items, as they would be in a divertissement, but rearranged so that they form a self-sufficient entity. These Events—lasting about an hour and a half, without intermission—employ musical scores and costumes different from those associated with the discrete pieces from which the movements derive; and, given the extent of the Cunningham repertoire and the almost infinite number of ways sections from it may be rearranged, it is likely that no two Events will ever be exactly the same. As for their intended effect, Cunningham claims that Events "allow for, not so much an evening of dances, as the experience of dance."

James Klosty's book *Merce Cunningham* (Saturday Review Press, 1975) indicates that Cunningham has grown increasingly fond of Events. Certainly, in recent years, his company has presented almost nothing but Events in the New York area. The first Event ever took place in 1964 in Vienna; the first I encountered was #25 at Brooklyn College in December 1971. A recent Event I attended at the Cunningham studio—in December 1975, only four years later than my first—was #151. These figures and dates in themselves attest to Cunningham's interest in Events.

One's first Event, if bewildering, may also be fun. It's a lark—"something different." But as Event follows Event, bewilderment may turn to dismay as it dawns upon one that Events, far from being regarded as mere novelties, have been legitimized as major endeavors by the Cunningham company. Moreover, they raise fearful questions, not only about the nature of Cunningham's art, but about art in general. The kinds of questions they invite are those implicit in the shocked exclamation of a friend a few years ago after attending some Cunningham Events: "He's dismantling his repertoire!"

As is often true of developments in the performing arts, Cunningham's current predilections may involve practicality as well as pure aesthetics. By mixing older works together, Cunningham may keep much of his repertoire active. Simultaneously, he can try out new composers and designers. The flexibility of the Event format makes it possible to adapt his choreography to each fresh performing situation he encounters: Events fit easily into studios, gyms, museums, and lofts, as well as into conventional theatres. Yet, ultimately, these are Cunningham's concerns, not those of the audience. Audiences always want a "good show." If a certain performance procedure cannot produce one, then it should be scrapped, no matter how otherwise practical it is. Thus, we are led from practical to aesthetic difficulties. And, to some dancegoers, they seem enormous.

Still, Events should not have prompted quite the amount of shocked surprise that they did, since they can be interpreted as logical outgrowths of basic Cunningham theories. Cunningham has always been fascinated by fluid performing situations, by live theatre as something inherently unfixed. In dance of any kind, even when choreography is scrupulously set, no two performances will ever be exactly the same because of the cast's differing physical and mental conditions at each of those performances. To go to the theatre is always chancy. Cunningham has long capitalized upon theatre's uncertainties. For instance, he has created dances consisting of several parts which can be performed in any number of possible orders. Similarly, the music and décor for his pieces occupy the same space and time as the dance but usually do not imitate or logically relate to anything in the choreography—a practice which makes Cunningham simultaneously a Diaghilevian and a non-Diaghilevian choreographer: Diaghilevian because he commissions composers and painters, non-Diaghilevian because he makes no effort to have all parts of a production lock tightly together like pieces of a jigsaw puzzle. Once the parts of a single piece are regarded as potentially interchangeable, one is only a short step of the imagination away from thinking that all parts of all one's pieces are similarly interchangeable, and when that step is taken the Event is born. But some audiences may wonder whether that step ought to be taken. Has Cunningham this time really gone too far?

Unquestionably, the Events intimidate. To begin with, there is often nothing—or very little—that one can say about them. We are such verbal creatures that not being able to come up with a well-organized verbal assessment of our perceptions can be frustrating. No wonder a few critics are particularly annoyed by Events, for critics are by necessity the most verbal dancegoers of all. But what is there to say about an Event?

Well, one could try to describe it. Most Events are open in form, but some exhibit simple structural characteristics which may be noted. Thus, one recent Event was, whether by forethought or happenstance, constructed according to a pattern which Louis Horst, after gnashing his teeth, might have classified as extended ABAB or rondo form: a group section was followed by a solo which was followed by another group, and so on. One could continue trying to say something about an Event by recording in exact detail each action as it occurred. If one possessed the necessary skills, one could even notate it.

But what really would be accomplished by that? For there might still exist an inexplicable gap between the actions themselves and one's responses of delight, horror, or befuddlement. At least, Cunningham's individual dance works, though abstract, do seem to be "about" something, because each establishes an atmosphere or emphasizes some quality of movement so that, say, *Summerspace* looks genuinely distinct from *Winterbranch*. The Events, however, remain impregnable. There they are: great hunks of theatre, seemingly unapproachable.

There is, though, at least one way of regarding Events which can make them less forbidding, a point of view emanating from the philosophy which produced them in the first place. Cunningham, John Cage, and other artists in their circle regard art as an imitation of nature—but not in any literal sense, for that might result in nothing more than a superfluous replication of objects. Rather, they wish to imitate nature in its manner of operation. For them, the universe is Heraclitean, forever open to metamorphosis. Events, then, are attempts to reproduce in miniature the workings of the universe. In Events things happen and are transformed into other things happening, images are born and disintegrate and reshape themselves into other images. Everything has its own form, yet form is always subject to modification. Frequently, even when the choreography is vigorous, Events somehow possess an overall feeling of imperturbability or even serenity. They resemble such phenomena as the running of rivers, the formation of crystals, the orbits of planets, or the flow of traffic through the streets: they partake of some process which can be related to the basic processes of earthly existence. The "experience of dance" which Cunningham says he desires Events to provide is thus very much like the experience of life itself.

Even the length of Events is significant. Ninety minutes, uninterrupted, is a sizable chunk of choreographic time. It is long enough to seem an eternity. It is also long enough to prevent one from thinking in terms of beginning, middle, and end, as those terms apply to Aristotelian tragedy or French boulevard farce. Like the universe, Events have some sort of beginning and, as scientists say the universe will, in due course they come to an end. Otherwise, they are all middle—which is how we usually perceive life: life is something we are in the midst of. And just as choreographic incidents melt away and are succeeded by others, so individual lives die while life itself continues. Cunningham has managed to capture the processes of the universe in artworks which are models of that universe and at the same time objects subject to that universe's principles of change. He has created an art which is abstract, yet absolutely realistic.

Viewing Events this way allows one problem Eventgoers often fret about to be put in its proper perspective: namely, must one be able to recognize the original dances from which the movements in Events derive? Certain passages are easy to identify if one knows the Cunningham repertoire: a trio in which one dancer carries a stick comes from *Signals*, as does a set of finger games; a swaying solo is out of *Second Hand;* when Cunningham inches about on little cat feet that's the solo called *Solo*, when his hands flutter like crazy that's *Loops*, and when the dancers start falling and dragging each other about, that just has to be *Winterbranch*. Being able to trace these episodes to their sources can be instructive, for one starts to realize how movements which have a certain character in one context may assume a totally different character in a new context, the most striking example being the movements which look so horrific in *Winterbranch* and which can also seem tame or gamelike in some of the Events.

Sometimes, however, I am unable to identify the sources of the movements I watch, even though the program note tells me that they come from pieces I have seen before. But perhaps that is nothing to worry about. Perhaps too great a fuss is made about the sources of the Events, whereas one's real attention should be focused not upon where the movement comes from but upon how it looks right now. It might be useful to compare Events with streets: if one knows the neighborhood, one can enjoy noticing that there goes Mr. Smith or Mrs. Jones, or that the corner store has a new window display. But if one is a stranger to the neighborhood, one may still find its buildings and people interesting to watch. Similarly, knowing the sources of an Event can come in handy, but not knowing them need not blunt one's enjoyment.

Nevertheless, the relationship of whole pieces to Events does prompt another worry, one less metaphysical in nature. The movements which comprise Events have to come from somewhere, and they usually come from previous Cunningham dances. Cunningham's preoccupation with Events can make one fear that any new dances he choreographs may not be terribly interesting as entities in themselves; they may only be repositories of steps he can later incorporate into Events. Such fears are probably groundless. In Princeton last January, the Cunningham company offered its first repertory performances in the New York area in a long time. The programs contained two local premieres and a world premiere. Each piece was distinct in mood, each had its own recognizable personality. Judging from the Princeton performances, it does not seem as though Events are leading Cunningham to choreograph inferior dances.

Comparisons with city streets or natural forces suggest that Events might be called, in a sense, dances about everything, while most conventional dances, like most artworks of any kind, concern some specific thing: some idea, story, or emotion, as in narrative dance; or some particular way of arranging steps in space and time, as in abstract ballet. Artworks, as we usually conceive them, allow us not only to focus our attention upon something, they also, through their very finitude, provide opportunities for breaks of attention—breaks provided, for example, by the pauses which usually separate dances in the theatre. The fluidity of Events prevents them from having this quality of focus which is ordinarily so important to art and which is one reason I hope Cunningham will never totally abandon programs of clearly separate dance works.

By their very sprawl, though, Events are reminders of the importance of paying attention and staying mentally awake. Just as we cannot truly savor the objects we pass while walking down the street unless we really pay attention to them, so we cannot enjoy Events unless we carefully observe everything which happens in them. No wonder they can be exhausting to watch. Curiously, one may need to pay more attention to Events than to individual pieces. The reverse would initially seem to be true: theoretically, because Events are so long one should be able to let them wash across one's consciousness, whereas the brevity of pieces should require intense concentration. In actuality, it is the Events, not the pieces, which usually require the greater concentration. The pieces may soon declare what sorts of things they are about, while the Events, simply because they are potentially about everything, must be scrutinized for new revelations at every moment.

In his separate pieces, Cunningham has tried to get us to look at things as they are. Now, through his Events, he wants us to look at everything at every instant. The task he has set us is far from easy. And rebelling against him on occasion are both our love of sloth and our love of art. For there are occasions when we do not want or need to look at everything but at one particular thing only. These are the occasions when we desire whole individual works, not Events. Yet having sharpened our eyes by looking at Events, we may, in turn, be better able to see the individual works. Similarly, by paying attention to Events, we realize that they, like all things around us, consist of one particular thing after another. Everything is but the sum total of some things.

By maintaining both pieces and Events in his repertoire, then, Cunningham has established a dialogue between everything and something. He not only provides us with different kinds of things to see, he reminds us that the same things may be seen in different ways. The pieces isolate and frame, the Events are all-inclusive. If we want to, if we need to, we can even put up our own frames of attention around the action in Events. Cunningham probably won't object: he gives us the freedom to make up our minds.

*Ballet Review* 5/4 (1975–76): 56–60

# MOMENTS CALLED NOW

Merce Cunningham and Dance Company presented a series of Events at their Westbeth studios during December 1975. The "score" for the Event of 27 December was an essay by Yasunao Tone read and discussed by Tone and Jeffly Lohn. As they read, three television screens showed images of a room with a woman posed inside it, the cameras slowly circling the room and returning to the woman.

Ostensibly about photography, the essay became so metaphysically abstruse that I started tuning it out. Suddenly, however, I found myself paying attention. One of the commentators was speaking of "Momentism . . . a moment called now."

It struck me that all of Cunningham's choreography might be regarded as celebrations of moments called now. These days in New York—I suspect for mixed reasons involving aesthetics and economic practicality—Cunningham devotes himself primarily to Events. Yet he also maintains a repertoire of dances. An opportunity to see several of them, including a revival and three premieres, came 13 and 15 January 1976 when, prior to a foreign tour, the company appeared at Princeton's McCarter Theatre. Seeing these performances shortly after I had attended an Event was instructive, for they made me realize that Cunningham devises at least two radically different kinds of works. While his Events consist of unbroken successions of moments, the dances hold moments under a microscope, for each separate piece favors a specific type of movement or spatial arrangement.

Having said this, I cringe with apprehension. Perhaps what I thought I saw happen happened only in my head. Nevertheless, it did seem that each dance shown in Princeton had a distinct personality. Thus, *TV Rerun* is an ensemble piece in which the dancers, except for a brief instant, never touch. The piece is also photographed as it occurs by a camera crew, their utilitarian actions contrasting to the company's abstract dance movement.

As its title implies, *Signals* involves signaling, making contact. At the beginning of one duet, Susana Hayman-Chaffey and Charles Moulton sit looking at each other, establishing psychic contact before they ever establish physical contact. Other episodes explore further ways of establishing contact: Cunningham appears to control the motions of his dancers by clapping or grunting and, in one ingenious section, first Cunningham, then Chris Komar, uses a pole to come between and manipulate the bodies of Moulton and Ellen Cornfield. Cunningham's handing over of the pole (and the implied power it possesses) to Komar may be itself a signal that this young dancer, notable for his authority, elevation, and gestural precision, is being regarded as an increasingly important company member.

The laconically titled *Solo* for Cunningham is pure animal attentiveness. Holding his hands like paws, Cunningham inches onstage. Repeatedly, he looks around, gazing at something invisible to us but clearly real to him. Stretched on his side, he brushes his arm against his head like a cat cleaning itself until he is interrupted by a noise only he can hear. Until now, all movements have been small. But then he starts scratching furiously at the air, as though enacting some kitten's dream of leonine glory. That done, he inches offstage with the same minuscule steps with which he began.

The program note for *Rune* states that this dance, dating from 1959, is arranged so that "it can be changed from performance to performance." The Princeton version, to shards of piano music by Christian Wolff, seemed to be preoccupied with time, with time slowed down or speeded up, and with different things occupying the same units of time. Solo figures were pitted against a small ensemble, the soloist leaping while the ensemble huddled, the ensemble bouncing while the soloist strode solemnly. There were also occasions when everyone's gestures slowed to near immobility, as though the dancers were turning to stone before our eyes.

*Torse*, given its world premiere, also stressed the factor of time, but here time passed with an unvarying steadiness. There was musical steadiness, too, for Maryanne Amacher's score consisted of ceaseless waves of electronic sounds. Choreographically, *Torse* involved lines and blocks: dancers stayed in line or got out of line to join another line of dancers, or blocks of dancers traversed the stage in rectangular formations. Geometry also pervaded a trio in which Komar, Robert Kovich, and Moulton leaped about, making triangles in space. Brushing and skipping steps predominated until these motifs constituted a choreographic ostinato. Though much activity occurred, that activity was so similar in nature that ultimately it seemed tranquil, even lulling.

If *Torse* emphasized lines, the East Coast premiere of *Sounddance*, to wild electronic whirrings by David Tudor, concerned going around in circles. Whereas *Torse* radiated steadiness, *Sounddance* radiated turbulence, despite its perfectly symmetrical form. Gradually, the dancers entered one by one through folds of a curtain designed by Mark Lancaster, then one by one they left until the stage was empty. There were lots of turns, bodies were whirled in circles, there were ring dances with linked hands. These circles may well have been vicious, for almost everything was done in a rush. Once the company even ran furiously in place, as though they felt they had to hurry just to stay where they were. When the furious tempo abated, the dancers were arrested in tangled groupings as though caught in a gigantic spiderweb. In *Sounddance* even slowness had the agitation of high speed.

A rebus is a puzzle in which pictures of objects symbolize the sounds which constitute the word to be guessed. Thus, a picture of a windmill, a pathway, and a key might be a rebus for Milwaukee. Cunningham's *Rebus*, also given its East Coast premiere, is a kinetic rebus. Parts even look like the rebuses which can be found in children's puzzle books: for example, the opening in which Cunningham, in blue shirt and brown pants, points stiffly toward a metal bar from which coat hangers and clothing dangle. There is a riddling quality about the dance movement, as well. To a David Behrman score in which a soprano chants above organlike electronic sounds, the ensemble moves at a comfortable moderate tempo. There are many unison passages, making the dancers seem a chorus. Cunningham threads his way among them as though exploring a labyrinth, occasionally singling one dancer out for no discernible reason. Sometimes the action halts, enabling the cast to pose like statues— statues of what, though? Similar perplexities are aroused by the finale in which Cunningham, wearing red tights rather than street clothes, repeats the same pointing gesture he employed at the outset.

What does *Rebus* mean? What's the answer to this puzzle? Most likely, *Rebus* is simply nonliteral choreography. Still, it retains an air of mystery. Even Mark Lancaster's deceptively simple costumes for the ensemble— all are white, yet each has a touch of some other color—help intensify the dance's enigmatic feeling.

My own answer to the rebus is: there probably is no single answer. Life is a mystery and therefore art, being a part of life, can also be mysterious. Each person lives life in his own way; each person's moments of experiencing both life and art are uniquely his own.

*Dance Magazine* (March 1976): 30–32

# FOUR

# *Ballet Makers*

*Dancers of the Hamburg Ballet in John Neumeier's* Mahler's Third Symphony. *Photo: Holger Badekow.*

$\mathcal{B}$allet classes look remarkably similar everywhere. Individual teachers may emphasize different points of technique. Analytically minded ballet masters may codify their procedures in pedagogical manuals which can be used as the bases for carefully graded training methods. The persistence of certain approaches to ballet training in different parts of the world may help develop local or national ballet styles. Nevertheless, the basic structure of a ballet class scarcely differs from city to city or nation to nation. Although ballet students from one country who enroll in a foreign school may occasionally be puzzled by what they encounter, they seldom find their lessons totally bewildering.

But what is true of ballet in the classroom is not necessarily true of ballet onstage. The theatrical works that are known as "ballets" may all employ academic technique, yet choreographers can put that technique to many surprising or even shocking uses. And choreographic styles that please audiences in one city may be execrated elsewhere.

Ballet lovers everywhere can grow contentious as they champion their favorite choreographers. The critic Edwin Denby once remarked that the feelings of balletomanes can be as intense as those of "a passionate coffee-drinker newly arrived in a strange country and for the first time tasting the brew that there is called coffee." Although, like certain kinds of coffee, certain types of foreign ballets may never be to our taste, if we are not hopelessly bound by our predilections we may, through increased acquaintance with the ballets of other lands, come to have a renewed appreciation of ballet's creative possibilities.

However, stylistic differences are not the only issues troubling ballet lovers today. As a result of a worldwide ballet boom, we are blessed with scores of well-trained dancers. But, since creative artists are usually rarer than interpretative artists, we do not have enough talented choreographers to supply all those dancers with gratifying repertoires. Moreover, some bal-

*let choreographers do not appear to be sure how to develop the vast tech-nical vocabulary of steps they have inherited from the past. The reviews in this section examine the various ways in which some prominent choreogra-phers from several countries are drawing upon their balletic heritage.*

## GRIGOROVICH AND THE BOLSHOI

Even without Alexander Godunov's defection, the Bolshoi Ballet's engagement at the New York State Theater (1–26 August 1979) would have been unusual. This was a season consisting entirely of works by a single choreographer: Yuri Grigorovich, the Bolshoi's artis-tic director. Rarely has a visiting large-scale ballet company devoted itself to only one choreographer here, the few exceptions including Béjart's company and the Stuttgart Ballet under John Cranko's direction. However, the Stuttgart also offered a traditional *Giselle*, whereas *Swan Lake*, the one "classic" in the Bolshoi's repertoire, turned out to be Gri-gorovich's revised version of that ballet.

This was obviously a season that tried to demonstrate why Russian balletgoers value Grigorovich so highly. It was certainly an interesting season, although Grigorovich's choreography did not win universal ap-proval. But that was partly because Grigorovich was dealing with a set of choreographic problems rather different from those which concern our own choreographers. His solutions to them did not always amaze us simply because the problems themselves were not so pressing to us.

Grigorovich comes from a nation where the evening-long narrative ballet remains the norm. One of his problems, then, is to prevent his own evening-long ballets from sprawling. He has avoided sprawl by means of an almost obsessive concern for unity. In addition to *Swan Lake*, four of his major works were presented. Each was different in mood. Each was unified and stylistically consistent. Each, indeed, had its own special "look."

However, having achieved unity, Grigorovich was not always able to find choreographic variety within that unity. Either because his choreographic vocabulary was essentially limited or because, in his quest for unity, he deliberately limited his vocabulary, his ballets had the misfortune of getting off to a striking start and then gradually running out of steam.

The least satisfactory of them was *The Stone Flower*, which had not been seen here since the Bolshoi's first visit in 1959. Prokofiev's allegory concerns an artist's rejection of an art of merely formal perfection in favor of an art that somehow aids humanity. Curiously enough, the scenario theoretically ought to allow for considerable choreographic variety, since its scenes range from a gypsy festival to what is virtually an abstract ballet for some jewel spirits. But Grigorovich's choreography was weak throughout. He simply could not bring the allegory to life. The virtuous heroine spent the entire ballet mooning about in a nightgown, while the sinister Mistress of the Copper Mountain kept tying herself into knots. And the ballet of the jewel spirits, which ought to have been one of the work's highlights, was unimaginative in its choreographic designs.

If *The Stone Flower* was much too mild, *Spartacus* verged upon bombast. It is a ballet that impresses through its sheer force, through the way its mass movement matches Khachaturian's clamorous score. Yet it was hard to maintain interest in a ballet in which everyone was either terribly virtuous or terribly vicious and no one was interesting simply as a human being.

Or so it seemed to me, who had never seen *Spartacus* before. But friends who had seen the ballet with such dancers as Maya Plisetskaya and Maris Liepa (neither of whom appeared on the current tour) claimed that the characters in *Spartacus* could be made to seem very striking individuals. Here, however, they all looked like animated abstractions akin to the heroic figures in post office or courthouse murals. Although the people in those murals are usually depicted after their struggles have led to some sort of apotheosis, *Spartacus* appeared to be an apotheosis from the start. Yet there were exciting things about it: the marches and battles, of course, and, in the otherwise disappointing second half of the ballet, Aegina's surprisingly erotic dance of seduction with a shepherd's staff and Phrygia's Duncanesque lament before her husband's corpse.

Two works had never been presented before in America. One was Grigorovich's new *Romeo and Juliet*. And very new it was, for it received its Bolshoi premiere as recently as 26 July, although Grigorovich had staged an earlier production for the Paris Opéra Ballet. In Moscow, this *Romeo* has prompted controversy, for those who consider Leonid Lavrovsky's *Romeo* a modern classic fear that the Grigorovich will oust the Lavrovsky from the repertoire.

For different reasons, Americans may also find this *Romeo* controversial. Unlike most balletic adaptations of Shakespeare's play, this is not a retelling, but a complete rethinking of the familiar story. Therefore, it is more akin to the radical choreographic treatments by Oscar Araiz and John Neumeier than it is to the versions of Cranko and MacMillan.

Grigorovich turns the play into a romantic choreographic revery. At the outset, Romeo is discovered pining not after a flesh-and-blood Rosaline, but after an ensemble of wispy sylphlike ladies. They are idealizations of young love, and the ballet itself is an idealization of young love. Many of the characters are portrayed as being very young. Juliet's parents, for example, are young people (which, considering her own age, is perfectly plausible); even the Nurse is young (which, considering her store of worldly wisdom, is not quite so plausible). However, by trying to make his ballet a distillation of the essence of young romantic love, Grigorovich gets himself into difficulties.

For one thing, the ballet is terribly long; a three-act distillation is almost a contradiction in itself. Indeed, this *Romeo* is even longer than most, since Grigorovich has employed some music that is usually omitted. The ballet is also rather bloodless. Grigorovich's idealization of Romeo and Juliet has turned them into conventional balletic images of eternal youthfulness: they become a ballerina and a premier danseur, not real people from Renaissance Italy or Elizabethan England. This sense of unreality is emphasized by Simon Virsaladze's settings, which consist of nothing but heavy draperies behind which dim architectural shapes are occasionally visible.

Grigorovich's most curious innovation involves having a sort of Greek chorus of ten women appear at moments of heightened emotion. They look like fugitives from *Serenade* or *Les Sylphides* and some balletomanes have nicknamed them the "pink Wilis." Presumably, they symbolize the power of passion. But what meddling nuisances they turn out to be! They pop up everywhere. They wander into what would be the balcony scene, if this production had a balcony, and they even invade the privacy of Juliet's bedroom during her one night with Romeo. They are given wafty choreography. But so are too many of the other characters too much of the time.

*The Legend of Love*, Grigorovich's other unfamiliar ballet, fared better. Based upon a play by the Turkish poet Nazim Hikmet, it is, like *The Stone Flower*, a fable. A proud Queen gives up her beauty so that her Sister will be magically cured of an illness caused by a drought. When a Youth falls in love with the Sister, the jealous Queen orders him to build a canal through the wilderness. Then, repentant, she releases him from exile, an act of compassion that restores her own beauty. Nevertheless, the Youth determines to complete the canal and rescue the entire nation from drought. The story, of course, is a glorification of self-sacrifice.

Grigorovich has done something quite surprising with it. He has turned it into a fantastic, yet leisurely, spectacle that resembles a Hollywood film based upon the *Arabian Nights*. Arif Melikov's music even sounds like the sort of music that might accompany such a film. Grigorovich has tried to make the action suggest a set of animated Persian miniatures. Hence, many movements are done in profile and the ballet abounds in delicate curving gestures for the hands. Not all of Grigorovich's touches are successful. At several points, for instance, the orchestra stops and, to ghostly sounds from a loudspeaker, the leading characters try to dance out their thoughts—a device akin to the "danced monologues" in *Spartacus*. But these danced thoughts always remain vague. Nevertheless, *Legend of Love* was gently attractive.

The company included several dancers familiar from previous visits. Nina Timofeyeva was a powerful Queen in *Legend of Love,* while Natalia Bessmertnova's lyricism remained much admired (her sister, Tatiana, by the way, revealed herself to be a dancer of considerable dramatic flair). It was, however, some of the younger artists who attracted the most attention. Godunov's robustness was much liked. Ludmila Semenyaka has developed into a very exciting dancer. Although capable of the utmost delicacy, she can plunge into glittering choreography with almost reckless abandon. The public's favorites were Nadezhda Pavlova and Vyacheslav Gordeyev: Gordeyev, every inch the gentleman; Pavlova, a dancer who can attain almost ecstatic intensity.

There was much spectacular dancing, yet the Bolshoi never turned itself into a circus, as it has done on other occasions. There were no "Highlights" programs, no divertissements in which smiling women threw themselves at brawny men, then did it all over again as an encore. Whatever one may have thought of individual works, it was a serious season capable of being discussed and appraised with the utmost seriousness.

"New York Newsletter," *Dancing Times* (October 1979): 32–33

# TALKING TO MYSELF
# ABOUT ELIOT FELD

*D*espite pleasant dancing, I was disturbed by the Eliot Feld Ballet's season (29 November 1974–5 January 1975, New York Shakespeare Public Theater). I kept arguing with myself about it.

*Myself:* What's the problem? Eliot Feld is one of the brightest American ballet choreographers to have emerged in recent years, and his new company not only has such distinctive personalities as Lawrence Rhodes and Christine Sarry, it's a cohesive ensemble, as well. What more can you want?

*Me:* That's the trouble. I want more. Considering Feld's ambitions, I expect more. I demand more.

*Myself:* Aren't you the ornery cuss—wanting, expecting, and demanding things everywhere! But look at the variety Feld's already given you. There's the starkness of *At Midnight,* the Romanticism of *Intermezzo,* the homage to Jewish tradition of *Tzaddik,* the . . .

*Me:* I know, I know. But this very eclecticism is ominous. Feld's ballets are undeniably accomplished. Yet however serious the creative impulse behind them may be, the results often appear shallow. Everything is too neat. Feld seems afraid to let himself go. I'd almost prefer inspired awkwardness.

*Myself (frostily):* Could you give examples of just what you object to? (And they'd better be good!)

*Me:* Take *Intermezzo.* With its Brahms music and ardent lovers, it pays tribute to the Romantic spirit. Yet Feld also introduces jokes mocking that spirit, as though he were reluctant to display unabashedly rapturous emotions. And then take *Tzaddik,* in which an old rabbi exhorts two students. The ballet is largely static: photographs of key poses might have the same effect as an actual performance. But what disturbs me more is that, for all his exhortations, the rabbi never becomes a believable or even interesting character. He remains too generalized. Presumably, he symbolizes ancient wisdom. Yet I could imagine a skeptic interpreting the ballet as an attack upon organized religion. Without changing a single step, the rabbi would thereby become a demented fanatic, while the conclusion, where he wraps his disciples in the scrolls, would represent superstition enslaving humanity.

*Myself (aghast):* Come off it! Surely you don't think that's what *Tzaddik* is really about, do you?

*Me:* Of course not. My point remains this, though. *Tzaddik* never makes a complete enough choreographic statement. I am similarly disturbed by *The Consort,* the newly revived production from 1970.

*Myself:* Why? I thought it was nice. And craftily crafted, too. Five couples dance to Elizabethan music. At first, they are stately and, despite balletic extensions, their look suggests old court dances. Later, the

women remove their hair ornaments and raise their skirts and the dancing gets more vigorous. It's very Elizabethan, you know: the contrasts
between aristocratic manners and gutsy street life, between decorum and
passion.

*Me:* It's not Elizabethan enough. The contrasts are too tame, as though
Feld feared he might scandalize the Puritans. For all the skirtlifting,
these kids still resemble swains and damsels frisking on the green.

*Myself:* Couldn't the irony be intentional? Perhaps Feld is hinting that
sensuality is a problem only when it is accompanied by guilt. The kids,
though lusty, are still essentially innocent.

*Me:* Then they should be even more lusty! Here, again, Feld doesn't
go full-out in the exploration of his ideas.

*Myself:* But *The Consort* ends with the men clutching the women and
the women spreading their legs. If Feld went "further out" than this, the
theatre would have to post an "X" rating on the door.

*Me:* A mere socko finale. Just compare it with Paul Taylor's *Churchyard*, which shows a comparable progression from decorum to lust and
you'll see the difference. Taylor's progression is both gradual and chilling, and also raises moral questions without preaching. *The Consort* is a
sort of prettified *Churchyard*. Which brings me to another problem.

*Myself:* Oh dear. What now?

*Me:* Many of Feld's ballets are stylistically indebted to other choreographers. *At Midnight* suggests Tudor and the Balanchine of *Ivesiana*,
while *Intermezzo* suggests Balanchine and Robbins, and *The Gods Amused*
suggests the Balanchine of *Apollo*.

*Myself:* What, pray tell, is wrong with that? There is no such thing as
total originality in art. Precedents exist for virtually every artwork, and
to make a fetish out of "originality" can reduce art to stunts and conjur-
ing tricks. You're forever yammering that dancers today aren't aware of
their heritage, yet when Feld draws upon his heritage it upsets you. Feld
is teaching himself to be a choreographer as he goes along, and he's
doing it by assimilating the achievements of the masters. You must admit
that in Balanchine, Tudor, and Robbins he has certainly chosen fine
models. Think how you would holler if he went to (name deleted) or

(name deleted) for inspiration. Feld can be likened to a musician practicing five-finger exercises: he seeks control over his medium.

*Me:* However, musicians practice etudes so that they'll eventually do concerti. There exist few choreographic concerti by Feld.

*Myself:* What about his new piece—*The Real McCoy,* to Gershwin piano music. What's he accomplished there?

*Me:* Hmm.

*Myself:* What do you mean, "Hmm"?

*Me:* During the last moments of the ballet the protagonist scratches his head. That's what I mean by "Hmm." The ballet's a puzzler. Standing before a Rouben Ter-Arutunian backdrop of painted rainbows, a boy in modern sports clothes (Feld himself) plays with a top hat and cane, as though to indicate that any boy can dream of growing up to be Fred Astaire. A supercool beauty (Michaela Hughes) rolls in on a piece of furniture resembling a chaise longue or a psychiatrist's couch. By pushing the couch around, boy joins girl for what is intended as an urbane pas de trois in which the threesome's third member is a piece of furniture. Then comes a smoldering duet for boy and girl while a small male corps struts with canes in the background. Finally, the girl leaves and the boy is left alone, scratching his head. How did this strike you?

*Myself:* As an ingenious attempt to use the aura of nostalgia to escape nostalgia. Instead of settling for camp, Feld, out of the allure of showbiz, makes a rueful little ballet about how dreams don't always come true, and about how all that glitters may be only glitter-dust.

*Me:* A nice idea. Unfortunately, having set his ballet within the framework of a showbiz style, Feld proves unable to compose in that style. The perambulations of the rolling couch in the furniture pas de trois are not witty enough, and though Feld tries for Fred Astaire jauntiness and Veloz and Yolanda glamour, he possesses no mastery over these idioms. Tactically, it was probably wise not to introduce actual tap dancing, for inexpert tap steps in this context would be painful. Yet Feld cannot supply any satisfactory balletic substitute for tap dancing. Or for old-time chorus routines. Or nightclub adagio acts. The results look impoverished.

*Myself:* It occurs to me that one master of finding balletic equivalents for nonballetic forms—from classic Spanish dances to semiclassic Viennese waltzes—is Léonide Massine. And, more recently, Twyla Tharp and James Waring have done marvels with old American pop styles. Perhaps Feld needs to do a few more five-finger exercises.

*Me:* Perhaps. But even granting your point, I still wonder who—apart from his influences—Eliot Feld is as an independent choreographer in his own right.

*Myself:* You're at it again? Let's change the subject. What did you think of the first work not by Feld to be added to his repertoire, Glen Tetley's *Embrace Tiger and Return to Mountain?*

*Me:* I'm not sure we're changing the subject. For despite their differences, Tetley, like Feld, sometimes contents himself with the mere surface look of things.

*Myself:* Whoa! I must interject here that I think *Tiger* looks stunning. Nadine Baylis's setting of translucent hanging panels and a mirrored floor is a real beauty, and the cast's brilliant control is simply breathtaking.

*Me:* Yes, *Tiger* is stunning—on the surface. Tetley examines Chinese T'ai-Chi shadowboxing exercises and, to an electronic score by Morton Subotnick, blends them with ballet and modern dance. The Chinese elements he's borrowed appear to be slow stretches from a wide-legged stance and a shielding gesture in which the hands are brought before the face. These generate a succession of solos, duets, and group dances. The choreography is as slick and shiny as the décor but, eventually, I start asking what the point of it is.

*Myself:* Certain implications are there to ponder, if you're willing to seek them out. Thus, since he employs shadowboxing as his choreographic base Tetley introduces symbolic references to human combativeness. There's a duet which begins with a man controlling a woman by guiding her every step, but which ends with the woman pushing him to the floor. And there's another scene in which four men stalk about, as though in search of some prey—which turns out to be a woman who, though tossed around by the hunters, nevertheless gives the impression of being essentially unconquerable.

*Me:* Such scenes exist. But there is something excessively calculated about them, as though Tetley had listed possibilities in his mind and was mechanically checking them off: "Now we'll have a sequence implying this . . . now we'll have a sequence implying that. . . ." All the while, the sequences imperturbably unwind like endless rolls of wallpaper.

*Myself:* You grouch! Or maybe Groucho's the word for you. You remind me of that old Groucho Marx song: "Whatever it is, you're against it." Yet you keep coming back to see Feld.

*Me:* Yes. I admire the vivacity of Christine Sarry, the power of Lawrence Rhodes, the way Naomi Sorkin is acquiring considerable elegance, the way all these dancers work hard for Feld. And I come with high hopes. For instance, I hope that someday a choreographer will create a dramatic ballet for Rhodes which uses his full emotional range and abjures that hangdog air which he is perpetually required to assume. Most of all, I hope for a truly inventive new ballet by Feld. Certainly, few other choreographers in current American ballet inspire such hopes. Right?

*Myself:* Right. At last we agree about something.

*Dance Magazine* (February 1975): 21–24

# NEUMEIER IN HAMBURG

*F*ew new choreographers have attracted more attention recently than John Neumeier, the young American who, after achieving success in Frankfurt, is currently ballet director in Hamburg. However, one curious thing about Neumeier is that while many of his works are acclaimed on the Continent, those which have been presented in London and New York have occasioned raised eyebrows as well as applause.

This may be only natural since, though ballet is an international art, there probably does not exist a universal ballet taste. Different choreographers appeal to different temperaments and thrive best in particular environments. Yet accounts of Neumeier's ballets remain intriguing enough to keep one's curiosity aroused.

Hamburg's first Ballet Festival (10–22 June 1975) provided dance-goers with an opportunity to appraise his choreography. Although the festival included a choreographic workshop, a guest performance by Béjart's company, and a gala honouring Nijinsky, the emphasis was, appropriately enough, upon Neumeier. Regarding the Hamburg company, there can be little argument. Neumeier and a staff headed by Ray Barra and Ilse Wiedmann have trained a uniformly attractive and proficient ensemble. As for Neumeier's choreography, it both pleases and puzzles.

Visiting Hamburg during the festival, I saw two new works. Fortunately, both were plotless. I say "fortunately," not because I believe abstract dance is inherently superior to dramatic dance, but because these pieces acquainted me with an aspect of Neumeier's talent of which I had been previously unaware. Such ballets as the National Ballet of Canada's *Don Juan* and Ballet Theatre's *Baiser de la Fée* had impressed me as works which not only tried to contribute to our culture by means of imaginative choreography, but which also sought to comment upon our cultural inheritance through the use of myth, legend, history, and philosophical speculation. Since choreographers are periodically accused of being empty-headed, these ambitions are laudable. But the resultant ballets, to my taste, were ponderous and what I could divine of Neumeier's intentions was often more stimulating than his actual choreography. And, finally, choreographers must be judged not upon their ideas, but upon their ability to compose satisfying movement of some sort—be that movement "classical," "modern," "antidance," or what-have-you.

In his new abstractions Neumeier demonstrates that he does possess such an ability. The first of them was his contribution to a program bearing the overall title of *Makrokosmos*, in which three choreographers set ballets to scores by the experimental American composer George Crumb. Premiered last winter at the Hamburg Opera's arena-style workshop, the Opera Stabile, it was repeated there during the festival. The Opera Stabile is such a tiny space that, while one could picture a theatrical company using it for readings or intimate dramas, it was hard to conceive how it could serve such more extroverted arts as opera and dance.

Nevertheless, the choreographers managed to cope with its limitations. Scoffing at the cramped conditions, Sergej Handzic filled *Das Echo* with forceful movements which bombarded the eye. Fred Howald hinted at a dramatic situation in *Der Schrei*, in which a woman confronted an ensemble of dancers who seemed to personify unhappy memories. As can happen in such ballets, the precise nature of the memories remained obscure, yet Martine Giaconi danced the woman with compelling intensity, and there was one heartbreaking moment when she rushed against the other dancers who were standing impassive as a wall, whereupon a woman detached herself from the wall and collapsed like a child falling dead into her arms.

Neumeier created a dreamlike landscape in *Die Stille*, partly through tricks of stagecraft. He suspended a mirror from the ceiling which reflected the dancers' movements and gave the illusion of transporting them to some unearthly realm. At one point, where Crumb quotes a bit of Chopin in his score, Neumeier had the dancers move slowly in a dim light, then suddenly turned on the houselights while the dancers clutched each other, the differences of intensity suggesting an awakening from dream into the anxieties of reality. But there was more than stagecraft here. Neumeier's choreographic images often possessed real power, as when a man whirled a woman around and her movements turned increasingly inward until she had actually wrapped herself about him, or when a woman trembled because of some nameless fright until she lost her ability to stand upright.

Even more ambitious was the world premiere on the Hamburg Opera's main stage of *Mahler's Third Symphony*, a two-hour ballet presented without interval. It is tempting to praise Neumeier simply for trying such a thing and equally tempting to berate him for foolhardiness. When the ballet ended, though, I was rather glad he had been so brash.

Though plotless, the ballet seemed to depict the spiritual journey of a man (François Klaus) who abjures power in favor of love, for in the strident opening movement, set entirely for men, Klaus steps aside from militaristic swagger and combat. In the next two movements he beholds gentle young people and looks wonderingly at, and hesitantly tries to establish contact with, a young woman. A dirge interrupts this bliss. The only section in which Klaus does not appear, it consists of a trio for two men and a woman filled with off-balance steps evoking grief and despair. The music which follows the dirge grows joyous again, while a charming, but slightly gawky, young woman (Zhandra Rodriguez) dances happily alone, then turns self-conscious when she realizes Klaus is watching her. At last, in the movement Mahler subtitles "What Love Tells Me," Klaus and Rodriguez dance briefly together amidst an exultant ensemble, and then part, as though to suggest that while love may express itself through unquenchable desire, the particular objects of desire may be ever-changing.

Almost inevitably, considering the symphony's length, music dwarfs choreography. Because Mahler has two lyrical movements come one after the other, the balletic treatment of these sections threatens to turn saccharine. And I wonder whether the dirge, though impressive, is really an intrinsic part of the ballet. It was, in fact, originally choreographed by Neumeier in 1974 as a memorial to John Cranko. Yet, perhaps, its very unexpectedness could be defended, for it shatters the ballet—just as pain and sudden death can shatter the ordinary course of our days.

Despite its blemishes, the ballet contains enough imaginative choreography to confirm the impression that Neumeier is indeed a promising choreographer. If his literary ballets reveal that he has an inquiring mind, his new abstractions suggest that it is also a mind which can think kinetically.

# KYLIAN AND NETHERLANDS
# DANCE THEATRE

ne of the season's nicest surprises was the Netherlands Dance Theatre's visit to the City Center, 9–21 July 1979. The troupe has been here before, of course, and in the past its ballets by Glen Tetley, Benjamin Harkarvy, and Hans van Manen have been respectfully received; yet they have not always generated excitement. This time, however, the company aroused real enthusiasm.

There was a van Manen ballet in the repertoire: *Songs without Words* (Mendelssohn), an oddly ambivalent piece that sometimes seemed to be emulating and sometimes mocking the sentiments of such a work as Jerome Robbins's *Dances at a Gathering*. All the other ballets, however, were by Jiri Kylian, and Kylian soon became the most talked about young choreographer in New York.

When Netherlands Dance Theatre appeared at the 1978 American Spoleto Festival in Charleston, South Carolina, his *Sinfonietta* (Janacek) created a sensation. And his *Return to the Strange Land* was the only really successful new work shown in the Stuttgart Ballet's 1979 New York season. How strange that this Czech-born, Royal Ballet School–trained choreographer should succeed here, while the efforts of such expatriate American choreographers as John Neumeier and William Forsythe have sometimes failed to impress New Yorkers. Foreign Kylian may be, yet there is something about his choreography that is much to American taste.

Although he quite rightly insists that his ballets are not abstract, nevertheless, like many American choreographers, he seems fascinated by movement as a thing in itself. And his ballets are always on the move. They are filled with strange swivels and lifts, exultant leaps, and reckless swoops across the floor. This rhapsodic approach to choreography made *Sinfonietta* a paean to the joy of life and the power of dance. But each of his ballets was a work of genuine interest.

Given his choreographic bravado, it is probably fortunate that Kylian also loves serious themes. Otherwise, he might be tempted to settle for nothing but flashy divertissements. But one of the things that made him so fascinating was the way he united virtuosity with high seriousness in his works, the single exception being *Symphony in D* (Haydn), yet another spoof—but a truly funny one—of the conventions of classical ballet.

*Symphony of Psalms* (Stravinsky) was something of a choreographic dialogue between faith and doubt. The dancers both assumed postures of prayer and reverence and questioned religious traditions. *November Steps* (Takemitsu) was equally ritualistic. Yet whereas *Symphony of Psalms* ultimately praised a community of faith, the rejection of rigid religious tradition appeared to be salutary in the Takemitsu ballet. Similar dualisms abounded in *Glagolitic Mass* (Janacek), in which rapture was interrupted by strife until a martyr's heroic death mysteriously gave other people courage to continue living.

*Children's Games*, to an electronic score by Gary Carpenter that incorporated bits of Mahler's "Kindertotenlieder," was really a ballet about the games adults play, the deadliest of them being war. *Transfigured Night* (Schoenberg) concerned estrangement, infidelity, and reconciliation, and it was set to the same score that Antony Tudor employed for his *Pillar of Fire*. But because its dancers seemed to represent emotional states rather than specific people, it was not so much a dance-drama as a choreographic poem about the feelings and passions engendered by a dramatic situation.

So described, Kylian's ballets may sound lugubrious. Yet one of the amazing things about them is that the dynamism and propulsiveness of his choreography prevent them from turning stuffy. Still, judging from the sample of his work presented here, Kylian does have a few curious mannerisms: for example, an inordinate fondness for the duet as a form; even when he fills the stage with people, they are apt to seem not a group or a mass, but a collection of couples. Nevertheless, Kylian's talent seems so considerable that one longs to see more of his ballets.

"New York Newsletter," *Dancing Times* (September 1979): 784

# FIVE
## *The Ever-Modern*

*Lila York and members of the Paul Taylor Dance Company in Taylor's*
Esplanade. *Photo © Jack Vartoogian.*

*A*n art form that prizes individual creativity and aesthetic inquisitiveness, modern dance resists definition. Therefore, dancegoers fond of tidy categorizations have been suspicious of it; some have even tried to wish it away. Although its imminent demise has often been predicted, it always manages a miraculous recovery. But when it returns to life, it may do so in an unexpected manner.

Many of the early modern dancers were soloists—the most celebrated of them all being Isadora Duncan—and their solos were personal expressions in the most basic sense of those words. As dancers organized companies, their works perhaps inevitably began to concern the relationships, or outright conflicts, between people and, by the mid-twentieth century, many creations of such major choreographers as Martha Graham, Doris Humphrey, and José Limón were dramatic—or, at least, thematic. Yet, possibly because they found the sheer ubiquity of such works oppressive, other choreographers—among them, Merce Cunningham, Alwin Nikolais, and Erick Hawkins—began to champion a dance that was abstract rather than explicitly thematic, and evocative rather than literally descriptive.

Still other dancers, particularly those influenced by the experimental productions at New York City's Judson Memorial Church in the early 1960s, rejected both the grandiloquent rhetoric of the dramatic dancers and the obsession with technique that had begun to develop among certain abstractionists. Instead, these rebels experimented with many kinds of movement, including supposedly "nondance" movement, and they stripped choreographic structures down to their minimalist essentials. Such concerns made them seem so unlike their predecessors that critics wondered whether the term "postmodern" should be applied to post-Judson choreography. Some lovers of older types of modern dance have felt puzzled or even betrayed by the choreography that has developed since the 1960s;

*other dancegoers—and I am one of them, as this choice of reviews will surely suggest—find it stimulating.*

*However, in its development, modern dance not only tosses choreographic concerns aside, it can also bring them back, and dancegoers began to detect a new concern for personal emotion and social vision in the patterns of the minimalists. In their practice, modern dancers have adopted Ezra Pound's slogan, "Make it new," and for them that can mean renewing the old. It should come as no surprise, then, that modern dance currently offers choreographers a host of styles and techniques that they can adopt or reject as they please. It remains to be seen how well choreographers will be able to adjust to such a pluralistic situation and whether the diversity of compositional approaches available to them will prove stimulating or intimidating.*

*One thing is clear, however. Modern dance has not lost its capacity to amaze, puzzle, infuriate, and delight.*

# PAUL TAYLOR:

## SURFACE AND SUBSTANCE

One of the fascinating things about Paul Taylor is that he is never quite the sort of choreographer one assumes he is at any given moment. As soon as a rule can be formulated about him, he may provide his own set of exceptions.

Early in his career, he confounded audiences with dances which came close to being motionless (motionless, at least in terms of the canons of modern dance which prevailed at the time), while critics chided him for his weakness for Dada. But just as one was about to categorize him in terms of one avant-garde tendency, he increasingly began to choreograph another kind of dance, a kind which delighted new audiences even as it dismayed some old admirers. There were occasions, from *Orbs* (1966) and *Agathe's Tale* (1967) to so recent a piece as *American Genesis* (1974), when his apparent concern for creating modern dance character-ballets suggested he was trying to play Léonide Massine to Merce Cunningham's George Balanchine. All during this time he was being applauded by one set of dancegoers as the prophet who would lead modern dance out of the wilderness of Cunninghamism and the Judson Church, while another faction was denouncing him for being reactionary—neither group apparently willing to concede that several different dance styles could be equally valid.

Just as Taylor's choreographic development over the years provides surprises, so individual dance works are also surprising, for many are not at all the dances they initially seem to be. *Private Domain* (1969), with its stage space obstructed by hanging panels, suggests that it will be a treat for voyeurs, since the movement, with its embraces and undulations, is often implicitly erotic and can be seen only in the apertures between the panels. But nothing terribly scandalous ever happens, just as, I suspect, people rarely do anything terribly scandalous in the privacy of their own homes—or, at least, whatever they may do there, they don't think it's scandalous: it's merely what they do at home in private. A dance which starts by promising erotic titillation instead becomes a dance about obstruction, since the visible course of the movement is interrupted when the dancer passes behind one of the panels. Every movement has a blank spot in it. So, too, Taylor may suggest, is every life at least partially unknowable: man's private domain is not simply the realm of the erotic, it is the mysteriousness of the psyche itself.

At first, *Public Domain* (1967) seems easy to talk about: it's a funny dance set to a tape collage of musical snippets, all in the public domain, plus bits of *Medea, The Importance of Being Earnest,* and W. C. Fields. But now just try to answer this question: what makes these funny things funny? Any answer advanced will almost inevitably imply a whole theory of comedy. Judging from *Public Domain,* it appears that, whether or not Taylor may believe that any movements are inherently serious, he may not believe that there are inherently comic movements. What makes a movement comic is the context in which it is placed. There are some imperturbable adagios which seem not in the least comic in themselves; but when they are followed by balls rolling across the stage, the incongruity of this juxtaposition makes the total effect comic. Sometimes Taylor will combine two types of movement, neither particularly comic in itself, but in such a way that the combination makes them seem comic. Thus, finger-snapping, in itself, may be jaunty, but it is not necessarily comic, while a mass of bodies oozing across the stage may be downright threatening; but when the bodies ooze and snap their fingers simultaneously, this amalgam of two dissimilar types of movement becomes comic because the movements are preposterously unrelated.

Taylor also employs movements which are indeed related to each other, but which no "serious" choreographer would include because of associations they have in other contexts. In a sequence of arm gestures Taylor throws in the familiar hitchhiker's gesture; it's certainly an arm gesture and therefore theoretically appropriate to the sequence, but because it has such a specific meaning its presence renders the otherwise abstract passage ridiculous. Finally, Taylor fashions comedy by showing movements which might very well occur during a theatrical performance but which (like preparations for and recoveries from steps) audiences are not ordinarily expected to see. Thus, after imposing groupings and displays of movement, the dancers walk casually away: dancers might do this backstage or with the curtain down, but they don't usually let an audience see them doing it, for seeing it makes their "serious" emoting seem foolish.

Have students write about *Aureole* (1962) and, almost invariably, someone will call it balletic. Lots of people call it that. Critics even like to refer to it as a barefoot ballet blanc. Yet just what's so balletic about *Aureole?* Its lopes and big skips seem only distant cousins of the balletic jeté. Frequently, in contrast to the intricacies of balletic port de bras, hands are held simply up or simply down. And the body itself is often held parallel to the proscenium arch in such disdain of the subtleties of épaulement that the body's weight, size, and sheer bulk are inescapably visible. Bulk looked even bulkier when Taylor himself danced *Aureole.*

But even with the present cast there is no way to escape the sight of bulk. And how can a dance which displays bulk be called balletic?

Nevertheless, *Aureole* does seem balletic. What makes one compare it with ballet is that Taylor has bulk attain a state of grace. Though one remains always aware of physicality, the dance never seems to sweat; always, it maintains superb aplomb and lucidity. Calling attention to weight and bulk, Taylor also manages to transcend weight and bulk as his dancers cover space and conquer air. Mere physicality is transformed, weight seems light, the earth seems airy.

An equally unusual transformation occurs in *Esplanade* (1975). If you try to describe it in simple terms, the dance will probably sound like a different dance than the dance it actually is. The movement in *Esplanade* is based upon such purely ordinary activities as walking, running, sliding, falling, and jumping. It is a dance without a single conventional "dance step" in it. That suggests *Esplanade* resembles one of the "natural movement" pieces several choreographers were doing a few seasons back. Yet *Esplanade* could hardly be more different. The natural-movement choreographers, in their disdain of frills and their concern with movement in its most ordinary manifestations, not only called a spade a spade, they often seemed eager to call it a dirty shovel. Theirs were certainly dances that sweated. *Esplanade*, like *Aureole*, doesn't sweat, even though all its movements are movements which could be drenched with sweat. The ordinary movements of *Esplanade* are done with extraordinary vivacity, they are ordinary movements only virtuosos can perform, Taylor here having achieved (to borrow Cocteau's phrase) a "rehabilitation of the commonplace." This transfiguration of the ordinary is further enhanced by setting the dance to Bach, including movements of the same concerto Balanchine uses for his noble *Concerto Barocco*.

*Aureole, Esplanade,* and other lyrical dances, plus a host of comedies old and new have helped Taylor gain the reputation of being a genial choreographer. He is that. But to categorize him as being only that is to forget several grim pieces from *Scudorama* (1963) to *Big Bertha* (1971). Even some of his comedies can turn unexpectedly nasty: take that little scene in *Book of Beasts* (1971) in which imperious ladies march in with boys cringing like spaniels beside them; then one of the "spaniels" ups and rapes his mistress.

It is the genial pieces, though, which one usually remembers best, and it could be argued that Taylor is at heart a sanguine choreographer: he even presents the Fall of Man in *So Long, Eden* (1972) as no great catastrophe, but only a necessary pang in the process of growing up. Poets and prelates may have apostrophized the Fall as *O felix culpa*; only Paul Taylor has turned it into a square dance. Yet, almost because of this prevailing cheer, Taylor's grim works should not be ignored.

Through his choreographic clarity and charm, through his concern for measure and proportion, Taylor suggests he agrees with the maxim "nothing in excess." This is a wise, mature way of looking at things. One difficulty, though, is that of discerning just what constitutes excess. What differentiates abundance from excess? And if, in recognition of these difficulties, one makes choices with caution, can't caution itself become a form of excess? At least two Taylor dances concern themselves with questions of excess. Neither supplies simple answers.

*Churchyard* (1969) begins as a chaste gambol, continues as a robust romp, and concludes as a hideous debauch. The creepy thing about watching it is that one can never quite be sure where virtue leaves off and vice begins. The dance is a continuum, an arc: once one is on the far side of that arc, wherever that far side may begin, its curve is a slide straight to hell.

*Big Bertha* (1971) is similarly disturbing. It, too, is a horrid continuum, one of those inexorable progressions from sweetness to terror choreographers like to devise and audiences take an almost guilty pleasure in watching (witness the popularity of such a ballet as Flemming Flindt's *The Lesson*). In the Taylor, members of an ordinary family are driven to madness and mayhem by a nickelodeon mannequin, Big Bertha. But who is Big Bertha? Or, rather, what does she represent? It's easy to say that she represents the forces of commercialization, particularly those which make use of sex appeal.

But wait a minute. Big Bertha isn't an image from a billboard or TV commercial. She's a toy, a doll. Should one, then, never depict an attractive human body for purely frivolous purposes? Say yes and you may let yourself in for a wave of prudery. Moreover, the husband in *Big Bertha* has presumably come to the amusement arcade of his own free will. Because he eventually goes crazy there, shall we close down all places of amusement as threats to the sanctity of the American family?

What makes *Big Bertha* more than crypto-neopuritanism is Taylor's concern for free will. The husband may have come to the arcade of his own free will, but while there he gradually loses his will. He can no longer choose to enjoy the antics of a mechanical doll. He has himself become an automaton, swayed by an automaton. By the end of the dance he is behaving like a mechanical doll and also like a mad beast; and Taylor implies that there is no essential difference between mechanism and beast since neither is in control of a will. Big Bertha, then, may represent any force (be it sexuality, commercialization, or even a compulsion to overeat) which can dominate people to such an extent that they lose their powers of discrimination and control. Since different forces may affect people in unpredictable ways, distinguishing between an amusement arcade and a den of iniquity becomes a complex problem for moralist, policeman, and pleasure seeker alike.

As a satirist, Taylor is concerned with these matters and with the ways people manage to live together. "Man is a social animal" goes the Spinoza quotation which serves as epigraph for *Cloven Kingdom* (1976). The statement is rich with ambiguity, for while it asserts that man is social, it also leaves no doubt that man is animal. Taylor provides one commentary upon that quotation in an all-male scene, a view of male bonding in which men gather for a bull session, galumphing and snorting about as though they were real bulls and causing one to wonder whether, the moment they enter their Eagles, Elk, and Moose lodges, men just might turn into real eagles, elk, and moose.

Human social patterns perfectly comprehensible to those who live according to them may absolutely bewilder outsiders. Taylor created a bewildering imaginary society in *Foreign Exchange* (1970). There were— or seemed to be—sporting events, warrior dances, mating rituals, and ceremonies of adoration. There were also peculiar native customs: a damsel emerged from a rock, a bossy woman chieftain ordered everyone about, and a curtain call occurred in the middle of the dance. It was all very strange—strange to watch, that is. The dancers went their way as though what they were doing was the most natural thing in the world—as perhaps it was. But only they knew it. In any case, while *Foreign Exchange* depicted an odd way of life, it nevertheless depicted a way of life which seemed real, though incomprehensible.

*Runes* (1975) does the same sort of thing. Like many of Taylor's dances, *Runes* is a work which is very different from the sort of work it superficially appears to be. Just as *Esplanade* may seem like something left over from an evening at the Judson Church, but isn't, so *Runes* may seem like a Glen Tetley ballet, but isn't. *Runes*, like many Tetley ballets, is ritualistic. But the way in which Taylor and Tetley differ may be seen by contrasting *Runes* with Tetley's *Le Sacre du Printemps*, as presented by American Ballet Theatre.

The Tetley *Sacre* is an anthology of references to mythic patterns and archetypes beloved by anthropologists, occultists, and psychoanalysts. During the course of the ballet one beholds the prophet or king who must die to save his people, the woman as life force, and the resurrected martyr (who, in the ballet's final moments, is specifically compared with Christ). *Sacre* is filled with references to culture. Taylor, too, makes cultural references—though much more indirectly. The big difference between the choreographers, however, is that while Tetley is content merely to refer to culture, Taylor actually creates a culture.

*Runes* shows the enactment of a ritual by a community. Just what this ritual is and just what the community is are left somewhat mysterious. If attending *Sacre* is like browsing through anthropology books in the library, attending *Runes* is like being an anthropologist out in the field. One must keep one's eyes open. Certain things about Taylor's ritual grow clear as it proceeds. With its motif of bodies falling to and rising from the floor, it is probably, like *Sacre*, some sort of ritual of renewal and regeneration. But as one keeps watching, this ritual starts looking increasingly odd. For one thing, the people involved apparently take turns at being victim and celebrant. At first, it is a man who lies inert on the ground, only to rise again, but as soon as he is risen his place is taken by a woman. Similarly, while there are times when the ritual is led by a male priest, there are also moments when he is replaced by a woman. The dance abounds with dualities and with sequences which unite dualities. Men cross the stage, women clinging to them as though these separate figures had merged into one androgynous whole. A man carries a woman, her arms and legs sticking out around his head like antlers: the body of a woman has here helped form the image of a male attribute. Similarly, there are both moments when the dancers crouch like beasts and moments when the men carry the women curved above them in idealized images suggesting crescent moons.

Victim and celebrant, priest and worshiper, male and female, flesh and spirit, real and ideal, life and death—*Runes* fuses these polarities. And because each dancer's role contributes to this fusion, Taylor's ritual becomes a peculiarly egalitarian ritual implying that all persons may make comparable fusions in their own persons. How this is to be done, though, is a matter each person must ponder in private. Instead of allowing us to nod with recognition at ready-made mythological symbols, *Runes* forces us to think about our own private mythology. It is a dance which ventures deep into a domain far more private than that disclosed in the dance called *Private Domain*. It is also a dance which reminds us how unpredictable Paul Taylor's choreography can be.

*Ballet Review* 6/1 (1977–78): 38–44

## TAYLOR'S RITES

The most important new work of many months was Paul Taylor's *Le Sacre du Printemps (The Rehearsal)*, which the Paul Taylor Dance Company offered during its 25th anniversary season at the City Center (15 April–4 May 1980).

Choreographers used to avoid *Sacre*. Now *Sacre*s are commonplace, and whenever new productions are announced one generally knows what to expect: there will be primitivistic paroxysms for dancers clad either in

Stone Age robes or in modern body stockings. Productions are so predictable that *Sacre* has lost its power to surprise.

Apparently realizing this, Taylor has created a *Sacre* unlike any other. He has turned Stravinsky's ballet into a thriller about a young woman with a baby who consults a detective, then goes off with him to a seedy waterfront dive, where a gangster's mistress kidnaps the child. After many adventures, including a jailbreak, comes a scene of mass slaughter that is both appalling and funny because it is performed in laconic slow motion.

At the same time, *Sacre* is also a ballet about a dance company rehearsing a detective-story ballet (hence the subtitle, *The Rehearsal*), and the imaginary troupe's rehearsal mistress is portrayed by Bettie de Jong, the Taylor company's actual rehearsal mistress. By using Stravinsky's own arrangement of *Sacre* for piano duet, rather than the orchestral score, Taylor evokes both the world of rehearsal studios and, in the detective-story sequences, that of silent films. The piano version emphasizes Stravinsky's percussive rhythms and Taylor, in response, has created a rhythmically complex work filled with staccato hops and jagged, propulsive thrustings. Since much of this choreography seems inspired by accounts of Nijinsky's ballets, Taylor's *Sacre* is simultaneously a novelty and a tribute to the first *Sacre*. The movement is also exciting in itself, so *Sacre* is interesting even after the initial surprise of its transformation into a thriller has worn off.

Actually, the surprise of that transformation never quite wears off. Taylor's *Sacre* is very peculiar. Whereas the incidents in its story are clear enough, Taylor deliberately withholds the motivation for those incidents. We never learn *why* the woman consults the detective, *why* her baby is kidnapped, or *why* anything else happens. Similarly, it is never clear whether the detective story is a costumed performance of the ballet that the troupe is rehearsing or the real-life incident that inspired that ballet. Moreover, de Jong's stern rehearsal mistress sometimes serves as a mirror image to the gangster's mistress. At such times, one cannot be sure whether she is simply coaching a dancer or whether she has become a sorceress, guiding someone's destiny. Or is Taylor slyly hinting that both crime and dancing are rackets?

Although everyone in *Sacre* resembles some character type from the ordinary world, what those characters do becomes as unfathomable as any primitive rite. Perhaps, then, Taylor's combinations of clear action with obscure motivation are ways of reminding us that primitive drives did not necessarily vanish with the dawn of civilization; they may have simply assumed new forms.

"New York Newsletter," *Dancing Times* (June 1980): 606

## AILEY'S *FLOWERS*

*Q*uite a lot happened at the City Center on 7 December 1980 when the Alvin Ailey American Dance Theatre offered the season's first performances of three works. A celebrity met her downfall. Lovers went in and out of love. Butterflies had tantrums. And the dancers' energy made everything exciting.

Yet the works shared a common choreographic problem. All three showed lots of things, yet revealed surprisingly little about what they showed.

A case in point is *Flowers*, Ailey's study of a doomed pop star, restaged in this revival by Ramon Segarra. Set to songs by Pink Floyd, Blind Faith, and Janis Joplin and possibly inspired by Joplin's life, it opens by showing the star thoroughly relishing her fame. Then she indicates that her private life is messier than her public image by throwing herself at man after man. When they reject her, she has an affair with a man who mistreats her and introduces her to drugs. The other men return, and, swooping like birds of prey, they lead her through a debauch from which she emerges a total wreck, hounded by photographers eager to exploit her degradation.

The work has impact, yet the motivation is sometimes hazy. Just what initially attracts the star to her cruel lover is unclear, and the avian fantasy is more visually striking than dramatically meaningful. Consequently, *Flowers* resembles a story in a scandal sheet.

Nevertheless, that story proved compelling. Alistair Butler, as the lover, was a sinister glowering presence, a man who was disturbing simply because of his perfect assurance, his awesome control.

As the star, Maxine Sherman started out by being so sassy that one could understand why audiences adored her. But there was desperation in her search for love, and gradually, and horrifyingly, the life force drained out of her with every step she took.

Problems of motivation also bedeviled *The Time Before the Time After (After the Time Before)*, Lar Lubovitch's dramatic duet to Stravinsky. Although it begins and ends with an embrace, between those embraces the man and woman the work concerns are never sure whether they should hug or hit each other.

But they exist in a vacuum. We never learn who they are or why they can neither get along nor stay apart. Indeed, the dramatic situation often appears to be only a pretext for spectacular movement and, in its own way, the duet is as much of a display piece as any old-fashioned pas de deux.

Fortunately, Donna Wood and Ulysses Dove danced and acted it to the hilt. Wood, who sometimes looked as cool as a classical ballerina, could instantly turn herself into a squabbling harridan, and then regain her composure. Dove's similarly unexpected changes of movement quality made the character he portrayed a man who could be both tender and bullying, and one suspected that he never quite knew which he was at any moment.

There was more splendid dancing in *Butterfly*, Rael Lamb's fluttery piece to electronic music by Morton Subotnick. Lamb's butterflies often got remarkably agitated for no apparent reason. Still, it was good to see Danita Ridout and Michihiko Oka in a stormy duet, Sharrell Mesh and Sherman as two rather seductive butterflies, and, perhaps best of all, the fragile Mari Kajiwara, whose balances beautifully suggested a butterfly's hoverings.*

*New York Times*, 9 December 1980

---

*A comparison of this review with the preceding one of Paul Taylor's *Le Sacre du Printemps (The Rehearsal)* may reveal that neither the presence nor the absence of any single quality can guarantee the sucess of a work, and that a quality which contributes to the effectiveness of one work may be a defect in another. By withholding motivation in *Le Sacre*, Taylor both creates a dance with a plot akin to the cryptic narratives favored by such writers of thrillers as Raymond Chandler and Dashiell Hammett and manages to comment on the essential mysteriousness of the human personality. However, because Ailey and Lubovitch wish to suggest a choreographic biography or create a character study, the absence of motivation makes their works less striking and convincing than they ought to be. Clearly, works must be judged on their own terms and not by a set of general rules.

## JUDSON REVIVALS: A FESTIVAL BENEFIT

New York's best-known center for avant-garde theatre is not a playhouse but a Baptist church, the Judson Memorial Church in Greenwich Village, which has a long tradition of upholding social reform and cultural freedom. A performance there resembles no other in atmosphere. In contrast to the staid patrons of the Broadway theatre, this audience is articulate, even cantankerous, about its artistic preferences. While uptown audiences tend to regard the arts as something for special (or social) occasions, the Judson audience looks upon art, not as something special, but as a necessary part of everyday life. If the atmosphere is usually informal, the intellectual ferment is often intense.

Most Judson presentations are free. But in the spring of 1966, to raise funds for the Judson Dance Theatre and Poets' Theatre, admission was charged for a performing arts festival. Although officially called a cycle of revivals, there were new works as well as old. One could object that too many comic pieces were programmed, while some worthy, but somber, works went unrevived. Yet this was, after all, a fund-raising event and, even among the avant-garde, comedy is notoriously "good box office."

Although certain dancers have been nicknamed "Judson dancers," dance there is surprisingly diverse. In general, however, these choreographers tend to be nonliterary, nonnarrative, nonmythical. They borrow freely from ballet, modern dance, or natural movement. They are more concerned with implication than with direct statement and prefer to stimulate the spectator's powers of perception, rather than stun with technical display or exciting stories. Sometimes these dances have the cheerful impersonality of hard-edge painting. Sometimes, influenced by assemblage artists, various media are so mixed that the results seem paintings that move or dances that don't. There is also a strong undercurrent of Romantic sensibility at Judson, manifested in picturesque or even slightly bizarre works.

The festival's most impressive dance composition was Yvonne Rainer's *The Mind Is a Muscle*, presented unfinished earlier in the year and now receiving its official premiere. A choreographic reminder that we are made of sinew and muscle, it began with William Davis, David Gordon, and Rainer fleetly performing movements related to calisthenics, gymnastics, and tumbling. They were succeeded by Becky Arnold, Barbara Lloyd, and Peter Saul, who, to the sound of hoofbeats, sprinted, jumped, cantered, and galloped.

Next, all six dancers performed acrobatic stunts (this was the one section in which they looked technically insecure), ran like gazelles on the veldt, then wheeled around and did finicky little movements, as though walking on eggs. Finally, as strips of wood dropped from the church's balcony to the side of the stage, Peter Saul danced a solo which fused the acrobatics of previous sections with the formality of classical ballet.

Event rapidly followed event, allowing little respite for dancer or audience. *The Mind Is a Muscle* demanded the same full attention of its viewers that they would devote to serious thought or hard labor. Yet its deceptively casual mood made it—to borrow terms from linguistics—a colloquial, vernacular dance. Other Judson dances were more deliberately elegant in idiom.

The best of these was the revival of Arlene Rothlein's *Morning Raga with Yellow Chair*. Utilizing mudras, modern dance, and yoga self-control, Rothlein moved around and upon a chair with almost feline agility, creating an aura of sensuality which grew until one woman and one ordinary kitchen chair evoked all the gaudy extravagance of our fantasies about the exotic Orient.

An attractive piece of Judson Romanticism was the revival of *April and December* (Tchaikovsky), a quasi-balletic solo choreographed by Remy Charlip for Aileen Passloff, who swept through it like a dryad in a woodland glade. The remaining dances were all curiosities of some sort. James Waring contributed two solos, his popular *Tambourine Dance*, in which he resembled a living *art nouveau* lampshade, and a new *March* (Mozart) which combined intricate arm movements, like those of a Rococo clockwork doll, with less interesting balletic movements for the feet.

In *What's the Big Idea 321*, excerpted from a long work not yet seen in New York, Katherine Litz, to Chopin's "Funeral March," frowned puritanically upon some flowers, dithered about like a moonstruck Ophelia, and cavorted like a chorus girl. In context, these antics may have comic point. Performed as fragments, they were just peculiar.

Sabina Nordoff's *Manu and the Fish* was based upon both an Indian myth and eurhythmy, a system of "visible speech" devised by the philosopher Rudolf Steiner (and distinct from the eurhythmics of Dalcroze). *Manu* was performed twice, each time producing a different effect. Danced to narration, it resembled mime. Minus narration, it seemed purely decorative. With its pulsating, expanding, and contracting gestures, its semicircular runs, its repeated use of hands encircling the head or palms held out to the audience, Steiner eurhythmy, as interpreted by Aileen Passloff and Remy Charlip, looked pretty, but also slightly monotonous.

Whether by chance or because their directors deliberately favor a single style, the plays were more alike in character than the dances. There was no trace here of the realism which has long been the trademark of American acting. No attempts were made to create illusion or to fool spectators into thinking they were someplace other than in a theatre. For the Judson actors, the major factor which distinguishes theatre from such comparable forms as TV or films seems to be the direct contact possible between performer and audience. The productions, often whimsical or fantastic, and filled with abrupt changes of tone, all employed dance. All also employed music, composed in every case by the Reverend Al Carmines, director of the Judson arts program. His scores ranged from the commonplace (*Home Movies*) to the delightful (*A Beautiful Day*).

Some productions were thin in content, being mere parades of theatrical devices. A case in point is H. M. Koutoukas's *Pomegranada*, a fable about how the animals succumbed to temptation along with Adam and Eve. Despite clever lines, lush scenery resembling a Rousseau painting, and whimsical choreography by Remy Charlip, it never really contributed anything provocatively original to the Eden myth. Similarly, Maria Irene Fornes's *Promenade*, concerning escaped convicts who wander into a fancy party, was as insubstantial as Viennese operetta. George Dennison's *Patter for a Soft-Shoe Dance* was defeated by Judson's unreliable acoustics. Choreographed by Charlip for George Bartenieff and Robert Frink, who commented upon the way of the world as they danced, most of the lines were inaudible. Rosalyn Drexler's *Home Movies*, a Pop Art portrait of the American home, was sometimes sharply satirical, sometimes merely strident.

The two most imaginatively conceived and brilliantly performed productions were also those with the most dancing. Gertrude Stein's comedy, *What Happened*, directed by Lawrence Kornfeld, had a cast composed almost entirely of dancers (Joan Baker, Lucinda Childs, Aileen Passloff, Yvonne Rainer, Arlene Rothlein, Al Carmines, Hunt Cole, Masato Kawasaki, and Burton Supree). The text, a succession of grammatical games, was used almost as a kind of accompaniment in the way that music accompanies an abstract ballet. The words, like melodies in a ballet score, were important, not for any literal significance, but for their ability to inspire and support choreographic action. Against the background of a clothesline hung with sky-blue laundry, the cast, like precocious children, played hopscotch, tag, and jump rope. Later, the audience was treated to the remarkable spectacle of Joan Baker trying to lower herself into a grand piano as though it were a bathtub.

Ruth Krauss's *A Beautiful Day*, a miniature revue choreographed and directed by Remy Charlip, also involved word games. But their ingenuities were less abstract than those of Stein. In fact, the revue was a tribute to the wonder of living. A quartet warbled the history of culture. Florence Tarlow vociferously lauded the mammary glands. David Vaughan read surrealist weather reports. Aileen Passloff was cryptically lured off by mysterious ladies in an oyster shell. And an octet turned a lullaby into a revel, asking, "Whom does the Little One favor?" and answering "The Little One favors the moon . . . the East River and the Queensboro Bridge . . . a beard full of butterflies," and finally, "The Little One favors astonishment."

So do the Dance and Poets' Theatres of Judson Church.

*Dance Magazine* (July 1966): 30–31, 62–63

# YVONNE RAINER:
# THE PURITAN AS HEDONIST

When I arrived in New York in 1964, I had already heard of her. Yvonne Rainer had the reputation of being a ferocious young woman who writhed to the squeaking of chairs being dragged across the floor. Before long, I saw her. She was not what I expected.

I saw her at the now defunct Washington Square Gallery where with Robert Morris she performed a duet called *Part of a Sextette*. Set to a poetic meditation on sleep, it was implicitly sexual in feeling and hypnotic in effect. But there were no writhings or squeaking chairs. The next week at the gallery, she did an improvisation with Jill Johnston to the Handel-Beecham *Love in Bath*, in which she repeatedly jumped into the laps of men in the audience. She did not jump into my lap, but I liked the dance anyway. Again, no writhings, no chairs.

What I was not aware of until I had been in New York for a while was that Rainer was undergoing a change of style. As she herself put it, she was trying to stop deriving her inspiration from the loony bin. She was becoming the Yvonne Rainer she is today. She went about it by stripping from her choreography most of the ingredients which usually make up dance productions: not only such obvious and easy to get rid of ones as plot, characterization, musicality, and theme, but climax, tension, suspense, development, and even the beautifully effortless or artfully effortful look custom has made us associate with professional dance theatre.

Rainer settled upon an open-ended form which prevents a dance from building to high points or getting anywhere logically. To a great extent, any part of the dance could precede or follow any other part without damaging the total effect. Rainer's recent dances have employed, recombined, and rearranged sections from previous works. For instance, her *Rose Fractions* at the Billy Rose Theatre in 1969 contained a film and a monologue previously used in *Two Trios*, and it concluded with the irregular canon which has come to be regarded as virtually the "signature dance" of the innumerable versions of *The Mind Is a Muscle*. Instead of violence, Rainer is now associated with coolness at its most cool.

This rejection of conventional theatricality suggests a Puritan temperament. Writing in the *Tulane Drama Review* (10/2 [Winter 1965]: 178), she pronounced a resounding "NO to spectacle no to virtuosity no to transformations and magic and make-believe no to the glamour and transcendency of the star image . . . no to style no to camp no to moving or being moved." In a program note last year, she confessed to a "rage at the impoverishment of ideas, narcissism, and disguised sexual exhibitionism of most dancing. . . ."

Rainer's Puritanism is a carefully considered choice. She did not have to be that way. Statuesque and blessed with a compelling stage presence, she could have been, had she wanted, a fine Expressionist dancer. She is also capable of charm, as evidenced by *Three Satie Spoons* (to the "Gymnopédies"), a solo dating from 1961 which remained until recently in her repertoire. While performing movements which seemed to be inspired by some imaginary classical frieze, she unexpectedly made "beep-beep-

beeping" noises while she danced and repeated banal statements about grass and sunlight. Her dance, like Satie's music, was simultaneously elegant and eccentric.

It was a lovely dance, but Rainer said "NO" to all that. The first theatrical manifestations of that "NO" I encountered baffled me: for example, *Parts of Some Sextets* at Judson Church in 1965. While I realized it was a sign of a struggle to exorcise overt Expressionism, I did not in any way enjoy it. Ten dancers lugged piles of mattresses about and flung themselves upon them for what seemed like a long, long time. The accompaniment was a droning recitation from the eighteenth-century *Diary of William Bentley*. Although the dancers moved, the composition never moved from its *idée fixe:* it was absolutely unbudgeable. As Rainer rightly put it in her *Tulane Drama Review* essay, it "progressed as though on a treadmill or like a 10-ton truck stuck on a hill: it shifts gears, groans, sweats, farts, but doesn't move an inch."

I was similarly perplexed by *Carriage Discreteness*, presented during the 1966 Theatre and Engineering series at the 25th St. Armory. Seated on a balcony above the action, Rainer gave movement instructions, selected from a predetermined set of possibilities, to her cast by means of a walkie-talkie. The dancers thereupon carried out her requests. As an idea, *Carriage Discreteness* was reminiscent of the living chess game with which a Renaissance prince might amuse himself. Yet it was more interesting to me as an idea than as a performance. The dancers could move only when given instructions and the gap between instruction and execution caused the piece to seem perpetually in danger of coming to a dead halt.

Fortunately, while Yvonne Rainer was boring me with her Puritanical strictness in some works, she was pleasing me very much in others—specifically, *The Mind Is a Muscle* series which began in 1966. From then to *Rose Fractions*, Rainer's Puritanism has been pushed to such an extreme that it has reversed itself to become a kind of hedonism. For once she has stripped away all spectacle from the dance, she is left with choreography's irreducible minimum, the dancer's body. She loves the body—with all its nerves, muscles, bones, and sinews—as a physical instrument which can accomplish a multitude of things. Her dances are tributes to the corporeal reality of human beings.

This love, however, is inextricably bound up with her distrust of showiness. She says in a 1968 program note, "I love the body—its actual weight, and unenhanced physicality." Unenhanced physicality: these words, I think, identify the peculiar quality evident in Yvonne Rainer's recent choreography. The performers are obviously agile (Rainer seems uninterested in physical failure), but the movements they are called upon to do look as though they have been taken from other than conventional dance sources. Often, they are task movements, game movements, movements used to accomplish something, yet removed from their functional context. A clue to the kind of unenhanced movement she favors is provided by a *Lecture* reprinted in the January 1969 issue of the literary magazine *0 to 9*. Here Rainer explains the development of a syntax of dance movements based upon the physiological fact that a person is able to move several parts of the body simultaneously, a simple example being one's ability to pat one's head while rubbing one's belly. Enormously complicated and difficult movement patterns can be developed from these simultaneities, but they are patterns which suggest physical fitness exercises rather than ballet or the technical systems codified by the older generation of modern dancers.

*The Mind Is a Muscle* employed such movements almost exclusively. In January 1966 the title was used for a short brilliant trio. By May of that year it had become a longer dance for six. In April 1968 it was presented in a full-evening version by a cast of eight. Whatever form it has taken, *The Mind Is a Muscle* has always been the same kind of dance: a dance which celebrates the body's capacity to be active.

In the *Village Voice* Jill Johnston has speculated whether a passage in which dancers clutch their abdomens might have been suggested by Rainer's own battle with a serious illness. If so, this passage represents, not disease, but the triumph of the body over disease, for although the dancers contort themselves, they are never vanquished. Throughout the dance, frequent use is made of obstacles with which the cast must cope.

Three dancers run on a floorcloth which crunches underfoot. Others climb a staircase and jump from the top. A juggler juggles balls, clubs, and torches. Dancers tumble on mats and later carry the mats about with them; still later, they lift each other.

Conceivably, these feats could be performed with the swagger and flourish of circus tricks. But Yvonne Rainer avoids exhibitionism. As a result, *The Mind Is a Muscle* is dynamically odd. Unrhetorical in tone, the choreography, even at its most complicated, makes no attempt to dazzle the audience. The action flows by with such rapidity and lack of emphasis that one must struggle to concentrate upon following the course of the dance. In that struggle to concentrate, the audience, too, is dancing—dancing with the mind. Rainer says, "The mind is a muscle," and just as the dancers are physically working certain sets of muscles, the audience is mentally working to keep up with them.

One of the first things I noticed about *Rose Fractions* was that the dancers looked as though they were having a good time. Although it lasted nearly three hours and utilized three dozen people (including those in the section choreographed by Deborah Hay), it seemed less austere than some of Rainer's previous compositions. Symptomatic of this was the fact that the excerpt from *The Mind Is a Muscle* this time was danced to the Chambers Brothers.

An amazing thing about the movements was that they all looked like things I fancied I might be able to do (although, quite likely, not as engagingly). The dancers mill about, tussle, huddle, scramble, walk, skip, turn somersaults, carry packages, trays, and each other, scatter gravel to a film of fidgety chickens, nudge in crowded groups, break into runs, hop, hobble, pick up books, and balance on a bar. There were those who found these activities stultifying. I found them a refreshing tribute to the ordinary human body—not those glorious bodies we see in, say, the *Nutcracker* pas de deux, but the bodies we actually have.

Rainer has said she rages against the "disguised sexual exhibitionism of most dancing." In *Rose Fractions*, off went the disguises. At least since the days back at Judson when she ran around naked in a few dances, Rainer has been concerned with the problem of the erotic and pornographic in art. Her ventures into this area suggest that she believes that the body is not (morally) dirty, it is dirty thoughts about the body which make the body seem dirty. As though corroborating the implications of the theory of pornography advanced by Arlene Croce in a *Ballet Review* article on Martha Graham (in which Croce argues that "estrangement is at the core of all lust"), Rainer appears to be trying to demonstrate that the greater the separation between thought and body, the dirtier the thoughts get and the body seems.

Toward the end of *The Mind Is a Muscle* occurs the recitation of a pornographic poem by John Giorno:

> . . . one fucked me
> in the behind,
> another in the mouth,
> while I jacked off
> one
> with each hand
> and two
> of the others
> rubbed
> their peckers
> on my bare feet . . .

And so on in like vein. Amongst the wholesome gymnastics this suddenly sounds thoroughly preposterous.

*Rose Fractions,* like *Two Trios* before it, contains a monologue by Lenny Bruce, effectively delivered in an understated comic style by Rainer. She tells us that she is about to say the dirtiest word she knows, a four-letter word beginning with "s" and ending with "t." Then she says it: "snot." Next, we hear all sorts of vile, dirty things about snot; for instance, you can't get it off suede. Pornography is here exposed as a way of thinking. It need not have any reference to truth and reality; a certain way of structuring thought is itself sufficient to make anything pornographic.

The "shockers" of *Rose Fractions* were films of a naked man and woman playing with a balloon and of a man and woman having sex. From a purely formalist standpoint, it could be argued that since choreography involves movement and sex involves movement, the sex film is appropriate for a dance concert. But that argument alone is either far too naive or far too sophisticated (I can't make up my mind which).

I suspect that Rainer, Puritan that she is, has a moral point to make. She wants us to contemplate the body without flinching or fantasizing. She has taken a secret thing—a stimulus for masturbation—and has made it public. Look: people do have sex, that is part of human nature and, despite the crude films shown at unsavory parties with the blinds drawn, there is nothing really so terrible about that, is there? Sexual agony is condoned as a theme in our theatre (as a whole genre of ballet and modern dance attests), sexual pleasure is taboo. However, to dwell obsessively upon either sexual joy or sexual pain suggests an unwholesome or ill-at-ease mind. Rainer showed the film once in *Rose Fractions*, made her point, and never returned to it; thus, the piece as a whole retained its artistic equilibrium. She again employed good sense by showing it near the beginning, with no self-conscious editorializing about sexual freedom, rather than saving it for a socko finale.

Stirring among many people—from hippies to gurus like Norman O. Brown and the apostles of sensory reawakening—is a feeling that our society is, at the very least, excessively oriented toward pain. The pronouncements of these people are often insufferably self-righteous, yet their basic contention cannot be shrugged off. One can find reflections of it in much current art, including some of the controversial dances presented during the final week of the Billy Rose season. Meredith Monk's *Untidal: Movement Period* can be viewed as a call for an end to racial strife; in all of her dances, Twyla Tharp seems to be upholding the integrity of pure movement as a good in itself which should not be corrupted.

Yvonne Rainer is jealously guarding the human body. In order to do so, she has had to rush into the playhouse and knock down the idols of the theatre, and if that action sometimes seems extreme to those of us who also enjoy other dance forms, the result for Rainer has been a way of dancing in which the body looks at once ordinary and exhilarating. Now that she has achieved this, I am curious about what she will do next.*

*Ballet Review* 2/5 (1969): 31–37

*What she did only a few years after this article was published was to give up dancing altogether and devote herself to filmmaking. But, by that time, she had influenced innumerable dancers and dancegoers.

# STEVE PAXTON'S IMPROVISATIONS

Questions, questions. The performance, 30 October 1979, by Steve Paxton and David Moss at Camera Mart/Stage One prompted lots of questions. And those questions sprouted other questions. What happened?

Paxton danced. Moss played an array of percussion instruments and sporadically burst into vocalizing. Their performance—an attraction in the Dance Umbrella series—was entirely improvised and, although the program labeled the part before intermission "Going On" and the next part "Going On Two," the evening was one long dance.

Paxton, who in recent years has become increasingly preoccupied with improvisation, began his dance with bouncy little movements akin to warmups. Many of the sequences that followed emphasized twists and shrugs and alternations of tension and relaxation. And yet, although Paxton might tense himself, he never became rigid. Energy was always able to flow through his body. The performance itself could be called a flowing. As its title suggested, it was a "Going On."

But—and here the questions tumble forth—where did it go? How satisfactory is improvisation, anyway? Because it requires dancers to invent everything afresh, is it merely a stunt? Can't the necessity of improvising turn dancers either into court jesters desperately trying to amuse or into aloof personages apparently indifferent to whether their audiences are bored or not? Besides, because the creative spirit is elusive, why tempt fate? What if one's muse refuses to come?

When we watch improvisations, what should we look for? What can we do other than admire someone's ability to keep going? But what if things don't seem to be going anywhere? What if, as happened in Paxton's concert, phrases are introduced but seldom developed?

Yet why should phrases always be developed? Why can't we just enjoy them for their own transient beauty? Because Paxton did everything from walk on his hands to scratch his ear, can't it be said his improvisation was as varied as life itself? And because, in life, prolonged calm may be followed by crisis after crisis, why can't a dance also have its Sargasso Seas as well as its windy Himalayan summits? Why can't a dance be as untidy as life?

Yet because, in life, we not only experience things, but also place value judgments on our experiences, how lifelike was Paxton's dance? Because all events in it were apparently given equal importance, was it lifelike at all? Or was Paxton trying to make us aware of the preciousness of each separate fleeting moment? Nevertheless, if every event is as important as every other event, don't all events become equally unimportant?

Questions, questions. But what's wrong with that? Because Paxton did stimulate thought, wasn't his dance of real importance, after all? Perhaps. But should a dance be more interesting to think about than to watch?

*New York Times*, 1 November 1979

# THE CHANGING FACES

# OF TWYLA THARP

*T*en years ago, some dancers spaced themselves out on a lawn in the twilight of a summer evening and began to move very slowly— so slowly, in fact, that they scarcely seemed to move at all. Yet they were moving, moving as if a sculpture garden had come to life. And as they moved, they faded away into the gathering dusk.

This magical moment concluded *Medley*, a long dance by Twyla Tharp that was first presented outdoors at Connecticut College during the American Dance Festival of 1969 and later repeated on the Great Lawn of Central Park. On both occasions, it attracted unusually large, enthusiastic audiences. It was, perhaps, the first work by Tharp to do so.

Others have followed. Tharp, once considered formidably esoteric, has become extraordinarily successful. She has not only choreographed for her own company, she has choreographed for the Joffrey Ballet and American Ballet Theatre, for Mikhail Baryshnikov and for John Curry, the ice-skating star. And she recently choreographed the movie version of *Hair.*

In some ways, Tharp's basic choreographic style has not changed. She remains fond of sudden stops and starts, twists and swivels, and abrupt changes of weight. What has changed, however—and changed significantly—is the way she packages and presents these materials.

Before 1969, her dancers were a severe bunch with resolutely blank faces. Or when they did show signs of feeling, they turned tough and faintly aggressive. The company, moreover, consisted entirely of women, for Tharp did not wish sexual distinctions, with all their erotic, dramatic, or emotional potentialities, to divert one's attention from the formal complexities of her choreography.

Filled with mirror images, inversions, and contrapuntal devices, that choreography was indeed complex. One section of *Re-Moves*, for instance, was exactly the same as the work's opening section, except that all the steps were danced backward. Tharp herself described *After 'Suite'* as a septet "performed in three adjacent squares. As each section of the work is completed, it is immediately repeated in an adjacent square as a variant of itself (retrogrades, shifts of focus, repatterning) while the next section is being introduced."

Today, Tharp's works may be equally intricate, yet the old severity is gone. Not only are there men as well as women in her company, her dancers look chic rather than truculent.

Two things helped bring about this "new look." First of all, as the mysterious finale of *Medley* suggested in 1969, Tharp has become interested in theatrical effects. In the Joffrey Ballet's *Deuce Coupe*, for instance, the scenery was created on the spot at each performance by a team of graffiti artists, while in *Chapters and Verses*, presented by her own company in 1979 at the Brooklyn Academy of Music, a miniature hot rod rolled onstage.

Even more important to Tharp's success has been her choice of music. Although she occasionally used musical accompaniments when she began to choreograph, most of her best-known early works were performed in silence so that nothing would distract from the movement. In 1971, however, along came the goofy *Eight Jelly Rolls*, to Jelly Roll Morton, the first of Tharp's successful utilizations of popular music.

Since then, she has turned to ragtime, jazz, rock, country fiddling, and military marches. Last season, she even choreographed the Mickey Mouse Club theme song. These accompaniments have helped sugarcoat her choreographic complexities. Sometimes she makes points by combining pop with classical music. *The Bix Pieces* found rhythmic vitality in both Bix Beiderbecke and Haydn, while *The Raggedy Dances* demonstrated that certain compositions of Mozart and Scott Joplin shared a comparable aplomb.

These dances had real points to make. More recent dances, however, seem to lack strong choreographic points. They simply combine wacky movement with unexpected music. Thus, whereas most dances to Sousa marches would probably show people keeping in step, *Give and Take* showed people getting out of step. But is such a slender comic idea sufficient for a whole dance? If *Give and Take* had charm, it was also slight. Charm was something people used to say Tharp's choreography lacked. Now charm may come too easily to her.

Tharp has choreographed herself into an odd corner. She and some of her fanatic admirers often seem to consider her style as a good in itself apart from any specific creative use to which it can be put. So regarded, her style becomes an all-purpose form of ornament that can decorate any occasion. If great stylists can sometimes also be moral forces because their chosen way of appearing before the world manages to confront, defy, or transform the world, Tharp's style is too often only something that enables her to fool around.

When she first started using music regularly, her excursions into pop appeared to liberate her. Now they may limit her. If only the most snobbish cultural mandarin would maintain that pop music is inherently inferior to classical music, surely it can be argued that pop music is of unequal value, that, despite its jauntiness, the Mickey Mouse Club song, for instance, is not as musically interesting as either Scott Joplin or Mozart.

Tharp's present willingness to employ even banal music simply because it somehow amuses her can lead to cuteness or cheap nostalgia. She may be tempted to choreograph froth and audiences may come to expect nothing but that from her. She will then have locked herself into a formula, just as television comedies can lock themselves into formulas because their fans may come to expect certain characters to appear each week displaying the same quirks of personality and repeating the same characteristic comic taglines.

This season, Tharp hinted that she may be trying to avoid formulas. Two of her new pieces were stabs at social commentary. Neither was successful, however. A suite of dances from *Hair* was vehemently antimilitaristic. But it was also gauche.

*Chapters and Verses,* a dance about American youth, showed, in some of its episodes, cheerful kids full of pep, while in other scenes it suggested that young Americans are superficial and violent. Yet, having established this dichotomy, Tharp declined to speculate upon whether or not American virtues outweighed American vices.

She thereby managed to toss out piquant choreographic notions without stirring up controversy and without offending either the advocates or the critics of youth culture, just as when she put graffiti onstage in *Deuce Coupe* she refused to indicate whether she considered graffiti a valid form of street art or a vandalistic desecration of public space. If refusing to propagandize may be admirable, a refusal to venture any opinion suggests superficiality.

Fortunately, Tharp can still commit herself at times to creative inventiveness. Her *Baker's Dozen* of last season contained some of her best choreography of recent years. Indeed, this sprightly, yet elegant, work about the joys of sociability may be her finest effort since *As Time Goes By* of 1973. Interestingly enough, neither dance contains gimmickry or odd musical juxtapositions. *As Time Goes By* is set to Haydn, and to nobody else, and *Baker's Dozen* utilizes jazz piano music by Willie ("The Lion") Smith.

Tharp's fondness for Haydn and Smith soon becomes choreographically apparent. She has taken a risk; she has dared to commit herself to showing us what she likes about this music. By so doing, she not only entertains, she also refreshes our eyes and makes us hear things anew.

*New York Times*, 9 September 1979

## TRISHA BROWN'S MINIMALISM

*T*risha Brown has been called a postmodern choreographic minimalist and that's a fearsome-sounding thing for anyone to be called. The "postmodern" part of the appellation refers to the fact that she has allied herself with those choreographers who over the past two decades have rejected both the Expressionist concerns of an earlier era of modern dance and the codified systems of dance technique developed by several of the modern dance pioneers. And because she disdains theatrical frills and prefers a no-nonsense kind of movement, she may be called a "minimalist." Moreover, like certain minimalists in the other arts, she is fascinated by rigorous structural principles. So she is, then, "postmodern" and "minimalist."

But, oh dear, how dull that makes her sound, and she is anything but dull. Perhaps, then, it might be better to find some other way to describe her. Brown herself has even given a clue as to how one might go about it. Significantly, on one occasion she defined herself as "a bricklayer with a sense of humor."

That she is. She builds dances carefully, thoroughly, methodically. But an architect who examined those dances might find them related not to the structures of Le Corbusier or Mies van der Rohe, but to such architectural curiosities as the Watts Towers or the Brighton Pavilion. An architect might also raise his eyebrows at some of Brown's sites for building dances. Her company has performed on the roofs of buildings in New York and on rafts floating on a lagoon in a Minneapolis park. Yet, even when she dances in conventional theatres, Brown's choreography can combine impersonal logic with personal idiosyncrasy.

Take, for instance, *Locus*, in which each dancer in the cast of four women imagines that she is standing within an imaginary cube on which there are twenty-seven points. The movements in the dance consist of progressions from one of those specific points to another. Such a structure might please the most ardent lovers of strict artistic form.

But what would they make of this next bit of information? Brown established the order of movements in *Locus* by writing an autobiographical statement beginning, "Trisha Brown was born in Aberdeen, Washington . . ." Then she assigned each letter a numerical equivalent (A = 1, B = 2, etc.) corresponding to one of the points on the cube. She translated the entire statement into numbers and let the twenty-seventh point on the cube represent the space between words. By going to the proper numbered positions, a performer can turn every word in that autobiography into dancing.

*Locus* is meticulously assembled. But it's a curiosity. Of course, to realize how truly curious it is, a viewer must know something about how it was made. Yet one can enjoy Brown's dances as lively movement experiences without possessing any advance knowledge about them. And the structural principles upon which many are built gradually become apparent; indeed, puzzling over the structure can be part of the fun of watching the dance.

*Line-Up* is a suite of little dances, each dance having something to do with staying in line or getting out of line. So described, the dances may sound dull; yet several can generate real suspense. In one, dancers are poised like racers on a starting line. First they must take one step out of line and get back in line within five seconds. Then they must take two steps out and back within the same time limit, then three steps, then four steps, and so on, the five-second intervals being marked by a gong. Should dancers fail to complete the movements within the allotted time, they are "out." The dance ends when everyone is "out."

In another episode of *Line-Up*, dancers holding sticks are stretched out in a line on the floor. Each dancer's stick must touch that of the next dancer at all times. Yet the dancers are also required to move around and under the line of sticks.

Beneath Brown's passion for order lurks a fondness for absurdity. There were touches of the absurd in *Glacial Decoy*, a work designed by Robert Rauschenberg. Much of it looked very orderly. Slides were projected upon four screens, each projection progressing from screen to screen until it had appeared on all four.

The projections, however, seemed unrelated. They simply showed things that apparently struck Rauschenberg's fancy: such things as cliffs, piers, light bulbs, dogs, boxcars, ferns, clouds, and clocks. The choreography possessed its own oddities. Two dancers rushed in. Then, as though the wings exerted a magnetic attraction, they rushed out again.

Later two women were joined by a third. Yet the magnetism of the wings always drew the newcomer away. Finally, as the two women kept dancing, two more were also occasionally visible dancing in the wings. Now it looked as if all the women were doing the same dance, except that two of them were doing it offstage.

Another work at a recent concert that demonstrated what a witty bricklayer Brown can be was *Accumulation with Talking Plus Water Motor*. It was the newest version of *Accumulation*, a solo that requires Brown to repeat movements and, with each repetition, to complicate the sequence by adding new movements, just as new words are constantly added to the repetitions in the song about the twelve days of Christmas. To complicate things further, while she moves Brown must tell stories. She even tells two stories at once, switching from one to the other.

In her new version, she did all this and more. Into *Accumulation* she inserted phrases from still another solo, *Water Motor*, so that she was eventually telling two stories and dancing two dances simultaneously.

*Accumulation with Talking Plus Water Motor* was quite a structure, a real feat of choreographic bricklaying. But even though each separate movement in it was a plain unadorned gesture, the dance that resulted was so fancy and complex that it recalled the architectural follies—all turrets and spires—that English eccentrics built for their amusement in the Romantic era. Brown may be methodical; yet there's a wonderful madness in her method.

*New York Times*, 15 July 1979

# NEW DANCES
# THAT MADE AUDIENCES THINK

*T*he Brooklyn Academy of Music's Next Wave Festival helped make the autumn of 1983 rich in modern dance and multimedia theatre. Productions were unusual and often surprising, and as a result of the emphasis upon collaborations between choreographers and visual artists, Next Wave productions were good to look at. In addition to giving visual pleasure, they also provided food for thought.

Thus, three works that received their New York premieres during the festival—Molissa Fenley's *Hemispheres*, Trisha Brown's *Set and Reset*, and Lucinda Childs's *Available Light*—posed fascinating problems of perception, and even though they told no stories and preached no sermons, they expressed some interesting ideas about life in this world.

*Hemispheres* invited viewers to think about one thing while watching something totally different, thanks to what could be called the "portable décor" devised by Francesco Clemente, an Italian artist. The stage space was empty, except for the cast of three dancers and the members of Episteme, the musical group that played the score by Anthony Davis.

Yet, as the program note promised, the work did contain a visual element. As they entered the theatre, spectators were given a packet of prints by Clemente and were free to examine those prints at leisure and to take them home or dispose of them as they wished.

Few spectators, I suspect, used them to decorate their walls, for the prints depicted bound and mutilated bodies. The dance, however, was in the athletically exuberant style for which Fenley is noted. Therefore, *Hemispheres* could be said to contrast the degradation of the body, as symbolized by the prints, and its liberation, as symbolized by the choreography. Presumably, as one watched the dance one may have recalled the prints; and if one glanced at the prints again after *Hemispheres* was over, one may have recalled the dance. And letting one's mind run back and forth between the dance and the prints may have prompted ideas about human shame and glory.

*Hemispheres* was as much a mental event as it was a demonstration of physical skill. If anything, it was too much of a mental event. With its repeated runs, turns, and flingings of the arms, the choreography lacked invention. Its limitations may have been deliberately imposed upon it by Fenley in order to emphasize the energy, rather than the intricacy, of the steps. Yet the steps she employed had little cumulative power.

In order to demonstrate their stamina, the dancers had to keep going on and, in order to appreciate that stamina, one had to keep on watching them. But watching the dancers became almost as much of a trial as doing the dance must have been, and when Fenley attempted to inject variety into the proceedings by means of a section in a slower tempo, she merely demonstrated that, thus far in her choreographic career, she is more adept at allegro than adagio movement. *Hemispheres* was undeniably interesting. Yet it was sometimes more interesting to think about than to behold.

Brown's *Set and Reset* and Childs's *Available Light* seemed equally good onstage and when they were scrutinized by the mind's eye. Both gave viewers unusual freedom of perception.

Laurie Anderson's score for *Set and Reset* included clanging and thudding sounds and, significantly, repetitions of the phrase "Long time no see." The structure by Robert Rauschenberg that served as décor consisted of a rectangle surrounded by two pyramidal shapes. At first, this construction stood on the ground, then it was suspended in the air above the dancers and films were projected on its gauzy surfaces.

What were they films of? That question is extraordinarily difficult to answer. They appeared to be blurred newsreel images of people, animals, and machine parts. Or maybe they showed none of those things. But, whatever they depicted, they were so misty and they came and went with such rapidity that, no matter how long one squinted, peered, or stared at them, one could not be sure just what one was looking at. And if one puzzled over them too long, one missed the dance entirely.

The dance, though, was just as peculiar as the films. As if summoned by some mysterious power, the members of the cast were constantly drawn out of the wings toward stage center in knots and whorls of movement. Yet whenever patterns started to crystallize, they melted away again, and anyone trying to devote total attention to them would have had to ignore the films.

Working in collaboration, Brown and Rauschenberg created a dance that could not possibly be assimilated at a single viewing. Perhaps its events can never be fully assimilated, even after several viewings. Anderson's reiterations of "Long time no see" therefore emphasized the work's special nature: whereas several things in it invited one's attention, if one watched any specific thing for a long time one would not see anything else. Yet one always had the freedom to see what one wished.

Childs gave viewers comparable freedom in *Available Light*. For this work, John Adams composed an attractive rhapsodic score and Frank Gehry, a California architect, designed a setting dominated by a platform on which two dancers—but not always the same two—kept performing some of the basic steps from which the dance was made. While they did so, other dancers on the ground wove those steps into elaborate patterns through changes of direction and choreographic counterpoint. Childs herself was a variable in this formal scheme. She made two appearances among the performers on the ground, harmonizing with them without ever fully merging with their patterned activities. Yet, at the end of the piece, she was on the platform.

By having different kinds of events occur simultaneously on the platform and on the ground, Childs gave the audience the freedom to regard her dance either as a sequence of isolated steps or as a sequence of interwoven patterns. How one perceived it simply depended upon where one decided to look. Or spectators could create their own personal combinations of steps and patterns by switching attention back and forth at will between platform and ground. Childs, as a choreographer, had to be concerned with both steps and patterns. Therefore, it was only fitting for her to appear in both locations.

As their contributions to the Next Wave, Brown and Childs offered complex dances that could serve as fresh choreographic metaphors to express that old chestnut of a theme, the complexity of modern life. But unlike the artists who decry contemporary complexities and yearn for a simple life off in the woods or in some utopia, Brown and Childs delighted in a certain kind of complexity, and their attitude should not appear surprising or inexplicable to anyone who is a city dweller by choice. Indeed, some utopian visions, and even a few otherwise practical city planning schemes, often lack appeal because they propose a way of life so simple as to be boring. Although to survive in a city may occasionally require the stamina of Fenley's dancers, confirmed urbanites can be excited by the diversity of urban experience and even by the very fact that in a big city one can never see or do absolutely everything. Yet one always has choices.

The dances of Brown and Childs affirm that complexity need not inevitably involve chaos or mayhem and that there can be a complexity which is intellectually and emotionally stimulating and in which one can feel at home. Perhaps another word for this complexity is "civilization." And by stressing such complexity the Next Wave was a civilized festival.

*New York Times*, 18 December 1983

# PATTERNS AND SPINNING ARE ONLY PART OF IT

About a decade ago, Laura Dean staked out a bit of choreographic territory for herself and, since then, she has become known for dances involving constantly changing, but always clearly defined, patterns and extended passages of spinning.

These days, the members of Laura Dean Dancers and Musicians, Dean's company, are still forming patterns and they're still spinning, usually to rhythmically repetitive scores by Dean herself. But they have been doing other things, as well.

At the 1982 Spoleto Festival in Charleston, South Carolina, Dean, who had been associated with group choreography for so long, included important solo passages in her new *Sky Light*, and another premiere, *Solo in Red*, was a solo for one of her dancers, Angela Caponigro. The following autumn, for the Joffrey Ballet, she created *Fire*, which contained three duets. And in *Inner Circle* and *Enochian*, as well as in the revised version of *Sky Light*, which she presented in the spring of 1983 at the State University of New York at Purchase, Dean continued to explore the possibilities of solos and duets. In fact, Dean has become much concerned with the interaction between individuals and groups.

To some extent, Dean always has been, but we may not have been aware of it in our eagerness to fit her choreography into categories. The rigor of her work virtually invites such categorization. For instance, her emphasis upon pattern has led certain observers to call her a minimalist and to compare her meditative dances to what is sometimes termed "trance music." Similarly, her spinning has reminded some people of dervish ceremonies. But, whatever her private convictions may be, Dean has never publicly allied herself with any specific aesthetic, philosophical, or religious dogma in her interviews or published writings. What she offers, she once declared in a program note, "is simply the kind of dancing I like to do."

If one frees one's self from the tendency to enclose her choreography within tight theoretical limitations, then it can be seen that some of the things she is doing now were implicit in her older works. People took turns being leader in choreographic games of follow-the-leader in *Response Dance* (1974). Individuals momentarily stepped out of groups in *Song* (1976), and dancers paired off in both *Dance* (1976) and *Spiral* (1977).

Nevertheless, in Charleston it was startling to see only one dancer onstage in the serene *Solo in Red*, and it was even more startling to discover that *Sky Light* began with six solos. To emphasize that these were six different people, each wore a differently colored costume. Although in the Joffrey Ballet's *Fire* Dean did not always manage to blend her idiosyncratic modern-dance style with that of classical ballet, she did devise some intense duets. However, the last of them ended on a quiet, almost tender, note, so that it was possible to interpret the *Fire* of the ballet's title not as an apocalyptic conflagration, but as a tribute to the flame of the creative human spirit.

However one interpreted *Fire*, it was clear that Dean was doing more than being a choreographic Euclid in it. One could guess she had more on her mind than geometric patterns. In fact, no choreographer can be purely Euclidean, for patterns in dance are made up of arrangements of human bodies, and, as the abstractions of George Balanchine and Merce Cunningham have taught us, the ways those bodies are arranged may possess all sorts of significance. Thus, with their emphasis upon the relationships of individuals and groups and the way they temper fiery ardor with calming restraint, Dean's new dances, including *Inner Circle*,

*Enochian,* and the revised *Sky Light,* may be said to have social, even vaguely political, implications.

The dancers in *Sky Light* now wear identical yellow costumes, but the piece still begins with six solos. However, the remarkable thing about those solos is that they appear to move along as a single unbroken choreographic phrase. A new dancer may take over, but he does not disrupt the flow. Therefore, one could say that, far from being six solos, this sequence is one solo divided up for six people. A leaping dance, *Sky Light* also occasionally suggests a sports event in both its solos and group passages. But, though a sense of rivalry is sometimes apparent, there is no cutthroat competition.

*Inner Circle* begins with a solo for a male dancer. But, as he continues that solo, other dancers join in until six people are moving together. A solo has become a unison dance. Yet, paradoxically, this ensemble can still be viewed as a solo, for Dean implies that, at least at times, a unison dance is simply a solo that a number of people happen to be performing simultaneously. Later, in *Inner Circle,* other instances of interplay between individuals and groups occur when a soloist emerges from a unison group to do different steps and then returns to the group.

*Enochian* can be termed either a duet that looks like a solo or a solo for two people. At least in theory, it could also be done by a cast of one or by a cast of thousands. It begins as a solo for Ching Gonzalez that includes many upward stretches of the arms and high extensions of the legs. Significantly, the tempo often quickens, but there is no intensification of tension, Gonzalez proving that one can move rapidly without seeming anxious. When he leaves the stage, Dean enters and continues the dance without a break, just as the dancers of *Inner Circle* supersede one another without any sense of discontinuity.

Conceivably, a single dancer of great stamina could perform all of *Enochian.* Instead, Dean has two dancers perform it. Yet it could also be done by any number of people, each dancing a few measures, then letting someone else take over.

Dean's latest dances, then, depict individuals moving in harmony with groups and solo figures emerging from groups and returning to them. The soloists have their chances to shine, but never tyrannize the proceedings. The groups stifle no one, for their members are able to leave and come back to them. One individual gives way to another in the extended solo sequences, yet no one is oppressed. Nor do these comings and goings rend the social fabric. Events are often lively, yet never chaotic or violent. Given all this, one could imagine Dean saying that her new choreography "represents the growth of the individual in relation to his fellows in an ideal state."

However, Dean didn't say that—and, given her reluctance to philosophize, she probably won't ever say anything like that. Someone did say that, though. Back in 1935, Doris Humphrey, one of the pioneers of modern dance, said that in the program note for her *New Dance*, a plotless dance—in fact, a study in pattern—that was also specifically intended as a social statement. Its shifting group and solo passages symbolized democracy in action, and Humphrey took care that the roles she created for herself and Charles Weidman, her partner, never so dominated the proceedings that these two figures could be taken for dictators.

Dean, with her concern for design, and Humphrey, with her humanitarian zeal, turn out to share a similar vision. And it is equally possible that some of America's social prophets and founders of utopian communities would recognize kinetic images of their own ideals both in Doris Humphrey's *New Dance* and in the new dances of Laura Dean.

*New York Times*, 15 May 1983

# HOW NOT TO GET TRAPPED
# IN A CHOREOGRAPHIC RUT

One of the most likable things about Mark Morris as a choreographer is the way he romps through styles and forms like a frisky puppy. Since he began making dances in 1980, he has choreographed to Brahms, Vivaldi, rock, gospel songs, and traditional Tahitian and Indian music, and his themes have ranged from the intoxication of love to the social significance of wrestling. His refusal to limit himself to any single way of moving should gladden dancegoers who hate to see young choreographers fall into aesthetic ruts.

Morris has lots of ideas, including ideas about structure, and he enjoys trying out different ways of putting dances together. Take *I Love You Dearly*, which was offered during the Mark Morris Dance Group's 1985 season at the Bessie Schönberg Theatre. This solo for Guillermo Resto, to a suite of Rumanian folk songs, made one recall that Morris once performed with a Balkan folk dance group. In fact, the suite's first dance was like a folk song made visible. At the beginning of each new stanza of the accompanying song, Resto would pause in a corner of the stage. Thus, the dance, like the music, was stanzaic in structure.

Whereas that made *I Love You Dearly* choreographically logical, as well as true to the folk spirit, other dances over the years have been charmingly illogical. At one concert, *Etudes Modernes* and *Jr. High*, two unrelated works, were yoked together by having sections from each presented in alternation. In *Etudes* women twisted themselves into striking poses with the intensity associated with the great pioneers of modern dance. However, in *Jr. High* men portrayed ordinary kids trudging to school, answering questions in class, and trying to look macho in the gym. Just as the sublime and the ridiculous coexist in life, so Morris combined them in art.

The beginning of *Gloria*, to Vivaldi, contained a kinetic surprise. Two people were seen moving laboriously forward. As the music swelled, one expected bursts of activity. Instead, the lights faded and a whole jubilant vocal chorus went undanced. But let no one therefore assume that Morris cannot choreograph to choral music, for in 1985 he showed us *Handel Choruses*, to excerpts from oratorios. Such music would surely prompt many choreographers to devise monumental ensembles. Instead, *Handel Choruses* consisted of solos ranging in tone from the grotesque (a solo in which a dancer clutched and clawed at his body to a chorus about jealousy) to the gently whimsical (a solo in which a dancer wiggled sheepishly while the singers confessed, "All we like sheep have gone astray").

Morris has ideas about content, as well as form. Occasionally, his employment of them may seem strained. *Championship Wrestling after*

*Roland Barthes* was inspired by an essay, written in 1952, in which the French critic called wrestling a "spectacle of excess." However, whereas Barthes likened wrestling to classical tragedy, Morris suggested a somewhat different interpretation of the sport. After beginning as what might have been a parody of wrestling, the dance grew increasingly violent until one could easily conclude that Morris felt wrestling's "excess" to be akin to the debased spectacles of a fascistic regime. All these implications loaded down the dance—and wrestling—with unwieldy symbolic baggage.

Although Morris may veer between deftness and brashness, he is seldom heavy-handed in his best dances. At times, his concerns can be called spiritual, in the broadest sense of that word. *O Rangasayee*, in which steps derived from Indian dance are invested with a modern dancer's sense of weight and energy, resembles a sacred quest. The laborious movements of *Gloria* eventually give way to joyous leaping. But because one remains conscious of the effort required by these celebrations, one suspects Morris believes that though mortals find it hard to offer praise in this troubled world, when the impulse to praise is felt at last, it may be accompanied by fervor.

Other works concern the presence or absence of love and aspects of human sociability in general. Dancers swoop through *New Love Song Waltzes* as if head over heels in love. *My Party* shows people having a giddy good time. Both dances are fascinating for more than their conviviality. Like several other choreographers today, Morris cheerfully ignores conventions of sexual role-playing in his works. Some of his solos are danced by men at certain performances and by women at others. And, in his duets, women may partner men, or the two performers may both be of the same sex. Occurring in dances about social relationships, such partnering is more than a formal device: it is a sign that Morris envisions a utopia in which loves of many kinds are cherished.

One of Morris's strangest pieces is *The Vacant Chair*, a solo to three sentimental, even corny, songs. To the first—a song by George F. Root about death—the soloist, wearing a bag over his head, keeps lunging downward. Like a mask in a seventeenth-century ballet, the bag depersonalizes the performer so that his movements become not one individual's lamentations but emblems of grief itself. Then the dancer removes the bag, yet keeps his back to the audience and mimes the growth of a tree to Oscar Rasbach's once-familiar setting of Joyce Kilmer's "Trees." Finally, to Carrie Jacobs Bond's "When You Come to the End of a Perfect Day," he staggers mysteriously, and it is possible to interpret his staggerings as deliberate contradictions of the untroubled lyrics.

*The Vacant Chair* is ambiguous throughout, and Morris, by first covering and then turning away his dancer's face, prevents the solo's interpreter from establishing an emotional tone through facial expressions. To judge from their giggles, a few viewers consider the piece a spoof. Yet I find it poignant, as well as eccentrically amusing, for it demonstrates how simple, even trivial, things can trigger deep emotional responses. We have all been touched by sentimental songs, perhaps more often than we may care to admit; and, surely, one reason why some old songs remain popular is that, for all their emotional excesses, they still contain sentiments we recognize as genuine.

The solo makes something complex out of what could have been only a pretext for "camp" extravagance. Nevertheless, despite his achievement here, Morris would do well to guard against superficiality and cuteness, especially now that he is, in addition to being a prolific young choreographer, a popular one as well. Morris's choreography may range widely, but it does not always go deep, and there are times when his ideas prove foolish notions.

*Songs That Tell a Story*, to gospel songs, combined goofy gallopings with naive actings-out of the songs' dramatic content. If the songs were not really taken seriously, neither were they satirized. Religion thereby became little more than an excuse for a romp. *Love, You Have Won* can also be cited as an example of Morris being cute, for it depicts two vain courtiers posturing to a Vivaldi cantata. Their posturings possess formal complexity, for they involve movements that complement or mirror one another. But, finally, to match florid and heavily ornamented musical phrases with preenings and flutterings is to make sophomoric jokes about the Baroque period.

Curious about all sorts of ideas, Morris plays with good and bad ones alike, so one can never predict what he will do next. This in itself may be heartening, for it indicates Morris is blessed with inquisitiveness. If he resists the temptation to become nothing but an amiable prankster, one can expect further choreographic delights from him in the seasons to come. Right now, he is a choreographer obviously in love with movement.

*New York Times*, 5 January 1986

# SOME OF HER CHOREOGRAPHIC BRAINCHILDREN ARE REAL BRATS

*J*ust what can she possibly be doing? And why would anyone want to do something like that? Senta Driver's dances often prompt anxious questions, for Driver is one of the most exasperating choreographers at work today. Take the very name of her company. What does she call it? The Senta Driver Dance Company? The Senta Driver Dance Ensemble? Senta Driver and Dancers? None of the above. She calls her company Harry. Ask her what that name means and she may ask you why a name has to mean anything. Why *not* call a dance company Harry?

A highly respected teacher in the American regional ballet movement attended Harry's first concert back in 1975, and when it was over she said, almost in disbelief, "But all they did was walk." She was quite right. Driver's choreography for that concert was based entirely upon walking patterns. Since then, her step vocabulary has grown, but her choreography remains bizarre. To cite only one example, the sound of the dancers' own feet was the only "music" for *Primer*, one of the new works that Harry offered recently at the Brooklyn Academy of Music. Those feet, however, didn't go pitter-patter; they went thud-thud.

Other dances over the years have been equally odd. In her solo, *Memorandum*, Driver did nothing but trudge in a circle while calling out the names of famous ballerinas. The accompaniment for *Board Fade Except* was the recorded voice of a lighting designer reading the light cues for a dance by José Limón that had nothing whatsoever to do with Driver's own creation. In *Crowd,* Driver crowded the stage with ghostly looking white sculptures by Carol Parker and then had her dancers virtually ignore them.

Driver can be exasperating, indeed. And Harry certainly harries its audiences. Yet, no matter how puzzling Driver becomes, one suspects that she is being so for a reason. Very significantly, she once said, "A lot of my pieces are portraits of me thinking." A brainy, witty choreographer, Driver thinks about many things. But her thoughts return to several basic issues.

First of all, she thinks about thinking itself. If, as a dancer, she is constantly aware of bodily movement, so, as an intelligent dancer, she is also aware of the movement of thought, as she tries to explore the relationship between thought and action, between mental concepts and physical activities. Thus, *Memorandum,* with its constant trudging and its calling out of names, can be viewed as a choreographic depiction of the very process of cognition.

By yoking together one choreographic work and the lighting plot for another, *Board Fade Except* calls attention to the mind's capacity to follow several trains of thought simultaneously. The fact that a spectator may struggle to relate Driver's dance in some intellectual or thematic way to Limón's lighting cues attests to the mind's capacity to draw connections between things—only here, Driver implies, and not without a touch of malice, there are no logical connections to be drawn.

Driver's works frequently contain separate layers of meaning. It is possible to view one episode from a suite called *Gallery* solely as an abstract dance consisting of gestures for the fingers and hands. But as one watches that dance, one realizes that some of those gestures have acquired specific meanings over the years. There are gestures of greeting, for instance. There are even a few obscene gestures. Driver may have used them for decorative purposes; yet, at the same time, she does not want one to forget their everyday meanings.

Driver was playing with words when she called a dance *Sudden Death*, for that phrase can mean something totally different to criminologists and to sports fans. In the dance, a man and a woman, like members of an athletic team, go back and forth across a line on the floor with increasingly strenuous movements. The fact that they end *Sudden Death* by kissing may remind literary historians that in Elizabethan poetry "to die" can be a synonym for sexual intercourse.

All the steps in *On Doing* are related to a spoken text that makes persnickety distinctions among "hardly doing," "really doing," "not doing," and "overdoing" a movement. Driver's willingness to fuss over such distinctions is symptomatic of another of her choreographic concerns: she is fascinated by the nature of dancing. Often her choreography suggests that, even though she is a dancer, she remains skeptical about her art. Indeed, dancing may strike her as such a peculiar activity that she is compelled to ask questions about it. Why has convention favored some types of movements and not others? Why are certain movements considered graceful? Why, for that matter, is gracefulness considered good?

A student of dance history, Driver is aware that many of the modern dance pioneers were concerned with the choreographic effects of weight. But a sense of weight has vanished from much contemporary modern-dance technique, with the result that modern dance can sometimes be almost as light and airy as classical ballet. Like the modern dance pioneers, Driver has chosen to emphasize weight—but with a vengeance.

Her dances can be deliberately ungainly. Thus, two women clinging to one another lumbered about in *Pièce d'Occasion*. Later they scratched at space and scribbled on the air with their gestures. *In Which a Position Is Taken and Some Dance* may have been set to familiar, innocuous music by Gilbert and Sullivan, but the choreography was so grotesque that the dancers resembled animated gargoyles. And *Primer* is not the only piece in Harry's repertory in which feet thud on the floor.

As part of her choreographic skepticism, Driver has mocked the familiar theory that certain dance steps should be restricted solely to women or solely to men. Consequently, her dances contain many instances of unisex partnering. *Theory and Practice* was a male duet that explored possibilities of timing and attack, while in *Running the Course* the men carried one another and so did the women. It is not surprising, then, that at the Brooklyn Academy concert Driver choreographed a work in collaboration with Peter Anastos, one of the founders of the *en travestie* company Les Ballets Trockadero de Monte Carlo. No one danced *en travestie* in *Simulcast*. But *Simulcast* still looked strange. Blithely ignoring, or possibly transcending, conventions of male and female dancing, Anastos rose on the tips of his toes and later leaped in a fish dive into the arms of a woman.

For all its comic nonsense, *Simulcast* could not simply be dismissed as a prank. Driver is fundamentally serious beneath her jesting. A choreographic freethinker, she takes nothing on faith, preferring to test artistic dogmas for herself. Therefore, her works could be called a running commentary on dance aesthetics during the course of which she occasionally becomes so provoked that she proceeds to reinvent dance on her own terms. Some of her choreographic brainchildren are real brats. But those sassy, ornery dances are alive with their own ferocious energy. And because they are, one can become wild about Harry even when Harry is driving one wild.

*New York Times*, 2 December 1979

# DANA REITZ PERFORMS

*W*hat helps make the choreography of Dana Reitz so remarkable is its protean nature. Just as one thinks one has perceived the basic shape of a movement, that movement immediately becomes something else. Reitz's choreography is a choreography of perpetual metamorphosis.

Yet her dances are not based on mere whim. Both *Steps (II)* and *Single Score*, the solos that she presented 20 April 1981 at the Performing Garage, consisted of variations on certain gestures and actions that were introduced at the outset and then repeated with constant elaborations and modifications.

The complexity of her dances helped determine Reitz's stage presence. She began each solo by walking casually forward and nodding to the audience, as if to a gathering of friends. But once she started moving, her concentration suggested that she could have been solving equations as she danced.

Much of *Steps (II)* derived from a simple up-and-down movement for the hands. But out of that gestural seed grew a lush choreographic jungle. Reitz's arms curved and twisted. They jutted out, only to withdraw immediately and slither their way along her body. Her hands darted like fish or hummingbirds, and sometimes she could have been a juggler juggling invisible objects or a baseball player pitching an unseen ball or a warrior battling the air itself.

But she also allowed energy to dwindle and virtually fade away. She introduced pauses or rests into her choreography and would occasionally freeze a movement in its course, then transform it into another sort of movement altogether.

She kept going back and forth across the space in *Single Score*. Diagonals gave way to curves or zigzags. Brisk racings sputtered out into hesitant steps or little patterings. A rush forward was thwarted by a fierce stamp of her foot, whereupon her gestures calmed down and turned gentle for a moment. Nothing ever stayed the same. And to see Reitz's constant transformations of movements was like seeing all of evolution crammed into five minutes.

*New York Times*, 23 April 1981

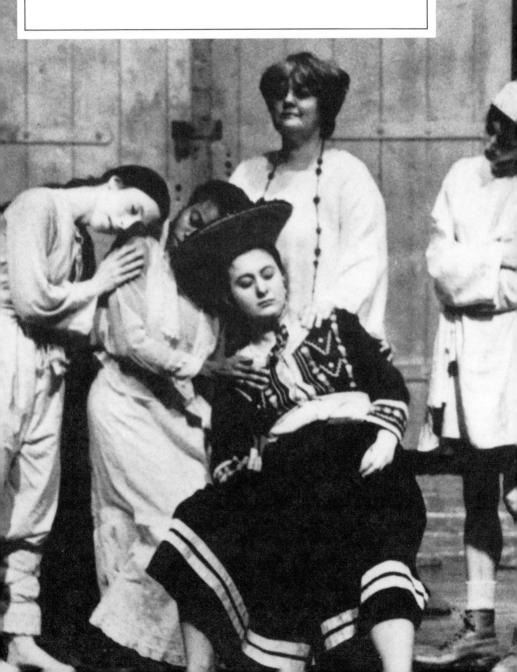

*Members of Meredith Monk's company, The House, in Monk's* Education
*of the Girlchild. Photo: Peter Moore.*

*S*ince the early 1960s, a choreographic form has flourished which, though related to modern dance, differs both from the solemn narratives that were so popular among modern dancers of the 1940s and 1950s and from the abstractions favored by some of the rebels against those narratives. Like the abstractionists, the exponents of this form have little use for conventional plot structure. Yet they are concerned with more than form and design, for they seek to create kinetic images that are intensely dramatic, in the broadest sense of that word, and emotionally expressive.

These imagistic productions have tended to be of two basic kinds. Some—for instance, the dances of Phoebe Neville—have relied upon movement alone for the creation of effects. These works descend in a direct line from the solos of such modern dance pioneers as Isadora Duncan and Mary Wigman. Other choreographers, however, ally movement with elaborate décor and, occasionally, spoken texts, and their offerings are often termed multimedia or mixed-media productions. The theatrical extravaganzas of such otherwise dissimilar creators as Meredith Monk, Ping Chong, and Robert Wilson are works of this sort.

Such productions have a tradition of their own, one extending from the multimedia theatrical experiments of the Cubists and Futurists early in this century to the "Happenings" of the sixties. An American pioneer of the form was the San Francisco choreographer Anna Halprin, who, in the late fifties and early sixties (when she was known as Ann Halprin) developed a personal style of dramatic, yet nonliteral, dance-theatre that intrigued younger choreographers and prompted several New York dancers to journey west to study with her. During the years in which I lived in the Bay Area she was the region's most important, and controversial, choreographic innovator.

*Occasionally in the arts certain related ideas can somehow seem to de-velop independently. Thus, in the late 1970s and early 1980s, it became increasingly apparent to Americans that Germany had produced its own Neo-Expressionist* Tanztheater, *and comparable Expressionist styles (the most famous of which was known as Butoh) had sprung up in Japan. Imagistic dance-theatre has become a global phenomenon.*

*Yet, like all artistic styles, it is not without its traps for the creatively unwary. The emphasis upon emotion can degenerate into hysteria. The dramatic rituals favored by some choreographers may lead them to stress the psychologically therapeutic aspects of their productions at the expense of theatricality (Halprin, for instance, increasingly devoted herself to communal rituals). And choreography may inadvertently be swamped by the other arts when media are mixed. Nevertheless, imagistic dance-theatre at its best is eloquent in its use of movement, and it can combine theatrical spectacle with high seriousness to offer both visionary fantasy and social commentary.*

## PARADES AND CHANGES

*U*ntil now, although she has influenced our own young avant-garde, Ann Halprin has been known to New York almost entirely through hearsay. Local dancers have gone to San Francisco, where she lives and teaches, to study with her. The Dancers' Workshop of San Francisco, which she directs, has toured Europe. But it had never visited New York before its performances on 21–22 April 1967 at Hunter College Play-house.

Consequently, these programs were eagerly awaited. For me, they also occasioned apprehension. As *Ballet Today*'s San Francisco correspon-dent some years ago, I had admired many of Halprin's creations. But I had not seen her group in four years—which can be a crucially long time in the artistic development of a dance company. Would this company still be interesting?

Happily, it was. In New York the Dancers' Workshop offered *Parades and Changes*, a ninety-minute "total theatre" work presented without intermission. It was the product of four collaborators: director-choreographer Ann Halprin, composer Morton Subotnick, lighting designer Patric Hickey, and costumier Jo Landor. The setting was the theatre itself with all its stage machinery and technical equipment fully exposed. This equipment was ingeniously rearranged throughout the performance, but never in an effort to create naturalistic illusion. The work began when, to the sound of electronic music, eight dancers walked through the auditorium to the stage. They stood in a line, facing the audience, and slowly took off their clothes to the point of nudity, then put them back on again. The action was repeated. Two men unrolled strips of brown paper and wrapped themselves up in it until they formed an impressive frieze of bodies and paper. After all the strips had been torn, each dancer gathered a mound of paper about himself and, looking like some fantastic flower or bush, rolled into the orchestra pit.

This sequence, because of the complete nudity involved, was inevitably the most discussed. What was astonishing about it was that it was in no way vulgar. Rather, it was the opposite; it possessed an almost chaste beauty and quiet joy.

Up to this point, the basic colors in lighting and costuming had been black, white, and brown. Brighter colors appeared as Halprin, clad in baggy yellow overalls, performed an eccentric dance accompanied by a one-man band and watched by a moon-faced dancer with a live goat on a leash. While the total effect was satisfactorily jolly, the choreography of Halprin's solo was not as comically pointed as it might have been. These antics seemed to be a cue for the rest of the cast, now clothed, to run up the aisles and descend on rope ladders from the balcony, creating a gaudy hubbub.

Movements gradually became percussive until the dancers were twisting and flailing like participants in an exorcism. Behind them marched a procession of other dancers and goat decked out with stage props and fabrics like a whimsical Mardi Gras parade. The dancers who had been flailing stretched out inert for a long time. Behind a scrim curtain a huge scaffolding construction was wheeled in with Halprin clinging to its top. The dancers rose from the floor and embraced each other tenderly. Wooden platforms were set in place, upon which the cast did a stomping dance, the wood resounding with a mighty thunder, the bodily energy of the dance expanding into vocal sounds, laughter, and shouts. Suddenly, on a scrim curtain appeared the shadow of Halprin gingerly taking a bath on the scaffolding. The image faded. *Parades and Changes* was over.

*Parades and Changes* was quite literally what its title said it was: a parade of events, a sequence of changing moods—all of it unabashedly theatrical and using the entire auditorium as environment for the action. Its elements—movement, music, décor—were meshed so that each separate element enhanced, and was enhanced by, the rest. Many new York dancers and artists have attempted "total theatre" or "mixed-media" events, but few have been as complex or imaginative as that presented by Halprin's company.

For all its multiplicity of happenings, *Parades and Changes* was never a muddle. It seemed to possess its own organic unity, the result, perhaps, of allowing a movement idea or emotional state to develop fully, to form, to expand, to subside, and then to be succeeded by a related idea.

Finally, what made *Parades and Changes* unusually pleasant was the goodheartedness it radiated. It never became a repellent or egotistical display. It never exploited its elements for sensationalistic purposes. Rather, Halprin and her associates managed to create an experimental work which was sensually beautiful, witty, and humane.

*Ballet Today* (July/August 1967): 26

# INITIATIONS
# AND TRANSFORMATIONS

lthough an admirer of many of Ann Halprin's previous dance experiments, I was slightly bored by her new evening-long *Initiations and Transformations*. And so I tried to ponder why.

Presented in three-sided arena staging in the City Center Ballroom, it began casually with Halprin and her company of seven men chatting and opening a bottle of champagne to celebrate their first night. Accompanied by a percussion ensemble, they embarked upon body awareness exercises (many of them done in the nude). Suddenly, briefly, there was an outburst of ferocity. Wearing boots and a red shawl, Halprin trembled, stamped, and twisted as though her body were bursting into flame. Proud solos for the men followed—then deep stillness. To the mesmeric sound of splashing water and the incantations of John Hopkins, the dancers transformed themselves into animals, prowling and lurking or pouncing upon each other in violent combat.

Theoretically, this should have been fascinating: the episodes were varied in mood, progressing from informality to primordial ritual. Yet much of it I found dull, and the production fell apart into aimless meandering. Finally, Halprin invited the audience to participate in some hop-and-shuffle sequences. Those who did appeared to be having fun. Here, I think, is a clue to my dissatisfaction.

Too much of the movement, though possibly interesting—or even therapeutically beneficial—to perform, was not interesting to watch. Conceivably, it did not even need to be watched; in fact, I have the disquieting hunch that an illustrated description could make it sound more effective than it actually was. Yet one of the glorious things about live theatre is its unique relationship between performers and spectators, the performers doing significant things for the spectators to contemplate, ponder, or savor. These performers were not inventive enough. There was not enough food for the eye (to borrow Paul Taylor's phrase).

If Halprin wishes to continue making theatre, then she must develop her company's theatricality, as well as its physical and psychic health. If, instead, she seeks to create new kinds of total participation rituals, then perhaps she should be bold enough to abandon theatre altogether.*

*Dance Magazine* (January 1972): 29, 73

*Devoting herself increasingly to rituals celebrating personal and social harmony, Halprin, in effect, did just that in the years following the publication of this review.

## MONK'S INIMITABLE IMAGES

*A*ll choreography appeals to the eye and the mind. But not all of it does so in the same way. Some choreography emphasizes design and pattern alone. The design represents nothing, the patterns are abstract. This kind of choreography delights the eye with its beauty and pleases the mind with its intricacy.

In another kind of choreography, the dancers' steps and gestures are not only attractive to watch for their own sake, they form images that somehow evoke ideas and emotions. The images may be fantastic, even outlandish. Yet, to borrow Ezra Pound's statement about poetic images, such dance images present "an intellectual and emotional complex in an instant of time." The choreographic works of Meredith Monk abound with images, and many of those images are powerful indeed.

A fine example of her imagistic theatre is *Education of the Girlchild*, a piece from 1973 that her company, The House, revived in 1979 at the Brooklyn Academy of Music. An allegorical account of life from birth to death, it seems sometimes a medieval mystery play, sometimes a modern comic strip.

It begins with a simultaneously comic and poignant birth image when some women pull aside a dust cover and discover not a piece of furniture beneath, but a shy, gawky, blinking girl. Later, senile dodderers hobble about, cackling defiantly while a stately figure passes among them, accompanied by a jester. Yet, one by one, the dodderers are silenced, for that stately figure proves to be Death and the jester is Death's henchman.

The entire second act might be called a single extraordinary image. This is a solo for a woman who, at the outset, looks incredibly ancient. But as she moves along a strip of cloth, she straightens up and becomes increasingly agile. The strip of cloth seems the road of life, while what we are witnessing is the course of one person's life. But we are seeing it in reverse, from old age to youth.

Unusual imagery began to appear in Monk's choreography shortly after her graduation from Sarah Lawrence College in the mid-1960s. Perhaps her most acclaimed early work was *16 Millimeter Earrings* (1966), a study of how outward appearances may reveal or conceal emotions. During the dance, Monk hid her face by covering it with a blank white globe. Yet on the globe were projected filmed images of her face. Another film showed a doll being consumed by flames. Finally, Monk took the place of the doll, the cinematic flames appearing to devour her real body.

There have been equally striking images over the years. Motorcycles raced through *Needle-Brain Lloyd and the Systems Kid* (1970). In *Vessel* (1971), a modern Joan of Arc was immolated in the light of a welder's torch. Masses of people did calisthenics in *Quarry* (1976). But the way they knocked over everyone in their way made these exercises a choreographic metaphor for a pogrom.

Usually, Monk's images combine movement with theatrical effects. Monk is not a minimalist or a choreographic purist who wishes movement to refer to nothing outside itself. Instead of excluding things from works, she includes, she combines, she draws parallels and makes connections. She tells stories (sometimes cockeyed ones) and plays with ideas. She does so by such various means that some commentators prefer to call her a mixed-media artist, rather than a choreographer.

And she really mixes media. In Monk's images, sight and sound, movement and stage design, are inextricably meshed. She not only choreographs her productions, she composes music for them and oversees their scenery and costumes. And, in addition to dancing, the members of The House may be called upon to sing, chant, mime, and speak dialogue.

A curious, but revealing, example of Monk's tendency to weave art forms together was her *Raw Recital: Roots* of 1974. First, she sang songs by composers ranging from Bach and Purcell to her pianist, Donald Ashwander. Then she danced to them—but very oddly. Ashwander played the accompaniments, as before. But he made no attempt to fill in the missing vocal lines. Rather, the melodies of the songs were replaced by Monk's gestures.

It didn't quite work, for one could not always see any direct connection between the vocal phrases and the movements she substituted for them. Yet the fact that she obviously regarded one set of phrases as the equivalent of the other is symptomatic of her desire to unify disparate theatrical elements.

Many of her works have been full-evening attractions. A few have been choreographic "serials" presented in installments over the course of several evenings. Monk's investigations of the evening-long dance coincide with a renewed interest by ballet companies in the creation of three-act classical works. But whereas most new full-evening ballets have been obvious and plodding, Monk's creations have been unconventional explorations of ways that events may be structured in time and space.

Thus, *Education of the Girlchild* plays tricks with time. The first act moves chronologically forward, whereas the second moves backward.

*Quarry*, based upon the fantasies of a feverish child, was deliberately enigmatic. Each separate incident resembled a piece of a jigsaw puzzle. The little girl may not have been able to fit the pieces together. But the audience could, and the pattern that emerged was dismaying, for all these events seemed portents of oppression and war.

On occasion, Monk has let the members of her audience decide how much time they wished to spend in any theatrical space. In *Co-op* (1968), performers scattered about New York University's Loeb Student Center repeated activities over and over. Spectators could come and go at leisure, devoting as much or as little time as they wished to the events. Monk also knows how to measure choreographic time very carefully. Because *Needle-Brain Lloyd and the Systems Kid* concerned journeys, the piece, staged on the Connecticut College campus, became a journey for spectators and performers alike.

It began in the afternoon in the college arboretum, where the audience beheld dancers crossing a pond in a boat. Then everyone moved to the campus green, where other events occurred. After a dinner break, events resumed—but now things happened in semidarkness. Finally, everyone returned to the arboretum to watch the dancers sail off again in their boat.

The three-part *Vessel* was both a fantasy about Joan of Arc and a study in expanding scale. The first part took place within the confines of Monk's own loft-apartment; the second, in an Off Off Broadway theatre. The third part was staged in a large parking lot across the street from a church. That lot became the square in which this St. Joan was burned.

*Juice* also consisted of three parts, and the parts were presented on three different evenings. But *Juice* exemplified diminishing scale. In the first part, performers utilized the great spiral ramp of the Guggenheim Museum. In the second, they were kept behind the proscenium arch of the Minor Latham Playhouse. The third part, presented in a loft, had no live participants in it whatsoever. Instead, audiences could watch performers on videotapes or stroll around exhibits of the stage properties used in the work's other two sections.

Monk is probably inimitable. One cannot expect the personnel of most dance companies to sing and speak, as well as dance. Nor would it be easy for most dance companies to appear in parks or parking lots. And, surely, only coyness would result if lesser choreographers tried to copy Monk's simultaneously childlike and sophisticated manner.

Yet if she cannot be imitated, she can serve as an inspiration and a challenge, for she has dared to explore fresh choreographic ways of treating thematic and narrative material. Her investigations have resulted in a host of memorable images.

*New York Times*, 18 February 1979

## LAZARUS, A MULTIMEDIA EVENT

*I*f a man sits at a table and eats a corned beef sandwich, no one watching him necessarily thinks, "How strange." Tables, sandwiches, and hungry men are all perfectly ordinary. But if that man eating that sandwich might just conceivably be Lazarus returned from the dead, one may think, "How very strange." The perfectly ordinary has been transformed by his presence.

*Lazarus.* That was what Ping Chong called the multimedia work involving movement, slides, and films presented by his Fiji Company on 7 March 1978 at the American Theatre Laboratory. Everything in it was both ordinary and strange.

First came projections showing urban scenes and a stairway inside a building. The screen was removed and a tape-recorded voice said: "This is a room. There is nothing in the room but a chair." And a chair was brought in. The voice named other objects, and those objects were also brought in, one by one.

A man (Tony Janetti) entered the room, a man who might have been Lazarus. His face was bandaged. He pulled change from his pocket and stared at it. He ate a corned beef sandwich.

Letters were read about children and an accident. A woman (Catherine Zimmerman) appeared holding a broken plate. The man lifted what resembled a cistern lid and peered inside. The man and the woman stared at each other. The woman started trembling. The man put a coat around her shoulders.

There were scenes from a science-fiction film about a monster from an alien planet. A puppet figure was seen ascending into the sky carrying a suitcase. Stagehands dismantled the set, brought in a smoking funnel, and scattered dead leaves about. One could hear wind blowing. Then someone announced, "The performance has ended."

And a strange performance it was. But the biblical story of Lazarus is also strange. It's a story that makes one wonder what it must have felt like to come back from the dead. How would the world look to such a man?

Chong's emphasis upon ordinary objects—that table, that sandwich—made one acutely aware of the sizes and shapes of things in this world. The way Janetti stared at everything—as if asking himself, "What can this be? What is it for?"—made him seem as much an alien as the monster in the movie.

But perhaps this man was only metaphorically Lazarus. Perhaps the world to which he was returning was that of memory. Perhaps these enigmatic episodes were memories resurrected from forgetfulness. Perhaps.

Chong's *Lazarus* invited such speculations. It was as carefully crafted as a poem, as mysterious as a dream.

*New York Times*, 9 March 1978

## PHOEBE NEVILLE'S ENIGMAS

Phoebe Neville choreographs enigmatic dances. And yet she never fills the stage with haze or fog. She has no ghosts wafting about in misty gauzes or flapping bedsheets. There is nothing blurred or smudged about her choreography. Each gesture has been carefully timed and pondered. Whereas some artists might try to create mystery by dropping veils upon objects, Neville choreographically lifts veils away in the knowledge that the more clearly something can be seen, the more easily one can tell just how strange it is.

In *Standstill*, one of the works presented by the Phoebe Neville Dance Company at its 1980 concert at the Washington Square United Methodist Church, a man and a woman warily approached each other. Even when they were virtually side by side, one could tell that they were not really together. Attempts to reach out and touch were followed by clenched fists and stamping feet. Then the man bent down and placed the hem of the woman's skirt in his mouth. But even this extraordinary gesture of contrition failed, and the woman was left alone, whereupon she forlornly placed the hem of her skirt in her own mouth. *Standstill* was an almost Strindbergian dance-drama of love and estrangement.

Other dances at that concert contained their own curious images. A caryatid from a Greek temple came alive in *Caryatid*. From the stiff way in which she moved, one knew that this was no human being, but stone in human shape. The opening of *Tigris* evoked the pomp we associate with ancient Assyria or Babylonia. Gesturing grandly, a haughty princess in a shining gown entered, accompanied by crouching figures who could have been either her handmaidens or her pet leopards.

Neville has been choreographing since the early 1960s. If, during that time, she has always been active in the modern-dance world, she has also been slightly apart from it. Although she participated in the experimental dance activities at the Judson Memorial Church during the sixties, she was something of an outsider even there. Her works were small-scaled, but never minimalist, and her craftsmanship left nothing to chance.

It is equally hard to relate her to current trends. Nevertheless, as interest grows in the sources of modern dance and as dancers and audiences are once more concerning themselves with such pioneers as Isadora Duncan and Mary Wigman, one can see that Neville is part of an important modern-dance tradition. She is—that rarity in today's modern dance—an Expressionist.* Neville uses movement to give objective expression to inner experience and manages to transfer the feeling of that experience to the viewer by the power and particularity of her movement.

At the same time, she is a miniaturist. Most of her works are brief, and few require more than three or four dancers. In terms of their emotional coloration, her creations over the years have almost invariably been dark. There have been exceptions—in *Dance with Mandolins*, for instance, she created a sense of giddiness simply by having her cast do nothing but repeat the scissorlike step known as the *sissonne* over and

---

*When this article was written, New York had not seen any examples of the Neo-Expressionist works so influential in Germany in the 1970s and 1980s.

over again. Usually, however, her dances conjure up states of melancholy or foreboding. And, like good lyric poems, they eschew hysterical rhetoric in favor of understatement and aptness of imagery.

They are so gesturally clear that moments from them linger in the mind. In *Triptych*, Neville held a rubber snake in her mouth as she made incantatory motions, thereby reminding viewers that the Delphic priestess was known as the Pythoness. In *Ladydance*, she wore a long green dress and walked primly until her strolling was interrupted by sudden turns and sharp movements of the arms. Then, her hair hanging loose, she started leaping and whirling like a bacchante until decorum returned at last.

Both *Passage* and *Passage in Silence* were unaccompanied dances about journeys. In the solo *Passage*, Neville shook her head from side to side and made curving motions in the air with her arms, after which she pulled her hands in tightly to her body, then walked and ran in circles. With each circle, she seemed to penetrate deeper into some recess of the mind or heart.

A woman standing behind a man at the beginning of *Passage in Silence* pointed resolutely onward, as if she were a goddess or muse urging him to set out upon a heroic quest. They began to move with a slow rocking motion. But as the man moved gradually forward, the woman moved backward until she vanished from sight, thereby leaving the man to complete his mission entirely alone.

*Memory* was a set of vignettes as fleeting as memories themselves. Each of its scenes was lighted by some lamp or candle manipulated by the dancers. In the most astonishing of the scenes, Neville, wearing asbestos gloves and a mask, literally held a burning fire and poured it back and forth from hand to hand.

In a later scene, the stage was left in total darkness. One heard the ominous sound of approaching footsteps, then saw a match flare and die. Again, one heard footsteps; again, a match was struck and, again, darkness prevailed. This gloomy nocturne was followed by a darting, rushing solo for a woman carrying a sparkler. When she finished her dance, a man entered with a candle, accompanied by a lurking figure who dogged his steps and finally extinguished the candle. In the last vignette, a woman lit a kerosene lamp and sat lost in thought at an ordinary table. She scarcely moved, but her concentration was enough to convince one that she was pondering some momentous matter for the entire length of a sleepless night.

The movements in *Cartouche* were spare but astonishing, and they were rich in implications. A man stood upon the back of a woman sprawled on the floor and made pompous oratorical gestures. Suddenly, the inert woman began to move. She reached out an arm, grabbed the man's ankle, and kept clinging to him as he tried to step forward. At last, she toppled him. Now it was she who stood upon his back. But instead of beaming triumphantly, she assumed that look of absolute despair that one finds on the face of Michelangelo's Lost Soul in the Sistine Chapel.

*Cartouche* could be interpreted in many ways: as a commentary upon relationships between men and women, for example, or as a meditation upon the nature of all power and the way that the glories of power, once attained, may inexplicably turn to ashes. It was an enigmatic, disturbing dance.

Indeed, most of Neville's dances could be called *Enigma Variations*, to borrow a title from another choreographer. Yet if they can be subjected to varying interpretations, that is because they are truly ambiguous, rather than merely vague. Their choreographic shapes are always distinct. One may not know what to make of them, but one can see what they are. Moreover, the gestures she devises do not simply convey messages. They can be savored for their own sake; they have their own beauty, intensity, and clarity. It is because they are so strangely clear that Phoebe Neville's dances are so clearly strange.

*New York Times*, 10 February 1980

# THREE VIEWS OF *ORPHEUS*

*O*ne of Europe's best-known festivals is the Holland Festival, which in the summer of 1975 emphasized the Orpheus myth with performances of Gluck's *Orpheus and Eurydice* and Offenbach's *Orpheus in the Underworld*. Götz Friedrich's raucous production of the Offenbach, choreographed by Erich Walter, was presented by what seemed a cast of thousands in the Amsterdam circus. A delectable musical soufflé was thereby inflated to aesthetically indigestible proportions.

Gluck fared no better. During his lifetime Gluck worked with such balletic innovators as Jean-Georges Noverre and Gaspero Angiolini, and his operas still challenge choreographers and directors. What a pity, then, that Rhoda Levine's production of *Orpheus* for De Nederlandse Operastichting was so feeble. Levine merely had an ensemble in long robes group themselves like church choristers giving their annual concert—and looking just as self-conscious. Of no help at all was the banal, shuffling choreography by Else Klink for the Stuttgart Künstlergruppe Eurythmeum, inexplicably imported for the occasion.

Fortunately, good Continental modern dance does exist, as evidenced by a truly imaginative German production of the same opera. This *Orpheus* was staged in Wuppertal, an industrial town which boasts the world's oldest monorail public transportation system and an opera house which has long been hospitable to dance.

Its current resident choreographer, modern dancer Pina Bausch, produced *Orpheus* as a choreographic opera. While the chorus sat in the theatre's side boxes, the singers portraying the three major characters moved about as though in a literal staging. But each character had a dancing counterpart, and these soloists, along with a dancing ensemble, interpreted the opera in an almost abstract manner, the singers telling the story, the dancers providing meditations upon its emotions.

During the mourning for Eurydice clusters of dancers huddled together like refugees, while the dancing Orpheus (Dominique Mercy) was wracked by grief. Journeying to Hades, he encountered a hell which suggested a madhouse guarded by brutal jailers. Amidst their ferocity a frail woman wandered, clutching a loaf of bread as though it were her sole remaining contact with earth's natural bounty. In contrast, the blessed spirits of Elysium glided in a ceaseless ebb and flow while other dancers simply walked across the back of the stage, the combination of tidal movement and ordinary walking creating an uncanny illusion of serenity. The pas de deux for Orpheus and Eurydice contained equally imaginative touches. There were the almost predictable coilings of Eurydice about Orpheus as he averted his eyes. But much of the time they moved apart from each other, aware of each other as though through a sixth sense, yet never able to confront each other, a limitation which gave to their actions—despite the great space in which those actions occurred—a feeling of restriction and frustration.

Only at the end did Bausch falter, her production sharing one of the peculiarities of Levine's *Orpheus*. Both versions, instead of using Gluck's conclusion in which Orpheus and Eurydice are eventually reunited, settled for a tragic ending by cutting the final scene and repeating the opening mourning chorus. However odd a happy ending may seem to us, that ending reveals much about how the eighteenth century viewed the universe, and to omit it is a failure to come to terms not only with Gluck's age but with Gluck himself. Moreover, given Bausch's imagination, it would have been fascinating to see how she might have interpreted the ending choreographically.

"Festivals and Phenomena," *Dance Magazine* (September 1975): 78–79

# PLOTLESS DANCE-DRAMA
# THAT DEALS IN EMOTIONS

An increasing number of choreographers are creating works that attempt to present dramatic situations in a nonliteral manner. These works lack conventional narratives and yet are charged with such intense emotional conflicts that they cannot be categorized as "abstract."

Several nonliteral dance-dramas were seen in New York during the spring of 1984, and two productions—Kenneth MacMillan's *Triad*, in its revival by American Ballet Theatre, and Pina Bausch's *Bluebeard*, for her Wuppertaler Tanztheater—can be cited as examples of the strengths and weaknesses of this approach to dancemaking. Whereas *Bluebeard* is richly evocative, *Triad* is annoyingly vague.

Set to Prokofiev's Violin Concerto No. 1 and first performed by the Royal Ballet in 1972, *Triad* purports to show how a young woman causes two brothers to become romantic rivals. But that is not quite what one actually sees onstage. In fact, one never knows what to make of the stage action. The choreography is in a slithery style that features lots of claspings and clingings. However, it seldom establishes any sense of characterization. Therefore, watching *Triad's* two men entwine may cause some viewers to suspect that this ballet is not about sibling rivalry at all; for these viewers, *Triad* may seem to concern homosexual or bisexual lovers whose affair is broken up by a woman.

Unfortunately, because they still must battle against vestiges of the puritanical notion that dance is "depraved," choreographers remain squeamish about treating certain sexual themes in a forthright manner. Therefore, *Triad's* men remain shadowy figures.

Just as MacMillan never establishes who his characters are, so he also fails to establish where and when his ballet takes place. Since the only setting is a cyclorama and the costumes consist of nothing but tights for the men and a little skirt for the woman, *Triad* appears to occur in no particular geographical location or historical period. Conceivably,

MacMillan may be seeking to emphasize that romantic rivalry is universal. However, though all behavior patterns may arise from the same emotional sources, such patterns differ considerably from place to place and era to era, and societies cope with the basic facts of life by blocking, unleashing, or carefully channeling human impulses and desires in many ways. Urban and rural societies are not alike; neither are repressive and permissive cultures. No two societies are exactly identical, and since dramatic dances consist of images of behavior, choreographers ought to have some clear idea of just what sort of societies they wish to depict.

*Triad* occurs in a void, and most of its plot developments are only pretexts for technically intricate, but inexpressive, choreography. However, one twist of the plot involves more than that. This is the moment when three unidentified companions of the woman suddenly beat up one of the brothers while the other brother watches for a suspiciously long time before intervening. This scene and its motivations are as obscure as anything else in the ballet. But whereas the other scenes are merely silly at their worst, the gratuitous violence of this one makes it repellent, as well.

Pina Bausch's *Bluebeard* is filled with violence. Yet, despite its unsavory people and unpleasant events, the work is not distasteful because its visual and kinetic imagery puts the violence into a context so that it becomes something to think about as well as to wince at.

Bausch takes pains to locate her dance. Rolf Borzik's setting consists of a crumbling house with a floor strewn with dead leaves. Although, surely, no such house exists on any block anywhere, the way its imagery combines domesticity with decay makes it a meaningful setting for choreographic action concerned with the crumbling of romantic relationships and, by implication, of a whole set of cultural patterns that control the ways in which men and women relate to one another.

What one beholds for nearly two hours is a man tormenting a woman— for convenience, let's call them Mr. and Mrs. Bluebeard, although they need not be legally married—and they are joined by a whole ensemble of tormented and tormenting* men and women in contemporary costumes. These suggest that Bausch feels romantic and sexual relationships are doomed to be agonized today. It soon becomes clear that, although Bluebeard is the principal offender, women are not simply helpless victims of male oafishness. Bausch's women can be as unappealing as her men. On occasion, they are hysterical. And they know how to lure men on, only to punish them.

In Bausch's world, physical beauty itself can be debased until it serves as a weapon. Thus, there are repeated muscle-building poses for the men and simperings for the women; rather than being evidence of a delight in the senses, these poses are ways of boasting about one's self and dominating everyone nearby. In another sequence, the women whip Bluebeard with their long, flowing hair. And still another episode finds Bluebeard draping Mrs. Bluebeard with ornate robes. But he places so many upon her that she can scarcely waddle. She has become a status symbol, just as, in some communities in the past, having a fat wife could be interpreted as a sign of one's material prosperity.

All the characters are clumsy, as if able to express few emotions other than violent ones, and their movements are almost invariably compulsive. That these people are trapped is evident in the way they let their bodies crash against the walls in one scene and in the way the women literally climb the walls in another.

An even more powerful sense of being trapped is created by the relationship between movement and music. *Bluebeard*'s full title is *Bluebeard Listening to a Tape Recording of Bela Bartok's Opera, "Bluebeard's Castle,"* and throughout the work the action starts and stops as Bluebeard keeps turning on and switching off a tape recorder, sometimes playing the same passage several times before moving ahead to a new one. By so doing, Bluebeard manipulates both the Bartok music and the people around him. But he, too, is manipulated by the music, which may symbolize such things as the power of social convention and the way conventions may be reinforced by the mass media. Although Bluebeard can stop the recorder, something inevitably forces him to turn it back on. He

*This phrase appears to be inescapable when discussing Bausch and I find I have employed it several times in my reviews of her.

is compelled to do what he does: he is programmed, a product of social conditioning.

So is everyone else, the production declares in its stunning final sequences in which the cast goes through what could be called a digest version of the work, repeating key images from various scenes again and again. Clearly, these people onstage are all programmed creatures. But then Bausch turns up the houselights in the auditorium. And by doing this she implies that we who watch inhabit the same world as her characters and therefore are just as conditioned as anyone onstage. At last, all the lights dim. Yet the dancers keep moving in the deepening shadows, as if to indicate that, unless changes are made, this is how things will always be.

Given the relentlessness of the choreography, one may well feel pessimistic about humanity's capacity for change. Or one may start wondering about what can be done to make humanity more humane. One may accept Bausch's view of the world and weep. Or one may scorn or defy that view.

Like it or not, agree with it or not, *Bluebeard* has to be taken seriously. Its imagery is too powerful to ignore and, though in no way naturalistic, it forces us to ponder human reality. In contrast, *Triad* is so choreographically blurred that it neither confronts us with a vision of the real world nor creates its own new world of pure imagination.

*New York Times*, 26 August 1984

## PINA BAUSCH'S HIPPO

What was a hippopotamus doing in Pina Bausch's *Arien* at the Brooklyn Academy of Music? Of course, it wasn't a real one, but only a construction with dancers inside guiding it. Nevertheless, what was a hippo doing in *Arien?*

Very possibly, affirming.

One rarely uses a word like "affirming" when speaking of Bausch.

Most of her productions are extraordinarily gloomy. There may be, how-ever, a sentimental side to her, for her works contain images showing both human depravity and the abundance, fecundity, or even benefi-cence of nature itself.

Consider that hippo. A placid, waddling beast, it was oddly endear-ing. And so it may have symbolized natural innocence.

Consider, too, a moment from *Kontakthof*, Bausch's depiction of a dance at a drab recreation center. Taking a break, the dancers—all of them lonely and tormented—watch a nature film about ducks on a lake, and when it is over they sigh sweetly. Again, all's well in the world of nature, but not in the world of human affairs.

A concern for nature may help explain why Bausch likes to cover the stage floor in productions. Thus, in *Bluebeard*, her powerful study of loveless marriage, she filled the stage with dead leaves, which may have been signs of her characters' deadened affections. Here both nature and human life have withered.

The stage for the almost totally despairing *Gebirge* was covered with dirt, which at times suggested a wilderness appropriate to the chore-ography's emotional desert. But the stage was not always barren. At one point, fir trees were brought in and a dancer cavorted gleefully. Nature had renewed itself, and a human being had found temporary solace in nature.

In addition to the hippo, the peculiarities of *Arien* included a stage flooded with water. This water may have represented the life force itself, and the hippo looked at home in it. The dance's neurotic human charac-ters, however, had to splash through it, and their exertions served as reminders that life requires effort.

Moreover, the way the water soiled the dancers' costumes emphasized that, for Bausch, life is a mess. Her dances may offer occasional glimpses of Eden. But it is an Eden in which only hippos can live.

"Critic's Notebook," *New York Times*, 21 November 1985

# KEI TAKEI

or several years, the modern dancer Kei Takei has been choreographing a cycle of nine works collectively titled *Light*. But not until this winter have the parts been performed together. On 27 February – 1 March 1975 at Brooklyn Academy of Music, Takei's company, Moving Earth, divided up the dances over three evenings, while on 2 March all nine were presented on a single program lasting six and a half hours.

Although, ordinarily, I dislike works of Wagnerian proportions, I chose to attend on 2 March, partly because of conflicting reviewing assignments, partly because I wished to discover whether the nine parts truly constituted a single work or whether they remained disparate items arbitrarily lumped together. *Light*, set to various sound accompaniments, poses an aesthetic problem which must be faced by anybody who choreographs a long abstract dance, particularly one not tied to a single score: lacking the obvious unifying devices of plot and traditional musical structure, what makes a dance a genuine organic entity, rather than an assemblage of separable parts?

*Light*, to my mind, does succeed as a unified entity—a quite impressive one, too—because of its movement style and its implications. Takei's images are as carefully ordered as stones in an Oriental garden, and this precision is emphasized by the white costumes worn by the dancers. But if the choreography is as clear as light, it is also as hard as light, for it is tight, tense, even oppressive in quality. Though Takei is a tiny dancer with a Japanese doll's face, the movement she devises tends to be weighted, the dancers sometimes having actual weights or humps attached to their costumes. This choreographic rock garden is as heavy as real stone. This *Light* is merciless.

Essentially, *Light* consists of vignettes showing people confronting adversities, never overcoming them, but never wholly succumbing to them, either. Gravity itself often seems their foe. Typically, in one scene coolielike figures slog about beneath the weight of burdens, while another figure stands proudly erect, only to fall as though crushed by an invisible burden. In another scene, three people—an obviously older man, a young man, and a young woman—cling to each other and gaze heavenward. Repeatedly, they sink to earth and struggle to rise again, some of their poses suggesting *pietàs*. Takei begins a solo naked from the waist up and, as she dances, keeps donning bizarre articles of clothing, each possessing humps or protuberances which progressively encumber her.

One sequence virtually induces claustrophobia. While dancers hop and flutter, a woman fills the performing area with white shapes resembling pieces of a jigsaw puzzle. Since the dancers can move only in the empty areas, their actions grow increasingly restricted as the filling of the stage continues with the inexorable progress of a glacier. Later, hordes of people remove the pieces of the puzzle, but even deliverance has the effect of constriction here, since the action proceeds by jerky fits and starts and the dancers, though they occasionally assume heroic tableaux, keep sagging and collapsing.

Nothing is achieved without effort, Takei suggests. And this seems true of art as well as life. A long episode juxtaposes images reminiscent of such agricultural activities as seeding and harvesting with scenes showing Takei portraying a choreographer rehearsing a company and revealing herself to be a ferocious disciplinarian. But even she does not have it easy. For though she is inspired by a sort of male muse, all energy and exuberance, she is hampered because, in this sequence, she is lame and so must labor painfully to communicate her ideas. The episode is weakened by excessive length, but it underscores the preoccupations of *Light* as a whole, particularly the emphasis upon struggle and the implication that the burdens of life may also contain the seeds of artistic creation. *Light* offers a peculiarly stoic view of existence; and though it is always harsh, it is also haunting.

"New York Newsletter," *Dancing Times* (May 1975): 420–421

# EIKO AND KOMA CONTROL TIME

lthough it is customary to define dance as an art of movement in space and time, audiences are often more aware of the way dancers cover space than of how they pass through time. Nevertheless, certain choreographers do much to create striking illusions in time. Among them are Eiko and Koma, the Japanese dancers who presented a collaboratively choreographed program on 20 July 1983 at Duke University's Reynolds Theatre as part of the American Dance Festival.

Usually, the two dancers slowed time down; but even when they moved quickly during their performance, they moved in a time scheme different from that of everyday reality. They rearranged time to suit their own creative purposes.

Their new *Beam*, to snippets of folk music, occurred on a mound resembling a sand dune. But it could have been Mount Everest, for it was the site of heroic struggles. Koma was revealed hunched on the dune, as if he were exhausted from having just climbed it. However, he soon lost his balance and fell down its slope. Then Eiko inched her way up the mountain. But having reached the peak, she let out a mysterious cry of desperation, and the lights faded.

When they brightened again, Koma was lifting her, and she attempted to straighten up in his arms and gaze into the distance. Because her face was turned away from the audience and his face was obscured by her body as he lifted her, the dancers seemed totally depersonalized at this moment, as if they were archetypal symbols of struggle rather than two real people.

Then Eiko once more became a vulnerable individual and slipped downward while Koma labored to stand erect and hold her again. But she finally vanished, leaving him in lonely splendor on the summit of a mountain.

Despite its moments of defeat, *Beam* appeared to affirm the dignity of effort. Its title was never explained. But the dance was obviously as sturdy as a beam of wood and as intense as a beam of light.

It shared the program with *Fur Seal*. Here Eiko and Koma did occasionally appear to be actual seals. Their glistening black costumes could have been sealskin. Feet often resembled flippers. There were times when the dancers stretched out on the floor like seals basking on a rock in the sunlight. And the work as a whole could be interpreted as an animalistic mating ritual.

Yet *Fur Seal* was choreographically more than a set of animal imitations. What made it remarkable was the way its human dancers invented and inhabited a totally nonhuman world. It could have been a world of seals. It could have been a world of other creatures. But it was not the world human beings live in.

All the movement was laborious and ungainly. Much of the action occurred in silence. But certain incidents were danced to a collage of sound effects and music, both classical and popular. Eiko and Koma also made sporadic snorting and grunting sounds.

Everything they did was heavily weighted. They toppled over and rolled on the floor. They scrambled along and hunched themselves up. They dragged themselves close to each other and clumsily embraced, then separated and staggered off on their own.

One never really knew why Eiko and Koma did any of these things. Yet they did them as if they meant much to the animalistic creatures they portrayed. Therefore, though the dance's events may have been inexplicable, they always seemed important.

One curious thing about *Beam* and *Fur Seal* was their length. *Beam* lasted only fifteen minutes, yet it virtually attained epic proportions, whereas *Fur Seal*, which was fifty minutes of slow motion, seemed to take no time at all. Eiko and Koma know how to make time pass magically.

*New York Times*, 24 July 1983

# HOW AVANT-GARDE WORKS
# RESEMBLE ROMANTIC CLASSICS

mong the glories of late-nineteenth-century Russian ballet were such spectacles as *Swan Lake*, *Nutcracker*, *The Sleeping Beauty*, and *La Bayadère*. These works, choreographed by Marius Petipa and Lev Ivanov, were grand in scale and lasted all, or most, of an evening. Today we call them classics and consider them in no way controversial in either form or content.

In recent years, a form of multimedia choreographic (or, at least, movement-oriented) theatre has developed that has generated much controversy, attracting both great praise and fierce denunciation. Among the examples of the form seen here in 1984 were *The Games*, by Meredith Monk and Ping Chong, the productions of Pina Bausch for her Wuppertaler Tanztheater, those of Ushio Amagatsu for Japan's Sankai Juku troupe, Tim Miller's *Democracy in America*, and, most elaborately of all, *Einstein on the Beach*, the extravaganza with direction and design by Robert Wilson, choreography by Lucinda Childs, and music by Philip Glass that concluded the Next Wave series at the Brooklyn Academy of Music. Some theatregoers might call these works innovative. Yet, curiously enough, in many ways they resemble the balletic spectacles of a century ago. In fact, they may be today's equivalents of those spectacles.

Like *The Sleeping Beauty*, which can last more than three hours if offered uncut, our own spectacles are panoramic and leisurely. As for their length, surprisingly many—*The Games* and all of Sankai Juku's, for example—are approximately ninety minutes without intermission, perhaps because movies often last that long and audiences may therefore be accustomed to spending ninety uninterrupted minutes in a theatre. Yet Bausch has created three-hour works, and *Einstein* lasted four and a half hours without intermission.

Long though it may be, *The Sleeping Beauty* does not bore ballet lovers. Similarly, our own spectacles hold the attention of theatregoers fond of mixed media. In every case, they do so because they present many kinds of movement and visual images. Just as Petipa's works did not simply contain balletic movement at its most academically pure, but were also rich in character dance and mime, so recent spectacles can be equally varied in their contents.

Set in the future, *The Games* juxtaposed a bleak vision of a society trying to recover from a cataclysmic nuclear attack with a set of ritual games celebrating such ordinary, but pleasant, aspects of our own life today as sidewalks, candlelight, and morning coffee. Amagatsu's *Jomon Sho*, a view of the evolutionary process, contained both physically grueling scenes, including one in which dancers, looking like seed pods or cocoons, were lowered on the stage with ropes attached to their ankles, and cerebral or allegorical episodes, including one in which dancers peered at one another through large rings, as if each were the other's mirror image. That scene thereby served as a metaphor for the discovery of self-identity. In her *1980* Bausch regaled audiences with parades through the auditorium, a tea party, monologues expressing the performers' hopes and fears, a beauty contest, and a magic act.

Miller's *Democracy in America* was a theatrical collage that combined movement, music, films, slide projections, video images, and spoken texts in what could be called a meditation upon how democratic ideals may grow tarnished. The texts ranged from high-minded statements about citizens' rights and duties to personal reflections by the performers on the meaning of democracy. The movement sequences included a depiction of milling rush-hour crowds, a little pageant of American history during which dancers carried cutout dates as if they were burdens, and a macabre game of volleyball played with the globe. Moreover, satiric social commentary was contrasted with poignant personal reminiscences, including scenes concerning the death of the choreographer's father. The result was a vision of decent people who found themselves genuinely perplexed by the world around them.

*Einstein on the Beach,* which had choreography by Andrew de Groat at its premiere in 1976, was rechoreographed by Childs. Yet Wilson's basic concepts and images remained unchanged. An aggregation of images of space, time, light, energy, and power, *Einstein* often resembled a set of paintings. Nevertheless, it achieved many of its effects through movement, and Wilson and Childs employed several kinds of movement in the course of making their points.

The most obvious spatial contrasts were those between closed and open spaces. Enigmatic little colloquies involving words and movement performed by Sheryl Sutton and Childs in a limited, confined space alternated with panoramic visions that covered the entire stage. In some of these, time was deliberately slowed down. Thus, as performers in one scene wrote invisible equations in the air, a train started to cross the stage, then vanished, then reappeared. What in real life would have been a steady, uninterrupted traversal was divided into segments through starts and stops.

Time was speeded up in other episodes, including the ensemble dances performed on an empty stage by members of Childs's company. The stage, usually filled with props and scenery, was now a vast uncluttered field as dancers swept in and out, jumping and whirling in waves of activity.

Still another scene created a remarkable illusion of movement through the virtual absence of movement. Two people were seen standing on the observation platform of a train. The pulsating ostinatos of Glass's score made it seem as if that train were hurtling into the night. Yet there was little actual movement of any kind.

Productions like *Einstein*—or those of Monk, Chong, and Bausch— bother some people because they are often unclassifiable, and one may not know whether to label them dance, theatre, opera, or performance art. Audiences fond of pigeonholing works find this disturbing. So, too, dancegoers used to abstract ballet or minimalist modern dance are disturbed by the fact that today's spectacles may make their points in other ways than through movement alone. For lovers of "pure" dance, spectacles are decidedly impure and even messy.

Yet they are most certainly lively. And they can be intellectually stimulating, as well. These days, few choreographers seem to be interested in conventional narrative dance-dramas, and abstract ballets are too often nothing but choreographic trinkets: strings of pretty, but inconsequential, steps to pretty music. In contrast, imagistic movement-theatre can be both unpredictable and imaginative. Today's spectacles are filled with things to look at. But even more than that, they can give audiences much to think about.

*New York Times*, 6 January 1985

*Members of the New York City Ballet's male ensemble in George Balanchine's* Kammermusik No. 2. *Photo © Steven Caras.*

ontemporary American dance is unusually rich. Two major forms flourish—ballet and modern dance—and there is an ongoing aesthetic dialogue between them. Major ballet companies exist from coast to coast. Modern dance is blessed with unusual diversity. The choreographers of some of its more recent manifestations have explored form and content, weight and energy, and, never willing to take anything on faith, innovators have questioned conventions of compositional structure and of sexual role-playing in the theatre.

Nevertheless, it is possible to worry about American dance. No unmistakably important new ballet choreographer has developed in recent years; in fact, given our growing number of companies, American ballet could be said to suffer from a choreographer shortage. It may also be threatened with artistic petrifaction, for many new ballets can all too easily be fitted into rigid categories. On the one hand, there are opulent evening-long narrative ballets retelling—and, in the process, often trivializing—familiar stories. Such productions tend to be favored by directors and board members of companies anxious to make an immediate impression in their communities. Other choreographers and dancegoers— particularly those who have been influenced by Balanchine—champion the abstract ballet. But, increasingly, such works tend to be slavish imitations of the master that preserve the letter and neglect the creative spirit of Balanchine's practices.

Modern dance has problems of its own. The popularity—and demonstrable efficacy—of ballet as a training method has caused some modern dancers to adopt a balletic lightness, even in works in which it is inappropriate. Thus, fascinating kinetic quirks may be smoothed out in the development of one all-purpose dance technique. Furthermore, the sheer multiplicity of compositional approaches may intimidate, as well as stimu-

*late, choreographers. In order to be noticed at all, choreographers may resort to gimmickry. Fads may follow fads, and possibly valuable new ideas may be discarded before their implications have had a chance to be fully explored.*

*If ballet were to cling to the tried-and-true while modern dance turned itself into a merely disposable, as distinct from a self-renewing, art, then American dance would have the melancholy distinction of being simultaneously successful and impoverished. Yet all these unfortunate tendencies can be reversed by choreographers of imagination. No one knows exactly how such choreographers can be nurtured; no one can predict where they may turn up next. But if it struggles both to keep itself open to ideas and to preserve its heritage, American dance may still be blessed with new choreographic visions.*

# CLASSICS COMICS

$\mathcal{O}$nly thirty years ago, Americans were skeptical about evening-long ballets. No company dared to present a bill consisting of *Giselle* or *Coppélia* alone, and when the Ballet Russe de Monte Carlo staged a three-act *Raymonda*, it was from the start always accompanied by a curtain-raiser or an afterpiece, while over subsequent seasons it was steadily trimmed until it had shrunk to a suite of divertissements. Audiences comparatively new to ballet wanted both value and variety for their money.

Then the Sadler's Wells Ballet came along with its full-evening productions, and a decade later the Soviets arrived with their own. Americans, like audiences around the world, developed a sweet tooth for spectacle. American Ballet Theatre, once famous for what George Beiswanger dubbed the "short story ballet," has increasingly devoted itself to full-evening attractions, while the trendy Joffrey Ballet has recently produced its own first evening-long effort. Across the country, multi-act creations are turning up everywhere. A board member of one company frankly admitted to me that, in her community, audiences dislike mixed bills and promoting them has driven press representatives to distraction. Theoretically, whether a particular ballet is short or long should not matter, provided it be good. However, most of the contemporary multi-act ballets I have seen are, at least to my taste, not good at all. Yet the multi-act form has acquired such prestige that a common term for it, "full-length," carries with it the implication that it is a superior form, that all ballets which are not evening-long are only snippets or sketches. Even some dance intellectuals argue this way. Peggy van Praagh and Peter Brinson maintain, in *The Choreographic Art* (Adam and Charles Black, 1963), "Mood and abstract ballets are one-act forms only, even though their special qualities may be combined at certain times in a full-length narrative work. So the mood ballet and the abstract ballet can never be more than secondary forms in the mainstream of choreographic development. The three-act narrative ballet, like the three-act play, must bear the main burden of development from period to period."

Yet to believe that "the three-act narrative ballet" is ballet's principal form requires taking much on faith. Historians might observe that in the past there may have been fewer evening-long ballets, in the literal sense, than we suspect, because many of the ballets which fill an evening today did not do so for nineteenth-century audiences. Theatrical programs back then could be whoppers containing a ballet and an opera and, sometimes, even a play. The contemporary equivalent might be a night's television fare from the situation comedy through the crime drama and on to the late movie. *Giselle*, at its premiere, shared the evening with an act from Rossini's *Moses*, *Nutcracker* was paired with Tchaikovsky's opera *Iolanta*, *Coppélia* with *Der Freischütz*, and not one of the Bournonville ballets we have seen can stand alone on a program, even in this day of shortened attention spans.* A century ago, theatrical bills were often very mixed bills indeed.

Length is by no means considered a virtue in every art form. Although

---

*Some recent revivals that have opened cuts in the scores of Bournonville's ballets now last an evening. However, these evenings are still short ones.

the novel retains more prestige than the short story, a respectable body of critical theory prefers lyric to epic length in poetry, while much post-Absurdist drama is relatively short. Should dance be compared with concert music, then the multi-act work may seem a freak, for Western music is dominated by the short composition—the composition as short as a one-act ballet—while such composers of sonic blockbusters as Mahler and Bruckner have been considered slightly odd in some circles.

History and aesthetics unite for one additional reason why the multi-act ballet cannot be said to represent the mainstream of balletic development—at least in the West since 1909. (In Soviet ballet the situation is different, and because Soviet artists have had to grapple with their own special aesthetic and social issues, I am confining my remarks largely to dance in America and Western Europe.) Since 1909 Western ballet has been profoundly influenced by Diaghilev's choreographers, particularly by Fokine. What makes Fokine important is not only his theory, but one aspect of his practice. Analyzing the old multi-act Russian ballets, he found that they contained two distinct types of movement: movement which furthered the development of the drama, and nondramatic movement which might convey mood or atmosphere, or be virtually a self-contained set of patterns in time and space. Fokine made this implied dichotomy explicit by dismantling the vast apparatus of Russian ballet. On the one hand, he choreographed ballets in which every instant contributed to the development of narrative or to the establishment of some essential dramatic effect; on the other, he choreographed one ballet, *Les Sylphides*, which, though it had innumerable emotional implications, contained no overt dramatic action whatsoever. Fokine invented the contemporary dance-drama and the abstract dance, the two forms to which most ballet and modern dance choreographers have devoted themselves ever since.

Despite their obvious dissimilarities, dance-drama and abstraction share important resemblances: both require unity of conception, and the more concise they are, the greater their impact; consequently, both forms tend to manifest themselves as single-act creations. Fokine took a big

Russian Easter egg apart. Now some choreographers are trying to put Humpty-Dumpty back together. Since that is no simple matter, it might be stimulating to speculate upon what materials may be usable in full-evening ballets and how such ballets may be structured.

The most familiar type of multi-act ballet is the narrative. Frequently, the source is literary (*Romeo and Juliet*), but it may also be historical (*Anastasia*), mythological (*Clytemnestra*), or even operatic (*Manon*— which is surely better known today as an opera than as a novel). Although some theorists scorn "literary dance," these sources are defensible, literature having inspired choreographers for centuries. In fact, a familiar scenario may help a choreographer cope with a vexing problem of dramatic dance. Advocates of dance-drama hesitate to talk about this, afraid of conceding too much to fanatic abstractionists. Nevertheless, the fact remains: not everything can be told in dance. Conceivably, everything and anything may be expressed, but not everything can be told— or, at least, told easily. Where a dramatist can convey information in a few words, a choreographer may have to have characters gesticulate wildly, and even then he cannot guarantee that audiences will grasp his meaning. Does anyone doubt this? Then let him try to choreograph and make clear to audiences absolutely unfamiliar with *Romeo and Juliet* the scene in which Friar Laurence explains the potion. All balletgoers eventually realize that there are moments in ballets which are meaningful only because we have read a program note or already possess certain background information. Acknowledging this does not invalidate dramatic dance, it merely helps us get past points a choreographer cannot easily relate and go on to something else he may express supremely well. The mime language Petipa used might even be termed a kind of kinetic program note, since the gestures are signs for something else in the same way that words are signs for something else. Now, if the program note proves more interesting than the actual ballet, then that ballet is bad. But program notes or familiar scenarios are not inherently objectionable.

Nevertheless, that so many recent multi-act ballets depend upon familiar stories seems worrisome, for it hints at a narrowing, rather than an expansion, of possibilities. Surely, other things can be done than to retell the same old stories. Why not tell a new story? Or why have any story?

The full-evening abstraction—a choreographic canvas on the scale of a Jackson Pollock—is a tantalizing notion. But, like the full-evening narrative, it brings with it special problems. One involves music. If music is to be used, what music? Should music be commissioned, the score is apt to be either one of two kinds, each of which may alienate a different set of dancegoers. If the score is in a traditional mode, some dancegoers will complain that it sentimentalizes the dancing; if experimental, other dancegoers will call it distracting noise. To set an evening-long abstraction to a piece of existing music virtually commits the choreographer to solemnity, since lengthy musical compositions tend to be vast symphonies or oratorios. Still, some honorable works have been set to grandiose compositions. Such choreographers as John Neumeier and Maurice Béjart have done surprisingly well with Mahler's Third Symphony and Beethoven's Ninth, respectively.

Or a choreographer may utilize several compositions, as Balanchine did in *Jewels*. There are those who claim that *Jewels* is not a full-evening abstraction but only three one-act ballets. They are right that the parts are detachable—but so is the second act of *Swan Lake*. What makes it possible to claim *Jewels* as a multi-act abstraction is that, while its parts may be lopped off, just as one could cut up a Jackson Pollock into several panels, when those parts are presented together they are presented in the same order: "Rubies" follows "Emeralds" and "Diamonds" follows "Rubies." This is how things are in the realm of *Jewels*. Another choreographer might want things another way. Balanchine wants them this way. Like any work of art, *Jewels* is arbitrary (someone else might have made it other than it is), yet it possesses its own internal structure which gives it its own character. Resembling *Jewels* in this respect are the multi-act mixed-media extravaganzas of Alwin Nikolais. Though they all have music by one composer, Nikolais himself, they, like *Jewels*, consist of separable episodes. But whereas Balanchine, by habitually scheduling all three acts of *Jewels*, apparently wants to emphasize that *Jewels* is a unity, Nikolais seems content to raid his extravaganzas, since he increasingly presents excerpts from them, rather than the works in their entirety.

Kei Takei's *Light* is a continually growing work which has attained such proportions that, no matter how long a program may be, it probably can only be seen in excerpts. Once dancegoers expected that this hypnotic, eloquent cycle would someday end and Takei would proceed to other projects. Now it seems as though each new dance by Takei is a further installment of *Light,* just as each of Ezra Pound's later poems was another "Canto." *Light* has gone on to become greater in the aggregate than any specific performance can be, for there remain parts we do not, cannot, see. This may be entirely appropriate, for, with its relentless variations upon images of people bearing burdens, *Light* is Sisyphean in nature.

Merce Cunningham's Events exemplify another approach to what might be termed the indeterminate evening-long abstraction, each Event being a new combining of materials from previously choreographed dances. With *Canfield,* Cunningham makes the same storehouse of movement the source either of various one-act works or of a single full-length production (and here, for once, that term is appropriate). Named after a form of solitaire, *Canfield* resembles an immense deck of cards, each "card" being a movement sequence. When *Canfield* shares a program with other ballets, Cunningham deals only a few of these cards; when *Canfield* is alone on the bill, he deals them all. Some dancegoers find *Canfield* and the Events exhausting. The way the choreography is divorced from overt theme, and even from a direct relationship to the musical accompaniment, can make the pieces a strain to watch. Conceivably, one could defend the difficulty of paying attention to the movement as a choreographic equivalent of the necessity in meditation of concentrating exclusively upon some object or word. With Cunningham, I am willing to force myself to pay attention, just as I am when I attend the deliberately repetitive long pieces of Laura Dean. Yet audiences unwilling to turn theatrical evenings into meditation exercises do have a point: nonreferential movements can become difficult to watch over a long period of time.

This human failing raises the possibility of another form of full-evening ballet: one which is somehow partly programmatic and partly abstract. Given their divertissements and vision scenes, many long nineteenth-century ballets were works of this type: the "Grand Pas" from *Raymonda* and "The Kingdom of the Shades" act from *Bayadère* are two familiar examples of abstract or near-abstract choreography occurring amidst a narrative. One problem about choreographing such a work is that of in-suring that the excursions into abstraction will seem emotionally and structurally appropriate to the moments at which they occur. Otherwise, the ballet will be a hodgepodge.

The full-evening ballet, then, is, with varying degrees of ease, ca-pable of sustaining dramatic, abstract, and partly dramatic, partly ab-stract choreography. Because most choreographers have chosen to be conventionally dramatic, the full potentialities of these genres are far from exhausted. Similarly, the ways in which materials may be arranged within long ballets remain largely unexplored.

To a great extent, choreographers appear to have trouble structuring multi-act ballets. Most such works seem too long, perhaps because their choreographers feel their ballets must literally fill an entire evening: otherwise, critics will not regard them as "full-length." Whatever the reason, many choreographers do run out of steam in multi-act works. Thus, Ashton's *Ondine* gets mired in a divertissement. Ashton may ar-gue that he includes that divertissement because he is deliberately cho-reographing in a nineteenth-century manner and nineteenth-century bal-lets contained divertissements. But if an *Ondine* is to be effective today, Ashton must revivify as well as research nineteenth-century style. Simi-larly, MacMillan finds himself with more time than drama on his hands in *Manon* and *Anastasia*. Because he has virtually exhausted his story before it is time for *Manon* to end, he introduces extraneous and rather lurid complications in the last act. In *Anastasia* he has, essentially, two stories to tell: one, the story of a seemingly tranquil imperial social order shattered by conflict; the other, the story of a tormented woman who be-lieves herself to be a survivor of that social order. These are both good stories, and each could be effectively told in an act. But MacMillan feels he has to have three acts. His solution is to try to spread the first story over two acts. But that so dilutes the story that when we finally meet Anastasia in the third act we may have lost interest in the problems of the Russian Revolution.

Long ballets often seem to have one act too many. Although "three-act" is a common synonym for "multi-act," it might be more profitable for choreographers to think in terms of two, rather than three, acts: one act to establish a situation, another to resolve it. *Giselle, La Sylphide,* and *Nutcracker* are all in two acts, as is one of the finest of contemporary long ballets, Ashton's *La Fille Mal Gardée.* Ashton's ballet bubbles along, partly because it lasts no longer than its story requires it to last and partly because Ashton keeps pushing things ahead choreographically. Although *Fille* contains what might be called variations, pas de deux, and ballabiles, they are frequently linked, rather than separated with formal pauses as they might have been in Petipa's day. Therefore, as soon as one thing ends, something new begins, and the action never lags.

Most contemporary choreographers of long narratives arrange events in simple chronological order. While this does help make action immediately comprehensible, it still disappoints me that so few choreographers have experimented with time. The dramatic approach of Martha Graham—the way she has her protagonists at some crucial moment of decision or insight relive their past as they go forward to accept their destiny—apparently has had little influence upon choreographers of long narratives. Indeed, one of the few major full-evening works to mingle past, present, and future provocatively is Graham's own *Clytemnestra.*

*Clytemnestra* can be exasperating, for it proceeds in an eternal vicious circle as Clytemnestra in Hades reviews the events of her tormented past again and again. Danced with conviction, however, *Clytemnestra* has enormous power because of its very insistence and length. We, like Clytemnestra, are trapped, snared by the repetition of terrible acts.

To insist that everyone choreograph this way would be to substitute one formula for another. In her own worst works, Graham herself uses fragmented chronology as a formula; this has the effect of making essentially simple action portentously obscure. But if fragmented chronology invites murkiness, simple chronology invites banality, particularly when a story comes from literature. Too many multi-act narratives are Classics Comics adaptations of novels or plays. The story is there, there is visceral excitement. But what may not be there is poetry or insight. Most versions of *Romeo and Juliet* are mere run-throughs of the plot. Despite touches of lyricism in the love scenes (as in the MacMillan) or a bustling robustness in the crowd scenes (as in the Cranko), they lack any real point. They are Shakespeare without Shakespeare and without the creative intelligence of anyone else who can freshen source material in the same way that Shakespeare revitalized his own sources.

Ironically (and the irony is a big one), even the most gifted choreographer who essays the multi-act narrative may find himself hampered by an impoverishment of resources. In some respects, the nineteenth-century choreographer could draw from a richer store of dance styles than choreographers can today. Though we live in an age of classic dance, modern dance, mixed-media dance, minimal dance, antidance, nondance, and heaven only knows what else, we tend to look upon these forms as mutually exclusive; or if choreographers do try to combine them, they homogenize them, as in the mergings of classic ballet and modern dance by Tetley and van Manen. This state of affairs comes about because of the way theories we have inherited from Fokine have been filtered through the further arguments of certain proponents of neoclassicism. Seeking concentrated, unified ballets, Fokine insisted that each ballet have its own style: *Les Sylphides*, *Schéhérazade*, and *Petrushka* look wildly different, yet each is internally consistent. With the rise of abstraction, the ideal of purity has been added to that of consistency. If the subject of a dance is to be dance itself, then the best kind of dance is ballet or modern at its most distilled.

While this is fine for a plotless ballet on pointe or for a dynamics study in sneakers, it will scarcely do for a three-act narrative. Nineteenth-century choreographers not only had classic dance, demi-caractère, national character, grotesque dance, and mime, they could mix these things up in a single composition, whereas our ideals of consistency and purity deter us from doing that. Our age is "classic" not only in its glorification of classic dance; it is classic in its concern for proprieties and levels of diction. Significantly, some balletgoers consider the lyrical first act of *Anastasia* its finest, while they call the Expressionist torment of the third "not really dancing." Whatever it may be "really," it is theatrically necessary as a visual, kinetic, and dramatic contrast to what has gone before. It helps give *Anastasia* whatever urgency it possesses. In three-act ballets absolute purity may invite monotony. All acts seem alike because all the dancing is, basically, alike. A horrific example of this was Peter Darrell's *Tales of Hoffmann*, recently in the repertory of American Ballet Theatre. This was a ballet choreographed in one all-purpose style, although each of its acts told a different fantastic story set in a different locale. This tendency toward purity is by no means confined to the West, Grigorovich having put on pointe the character dances in the third act of *Swan Lake*. But however and wherever it happens, the more "classic" a long ballet becomes, the duller it may grow. It is worth remembering that the great nineteenth-century triumph of Russian classicism, *The Sleeping Beauty*, is extravagantly "impure," being also a triumph of grotesquerie, mime, and character dance.

Just as some readers expect all poetry to be high-toned, so audiences may demand one single kind of dancing, even when it is inappropriate. And choreographers may feel obliged to satisfy them. When Bruce Marks choreographed a *Don Quixote* for Ballet West, he was faced with a literary subject not easily suited to "classic" treatment because its hero is a grotesque. Marks's solution was to have two Don Quixotes: the creaky old man and the handsome young knight he imagines himself to be. But instead of treating the two Dons dramatically or ironically, Marks employed the young Don primarily to partner the idealized Dulcinea (the ballerina) in rapturous classic adagios which, though they may have been "real" dancing, were also boring, since they never advanced the ballet.

Deriving as it does from attempts to make dance its own subject matter, contemporary "classic" dance is not always suited to the depiction of character. Much characterization in our long ballets resembles Classics Comics simplifications. Shakespeare's Petruchio and Katherine, two free-spirited beings, are reduced to animated cartoons in Cranko's *Taming of the Shrew*, where Petruchio simply swaggers and Kate does little more than either waddle in a goofy ducklike fashion or stab petulantly at the floor. An extreme dichotomy between "pure" dancing and dramatic movement exists in Cranko's *Eugene Onegin*, particularly in the pas de deux, which degenerate into displays of unusual ways of sliding or lifting the ballerina. If Onegin occasionally reminds the audience of his character traits by gazing coolly into space or striking his brow with his hand, these gestures are so obvious—they are cartoon gestures—that, rather than intensifying dramatic meanings, they make one conscious of their absence. What is being separated in *Onegin* (and in similar pieces) is not just dance and drama but dance and meaning of any kind, for the dance often cannot be defended in terms of such purely formal considerations as flow, design, or phrasing. This kind of dance is merely a technique display disguised as a classic pas in a costume show disguised as a narrative.

One interesting recent attempt at a long narrative, Oscar Araiz's *Romeo and Juliet*, presented by the Joffrey Ballet, may actually acknowledge that the pure classic dance style we prize most may not be ideally suited for the telling of stories. Unlike most choreographers who undertake a Prokofiev *Romeo*, Araiz does not adopt a variant of the Leonid Lavrovsky scenario. Rather, he has decided—as John Neumeier decided before him—to be idiosyncratic. But their idiosyncrasies are quite different. In his *Romeo* for the Royal Danish Ballet, Neumeier seems intent upon choreographing and giving his own personal twist to every last detail in the story. Not so Araiz. He assumes that audiences already know the story, just as Graham assumes audiences know Greek mythology. So Araiz feels free to omit Friar Laurence, Prince Escalus, Benvolio, and Lord and Lady Montague.

He begins abstractly. What the audience sees first is a plotless ballet with patterns suggesting attraction or antagonism. But then, at one point, when someone falls, it seems a real death. Drama has shattered abstraction, and the dancers return in Renaissance costumes to enact Shakespeare's story. But Araiz still consciously separates his dancers from his story: these dancers are not trying to live the story, they are relating it, a distinction emphasized by the Brechtian device of having the cast change costumes between scenes in full view of the audience. At various points Juliet is impersonated by three dancers. Yet these girls seem indistinguishable in personality (as, to a great extent, the female soloists are in *Serenade*). However, the fact that the doublings occur at moments of emotional intensity suggests that one of Araiz's themes is how passion may become obsessive and totally consume one. As the ballet proceeds, the dancers grow increasingly involved with the passions of the characters they portray. In the second act that identification becomes complete. Devoid of Brechtian touches, the sequences from the duelings of Mercutio, Tybalt, and Romeo to Juliet's "potion" scene are unabashedly dramatic and rush by with excitement. Touches of literal realism are introduced. Tybalt dies with an audible shriek. Juliet dries her eyes on a real bedsheet. (Because the ballet contains so few actual objects, those few which do exist gain increasing prominence.)

The "tomb" scene reverts to abstraction. The three Juliets stir from their biers into momentary life. As ever, they are indistinguishable; yet, collectively, they suggest a swelling of emotion. After dancing with Romeo they grow inert and, in what may be a macabre parody of Balanchine's Apollo and the Muses, Romeo has to drag their lifeless bodies across the floor, the home of these muses being not Parnassus but the grave. The ballet ends, as it began, abstractly. Effigies adorning other tombs in the vault come alive, divest themselves of their Renaissance robes, and dance an abstract mood piece which suggests that each man is a symbolic Romeo, each woman a symbolic Juliet. Here Araiz may be trying to emphasize that while all human lovers are inescapably mortal, art may immortalize their loves.

The Joffrey *Romeo* is full of surprises. While there is little real depth of characterization, Araiz has found a means to skirt this problem by making his ballet a series of commentaries upon passion and dancing. Whereas other choreographers have come up with Classics Comics, Araiz has devised a college casebook on *Romeo and Juliet*. That, at least, is an improvement. Yet if Araiz's precedent may challenge choreographers to do their own commentaries on literary classics, it may not assist any choreographer wishing to stage a straightforward dance-drama. Such a choreographer will somehow have to find a rich choreographic vocabulary which contains contemporary equivalents for character dance and mime.

One noteworthy attempt to provide a dance-drama with internal variety is Balanchine's *Don Quixote*. No matter how much Balanchine tinkers, its parts never cohere, and a few seasons ago Balanchine succumbed to requests for "more dancing" by introducing an interminable divertissement into the first act. Yet his *Don Quixote* remains worth studying because of its juxtapositions of classic dance, Spanish dance, court dance, and gesture in dramatically meaningful ways. Thus, after the second act's court dances, so stiff and artificial, comes the realism of the courtiers' tauntings of the Don, which culminate when, in a sadistic variation upon custard pie throwing, a woman smears the Don's face with cream. Much of the third act is devoted to a "vision scene," a near-abstraction much admired by lovers of "real" dancing. But note its placement. It is not a mere interlude. Following a humiliation and preceding a phantasmagoria of giants, pigs, and windmills, it is choreographic opium which tries to erase Don Quixote's pain. But, like any drug vision, it eventually fades, and then the pain seems all the more intense.

Since in the last century a multi-act ballet was often only one attraction on a theatrically mixed bill, a contemporary choreographer might find it rewarding to experiment not only with different forms of dance, but with the incorporation into dance of different forms of the performing arts. One of the most enterprising explorers of this sort of choreographic total theatre is Meredith Monk. Drawing upon dancing, miming, clowning, acting, utilitarian movement, singing, chanting, and spoken dialogue, Monk's productions are unusually rich. Yet, though often bizarre, they are not gluts of effects. Monk calculates her effects, squandering nothing. Not only does she put varied media to use, she finds considerable variety within each medium. Her recent *Quarry*, for instance, made considerable use of gesture. Yet she employed gesture in many different ways.

The central image was a feverish child whose illness eventually came to symbolize the fever of a society upon the brink of oppression and war, these larger meanings developing themselves piecemeal through gestural vignettes. Some were realistic: in separate pools of light (or rooms in a house) girls at a table share food, grandparents sit stoically, and a mother primps and seems distraught, while outside a stranger passes by, photographing people and checking names in a little black book. The grandparents—cultivated, educated people—discuss "academic jealousy" (from their tone of voice, it sounds like a euphemism), then freeze, pointing to something alarming occurring outside their window. The implications of these vignettes emerge only gradually and by accumulation; we must sort them out and make connections ourselves, just as a sick child lying sleepless in a bedroom sorts out and interprets the sounds filtering in from other rooms of the house.

Monk elsewhere employs caricature: a panorama of dictators contains an acidly satiric portrait of a vain, vulgar military leader and his entourage. On still other occasions, by following one type of gesture with a totally different one, Monk achieves startling effects. The coming of tyranny is suggested through a calisthenic drill in which the calisthenic actions are strong enough to stamp out or push aside anything or anyone in their path. This symbolism is followed by almost painfully stark realism. The stage now seems to be the waiting room of a deportation center in which the elderly academic couple are required to divest themselves of all personal belongings—coins, keys, jewelry, everything (the sounds of these objects dropped on the floor becoming the incident's horrifying "music")—before being sent—where? One shudders at the possibilities.

Monk's works also contain experiments with time and space. The first half of *Education of the Girlchild* proceeds chronologically forward, while the second goes backward from old age to infancy. *Vessel* and *Juice* spread themselves across time and space by having their installments occur on different evenings in different locations, the locations for *Vessel* increasing in scale from a small studio to an intimate theatre to a vast parking lot. Of course, such experimentation requires a specialized ensemble and probably cannot be duplicated by most ballet companies.

Unfortunately, most ballet companies have hardly experimented with full-evening forms at all. One of the most disturbing aspects of today's cultural scene is the way the rise of the full-evening ballet seems to herald an era when dance will be safe, tame, glossy, and vacuous. Dance has become popular and is growing increasingly respectable—not only in New York, but everywhere. Cities now want to display ballet companies, just as for generations they have been displaying art museums and orchestras. This is thoroughly admirable in terms of employment opportunities and dancers' security. Yet most art museums and symphony orchestras are conservative in policy. So are most opera companies. Dance, until now, has been more adventurous. Lacking a standard repertoire as extensive and as accessible in printed form as that of the symphony, dance has depended upon innovative choreographers. But while good dancers abound, choreographers are rarer, and now that scores of cities want their own ballet companies the shortage of choreographers is particularly acute. The full-evening ballet provides a curious but convenient solution to this set of problems.

While choreographing a truly good full-evening ballet, like choreographing any good ballet, takes genius, the full-evening form can allow the clever second-rank choreographer or ballet master to produce new works which are either gussied-up classics (*Swan Lake* or *Nutcracker* with titillating but never profound neo-Freudian touches) or ballets on familiar subjects (*Romeo and Juliet, Cinderella*) which permit the ballet master to bolster his own possibly limited ingenuity with adaptations of ideas borrowed from previous ballets on those subjects which he has seen. Good or bad, the results will at least be grand, since the typical three-act affair tends to last several hours, to use lots of dancers, and to be handsomely decorated.

All this will please managers wanting companies to gain instant recognition. It will please civic boosters who like to think and talk big—and how can you talk big about a company which does nothing but ballets for nine or ten dancers in simple leotards? And it will please audiences who like pleasant evenings in the theatre, provided those evenings don't make them think or feel too much. Big enough to "ooh" and "ah" over and long enough to intimidate, the full-evening ballet may have the look of importance, even when it has no substance. If the look is enjoyed so much that nobody misses the substance, then the full-evening ballet may soon effect drastic changes in American dance. I doubt that those changes will be for the better.

*Ballet Review* 6/4 (1977–78): 87–98

# THE RISE
# OF THE MALE ENSEMBLE

o one thinks it unusual if a dance work, be it narrative or abstract, classical or contemporary, contains an ensemble composed entirely of women. Nor is anyone really astonished if the entire cast of a dance is female, as the casts of dances have often been from the early works of Martha Graham to the early works of Twyla Tharp. Male-dominated ensembles, however, remain uncommon, and the mere production of an all-male work often sets dancegoers debating innumerable artistic and social issues.

An explanation for these debates is not hard to find. Male dancers have had to contend both with philistines who claim that dancing is not a fit profession for men and with an aesthetic attitude inherited from nineteenth-century ballet that tends to make dance the glorification of woman.

Curiously, however, male ensembles are not uncommon in musical comedy, films, or television. Thus, male dancers may appear when a choreographer wishes to establish a hearty or rough-and-tumble atmosphere. Or a female star may be supported by an all-male ensemble in an attempt to emphasize her allure. But these uses of men are often limited and formula-ridden.

In ballet and modern dance there have been attempts to devise genuinely imaginative works with male ensembles or all-male casts. Brief all-male sequences occur in such ballets as George Balanchine's *Stars and Stripes* (1958) and Jerome Robbins's *Moves* (1959). Among the works of the past two decades with totally male casts are Murray Louis's *Calligraph for Martyrs* (1961), Erick Hawkins's *Lords of Persia* (1964), and Gerald Arpino's *Olympics* (1966).

The pioneer in this field, however, was Ted Shawn, whose Men Dancers flourished from 1933 to 1940 and helped propagate ideas about male dancing that are still common. Yet Shawn's choreography also hints at fresh approaches to male dancing that choreographers are only now starting to explore.

The ways in which the male ensemble is used in recent works are often similar to the ways in which male ensembles have been treated in the past. Yet, if some of these works are examined closely, one may discern slight but important shifts of emphasis.

Previous male-dominated dances have often been preachy compositions specifically attempting to demonstrate the validity of male dancing. One strategy that many choreographers adopted was to relate dancing to three kinds of activity regarded as properly masculine: heroic struggle, work, and sports. Some of today's male-dominated dances may also be related to these activities.

Heroic struggle is certainly apparent in what may be the most surprising of these new pieces, George Balanchine's *Kammermusik No. 2*, for the New York City Ballet. Balanchine, after all, is not only the choreographer who has proclaimed that "ballet is woman," he once also declared that if a male ensemble were put on stage, it would look like "nothing."

Yet *Kammermusik*'s ensemble of eight men is the most noticeable thing in the entire ballet. These men are noticeable, first of all, because their presence runs counter to audience expectations and to Balanchine's own choreographic practice. Audiences are so used to seeing ensembles consisting of women in abstract ballets, particularly in Balanchine's abstractions, that the female corps de ballet has come to seem the almost impersonal instrument that enables Balanchine to make visible the designs he imagines. In *Kammermusik*, however, it is the men who constitute the corps de ballet.

Whereas many of the women of the New York City Ballet conform to a standard of long-legged beauty, the company's men do not seem to come from a common mold. Their differences are therefore particularly visible when they move as an ensemble. The men also stand out when they are compared with the soloists: two women and their male partners.

Here, again, Balanchine has defied expectations. One might expect that, for the sake of impact, Balanchine would contrast his ensemble with a single ballerina and a single danseur. Instead, he provides two ballerinas and two danseurs of equal importance. Such doubling gives to the soloists something of the anonymity one ordinarily associates with ensembles, while the visually startling ensemble asserts itself far more than ensembles usually do.

Balanchine's soloists, then, are almost anonymous, his ensemble almost individualized. Indeed, with its craggy choreography—its lunges and thrustings, and its groupings suggesting rock formations or friezes— *Kammermusik* might be a ballet about collective forces. In Balanchine's dialectical scheme of things, the soloists are one such force, the male ensemble another, and their interactions constitute a grandly scaled struggle which, though its exact significance is never revealed, brings to mind forces of history or nature.

If *Kammermusik* is heroic struggle, Rudy Perez's *According to What, or Is Dance Really about Dancing?*, which his all-male company, the Men's Coalition, offered at the Judson Church in February 1978, belongs to the tradition of the all-male dance in praise of work, a tradition that also includes Ted Shawn's *Labor Symphony* of 1934. Perez has always been fond of making choreography resemble tasks or work situations. There were many references to work in this piece, along with tableaux which, because of their muscularity, recalled those of mechanics and laborers in WPA murals.

One could relate the February 1978 programs of improvisations by Mangrove, a visiting all-male dance collective from San Francisco, to the tradition of all-male dances based upon sports. Certainly, much of the movement in these presentations at the O. K. Harris Gallery and Eden's Expressway resembled gymnastics and tumbling. But anyone who saw only that in Mangrove's improvisations would have missed something important, a quality explicit in Mangrove and implicit in some other new male dances that helps distinguish these works from many of their predecessors.

The young men of Mangrove looked as though they were having fun. They were not afraid to fool around. As they formed their human pyramids, they chatted or even giggled. Mangrove's improvisations resembled play—not labor or competitive sports, but simple play.

A sense of delight is comparatively rare in works for male ensembles. With its throbbing tempo, *Olympics* possessed a wallop that made sports seem almost combative. In Shawn's most famous all-male composition, *Kinetic Molpai* (1935), men celebrate the death and resurrection of a hero in episodes bearing such titles as "Strife," "Oppositions," "Dirge," and "Surge." No episode, however, is called "Rejoicing."

Now there are male dances that are unabashedly playful. The high spirits of Pilobolus were among the things that made this troupe seem distinctive when it was founded as an all-male company in 1971. Unlike the improvised feats of Mangrove, the acrobatic dances of Pilobolus, for mixed and all-male casts alike, are tightly structured. What helps make them a pleasure to behold is that the dancers keep huffing, puffing, and bluster to a minimum.

Even Perez, though concerned with work, is willing to add a bit of play to his choreography. There was a scene near the conclusion of *According to What* when, having just behaved like figures from post office murals, the dancers relaxed and slapped each other on the back the way athletes do after a game. One could never imagine the figures in *Olympics* or *Kinetic Molpai* unbending to such an extent.

Another possibly significant thing about many recent male-dominated dances is that they lack explicit themes or plots. Thus, *Kammermusik* evokes struggle, but the nature of its struggle remains unexplained. Instead, Balanchine invites audiences to enjoy the movement simply as movement, the sheer energy of his ballet suggesting that, for him, the very act of struggle may at times be a pleasure.

Balanchine, Perez, and the Mangrove collective may have abstracted male movement from struggle, work, and sports. But what remains onstage to be seen is male movement to be enjoyed as a pleasurable thing in itself.

Such recent developments in male dancing may have come about partly as a result of the efforts of advocates for the various sexual liberation movements and partly because such people as Shawn, however stuffy some of his efforts may now seem, did try to convince audiences that dancing was an honorable activity for men. He made people believe him when he claimed that male dancing was honest work and as vigorous as sports.

While he was best known for dances on heroic themes, he also experimented with all-male abstractions that he regarded as "music visualizations" of concert music. If Shawn's polemical pieces—his dances about workers and heroes—exerted a profound influence at the time of their creation, his studies in pure movement now take on new importance as foreshadowings of ways in which choreography for male ensembles may develop in the future if choreographers continue to investigate possibilities of male movement as something that may be enjoyed for its own sake.

Eventually, the day may arrive when the all-male ensemble, like the all-female ensemble, will seem thoroughly natural onstage. The implied subject of a male-dominated dance will not be the propriety of male dancing, as is often the case even today; that will simply be taken for granted. What then will matter is not how many male or female roles a given work may possess, but whether or not that number and type of dancers seem appropriate to that work. And essays of this sort will no longer need to be written.

*New York Times*, 19 March 1978

# IS BALLET
# DILUTING MODERN DANCE?

*F*orty years ago, there was a war on in the American dance world, a war between classical ballet and modern dance. Classicists accused the moderns of being technically limited and aesthetically eccentric, while the moderns charged that ballet was a European art form irrelevant to America.

Yet ballet thrived, and for many balletgoers the speed and energy of today's American ballet reflect the speed and energy of American life. The moderns, for their part, continued to glory in modernity. At least, they did so onstage. But when they sought out teachers, they sometimes sought out ballet teachers, for they realized that ballet classes could be beneficial to them, even though they had no intention of ever becoming ballet dancers.

So now there is détente. The great dance powers are managing to get along.

At first glance, it may seem that the balance of power slightly favors the moderns. Ballet stars, including Rudolf Nureyev and Erik Bruhn, appear as guests with modern dance troupes, and ballet companies have produced works by such modern choreographers as Doris Humphrey, Anna Sokolow, José Limón, Merce Cunningham, Paul Taylor, Murray Louis, and Twyla Tharp.

Nevertheless, some admirers of modern dance are worried. They fear that ballet is sneakily infiltrating modern dance and sabotaging it. What they dread is an increasing balletization of modern dance and, as evidence, they can point to several phenomena.

Martha Graham's present company is young and talented, yet its dancing is lighter and more flowing than that of Graham companies of the past. As for the ballet stars who go modern, critics—among them, Marcia B. Siegel—have accused some of "changing or merely disregarding the steps" of the modern works in which they have been cast.

Many young modern dancers currently take almost nothing but ballet classes. The theory seems to be, if you want to choreograph, then a modern dance composition workshop is the place for you; but if you want to be an adept dancer, study ballet.

Yet there are those who believe that modern dance's balletization has been carried to excess. One viewer with alarm is Senta Driver, who in the summer of 1978 informally discussed the state of modern dance with the participants in the American Dance Festival's annual Dance Critics' Conference, and she has returned to the issue in recent conversations.

Herself a ballet lover who has taken daily ballet class, Driver finds ballet training invaluable for developing speed, line, projection, brilliance of turns and jumps, and strength in the legs. But these are not the only things that dance training can develop; and if they are emphasized at the expense of others, then the stylistic differences that help make American dance so varied may disappear, leaving dancers with one all-purpose, semiballetic, but very bland, style.

There exist other worriers about modern dance training. A few years ago, Jane Dudley, the American modern dancer who now teaches at the London School of Contemporary Dance, recalled that some of the teachers of the 1930s who had been influenced by the choreographic Expressionism of Mary Wigman used to distinguish in class between sequences in which the dancer seemed the active master of the movement and sequences in which the dancer seemed to turn passive and be propelled by the sheer force of the movement: "movement that you control and movement that controls you." Such kinetic distinctions, Dudley thought, were being ignored today in modern dance and often seemed totally unknown to ballet students.

When these remarks were quoted to a ballet dancer who also admires modern dance, that dancer snapped, "Movement that you control and movement that controls you! That's just fancy talk! In any case, what's the big problem? If dancers are disciplined, they should be able to do whatever a choreographer desires."

Her response may derive from a conviction often held by ballet dancers that ballet training is superior to modern dance training because it is so comprehensive that it permits ballet dancers to "do more" than modern dancers can do. An example that ballet dancers often give is that whereas they can dance in bare feet, modern dancers usually have trouble moving in pointe shoes.

However, the problem involves more than being able to do this or that particular thing; otherwise, exponents of Bharata Natyam could easily scorn ballet and modern dance alike because neither teaches the subtle movements for hands, neck, and eyes that are known to Indian dancers.

Despite the admirable versatility of many dancers, it is by no means universally agreed that ballet dancers are the equal of modern dancers in modern dance compositions. Ballet dancers often tend to smooth out modern movements to their nearest classical equivalents, and when the Royal Danish Ballet performed Paul Taylor's *Aureole*, the company was accused of turning the choreography's odd tilts of the body into conventional arabesques.

Ballet training may not be as comprehensive as its apologists claim. According to Driver, there are things one probably cannot get from ballet exercises. Ballet is usually not concerned with asymmetry, off-balance movements, or weight. Ballet exalts purity of line. Yet line may be of little interest to nonballetic choreographers. On the other hand, ballet tends to ignore contractions and twisting and spiraling movements.

Unlike some modern dance experimentalists, ballet choreographers have made few attempts to redefine traditional stage space. Indeed, ballet's preoccupation with turnout suggests that the conventions of the proscenium theatre are built into the very premises of ballet technique.

Furthermore, modern dancers who take nothing but ballet classes may be unconsciously absorbing balletic notions that may ultimately contribute to the dilution of modern dance. There is a prejudice in favor of "prettiness" in ballet; one usually looks nonpretty only for dramatic effect. Yet looking pretty is not necessarily the only desirable way to look.

Ballet also idealizes certain body types. Whereas mere fatness is probably not countenanced in any style of theatrical dance, since fatness implies flabbiness and, hence, physical weakness, ballet also usually rejects the square body and, since rising on pointe provides one with extra height, the very tall body is suspect.

To prevent modern dance from totally capitulating to ballet, Driver does not urge modern dancers to stop studying ballet. The value of ballet training is indisputable. But what she does recommend is that there should be "no end to the number of techniques" open to students. "The important thing, though," she says, "is that all these techniques should be recognized as being distinctly different. Movement training should not be melted down."

Driver's remarks touch upon some of the significant issues in contemporary dance. If modern dance has remained unable to solve the problem of how to encourage diversity and individuality and at the same time assure a continuity of training and repertory, the advocates of ballet, as they have occasionally done in the past, may once again be treating their art's technical and aesthetic assumptions as though they were unassailable dogmas. And some people who would not profess to give intellectual assent to those dogmas are nevertheless dancing as though those dogmas constituted the absolute truth.

*New York Times*, 25 February 1979

# BALANCHINE'S CHOREOGRAPHIC INFLUENCE: PLUSES AND MINUSES

*C*horeographically, we live in the age of Balanchine. Through his works, the late George Balanchine significantly changed our ideas of ballet, and his influence continues to be felt by other choreographers.

Many recent ballets might not have existed at all if Balanchine had not provided precedents for them. As one might expect, the choreographers of the New York City Ballet, Balanchine's company, are carrying on his tradition. During the 1984–85 season, both Helgi Tomasson's new *Menuetto*, a gracious work to a Mozart divertimento, and Bart Cook's first ballet, *Seven by Five*, a romp to Saint-Saëns's Septet, could be described as Balanchinian abstractions to concert music. Abstractions of a similar sort are often staged by choreographers for regional groups.

When Fernando Bujones made his choreographic debut for American Ballet Theatre, the result was the bubbly *Grand Pas Romantique*. Although the ballet was inspired by the divertissements of the nineteenth century and was set to excerpts from a nineteenth-century ballet score, Adolphe Adam's *Diable à Quatre*, few nineteenth-century choreographers would have dreamed of creating divertissements so completely divorced from any thematic pretext. Thus, Balanchine's influence is being felt, indirectly as well as directly.

The works of such choreographers as Tomasson, Cook, and Bujones— and of the New York City Ballet's Peter Martins, as well—are often expertly constructed. Cook and Bujones may have been choreographic novices, but they put steps together with admirable confidence. However, simply because they are so competent, their ballets can in some ways also seem disturbing.

What is bothersome about many of the ballets by today's choreographers in the Balanchine tradition is the fact that, often, they do not seem to be about much. Of course, being plotless (or "abstract") they are not required to be about anything specific. Nevertheless, I miss the presence of some overall guiding concept or concern in them.

What one remembers most about these works are their details: for instance, in *Menuetto*, Kyra Nichols's bent-knee turns, the moment when Maria Calegari shields her face as if she were outdoors in the sun, and the double duet for two pairs of dancers during which the women sit on the floor with their backs to the audience while their suitors show off. And in *Grand Pas Romantique* there are such charming touches as the episode in which a duet is framed by two trios on either side of the soloists and the adagio that begins with the soloists stepping slowly toward each other as if in a dream of love.

These ballets sometimes seem to be all details. So, in a sense, are most works of art, since lofty concepts alone can seldom compensate for faulty craftsmanship. Yet it is possible for a work to possess exquisite details and still be inconsequential. Some jeweled ornaments are works of this sort: they are "precious" in both the good and the bad sense of that word. So are finely wrought knickknacks, whatnots, and trinkets. Considered in this light, certain Balanchine-influenced ballets could be termed choreographic bric-a-brac.

Given America's abundance of well-trained classical dancers, it is not surprising that choreographers delight in making beautiful bodies move as perfectly as possible. Yet this concern for pedagogical correctness can lead to a preoccupation with details for their own sake.

It is also conceivable that some young choreographers, in their understandable reverence for Balanchine, may be imitating him too slavishly. Whereas great artists can always serve as inspirations, younger artists should be careful about spending too much time in the shadow of a genius. T. S. Eliot once called Milton a bad literary influence; Eliot himself may be a bad influence, though both Eliot and Milton may still be great poets. In fact, Eliot and Milton may be bad influences in the same way: attempting to imitate the poetic organ tones of these two masters, younger writers may produce nothing but pretentious rumblings. And simply because Balanchine became celebrated for abstractions to concert music, young choreographers should not necessarily assume that they should therefore spend the rest of their days imitating them.

Defenders of these school-of-Balanchine abstractions occasionally justify them by saying, "At least, they are in the classical style," as if classicism were an endangered species. Such remarks puzzle me for, unless classically trained choreographers set out to be deliberately iconoclastic, I can't imagine what they could produce that would not reflect their background and experience. If anything, one may argue that certain rigid notions of classicism may be tyrannizing American ballet and that the abstract ballet, which for Balanchine was a vision in motion, is being treated by lesser choreographers only as an excuse for devising technical exercises. But displays of good schooling accompanied by nice music are not necessarily also significant works of art.

It would be unfortunate if young choreographers started to imagine that they had to seek permission from the ghost of Balanchine whenever they created a new ballet. It would be equally unfortunate if Balanchine's most ardent admirers regarded him as such a saint that they would pronounce any deviation from his choreographic practice a heresy. Making Balanchine a spectral censor is to ignore the fact that, while he was present upon this earth, he could be a cantankerous artist who often changed his mind about ballets and who always went his own creative way.

By narrowing the possibilities of classical ballet in a sincere, but misguided, act of homage to Balanchine, the time might well come when ballets will consist of nothing but strings of neatly arranged steps to symphonic music. The interest of these ballets would lie almost exclusively in the ingenious ways their choreographers had used classroom steps, and decorum would be prized as one of the greatest choreographic virtues. Ballet would thereby become a mandarin art, hermetically sealed from all contact with the ideas and passions of the world outside the studio and stage. Some balletgoers might conceivably welcome such a state of affairs and enjoy spending their time debating fine points of style. An art so seemingly impervious to human frailty might even be consoling in a strife-torn world. It might also be deadly dull; and if this is what ballet will be like in the future, I suspect I shall be enjoying ballet less and less.

Yet ballet need not be narrowed in this manner. The abstract form itself can perhaps be developed in unexpected ways, if choreographers would only be bold enough to experiment. Two of the New York City Ballet's most interesting premieres in the 1984–85 season were Jerome Robbins's *In Memory of . . .* and Peter Martins's *Poulenc Sonata.* Both were set to concert music. Neither told any sort of literal story. Yet they contained choreographic images that evoked dramatic situations and emotions. These were ballets in which, as in certain kinds of contemporary painting, abstract and representational elements were intermingled. Avoiding the perils of both the dance-drama at its most ponderous and the choreographic abstraction at its most trivial, this form of ballet may be worth exploring. And, given the age we live in, if precedents have to be found for it in the Balanchine canon, one can easily point to *Robert Schumann's "Davidsbündlertänze", Liebeslieder Walzer,* and *Serenade.*

*New York Times,* 1 September 1985

# NEW IS NOT ALWAYS BETTER

ot long ago at a party, an acquaintance came up and expressed amazement that I had enjoyed Ballet Rambert's recent engagement at Brooklyn College. "But how could you have liked it?" he demanded to know. "It was all so 1951!"

Now, to be pedantic about the matter, 1951 was not a bad year, for it was the year in which George Balanchine choreographed *La Valse*, Jerome Robbins choreographed *The Cage*, Frederick Ashton choreographed *Daphnis and Chlöe*, and Merce Cunningham choreographed *16 Dances for Soloist and Company of Three*, the first work in which he utilized chance methods of composition. However, what one says blithely at a party one may wish to rephrase more soberly on the morning after, and I suspect that my acquaintance was not referring to the Rambert's creativity. Rather, he was probably trying to say that he found the British company old hat.

To declare a company's works good or bad is one thing, and it can be fun as well as stimulating to argue over them. But when one pronounces a company outmoded, then one has introduced a whole new consideration into the discussion, for lurking in that pronouncement is the assumption that dance is inexorably moving forward in a certain direction. And this assumption, in turn, is usually accompanied by another: namely, that there is a readily identifiable avant-garde leading that moving forward.

Undeniably, our century has witnessed major avant-garde trends. But whereas there can always be vital creative work, there is not necessarily always an avant-garde, if by avant-garde we mean a specific group of artists who make such radical experiments that we are forced to question the very aesthetic bases of an art form.

Today, dance has no avant-garde.* Its last real avant-garde manifestation occurred twenty years ago with the establishment of the Judson

---

*Some observers speculate that choreographers influenced by recent trends in pop music and performance art may come to constitute a new avant-garde. Only the passage of time can determine whether or not this is true.

Dance Theatre, and there has been no new avant-garde since then. People occasionally still call certain choreographers avant-garde, but that designation usually turns out to be a convenient way of referring to artists who are working in the Judson tradition.

Some people may deplore this state of affairs. However, it can be argued that our lack of a choreographic avant-garde is by no means a catastrophe. Too often, those who proclaim themselves or their friends avant-garde appear to believe that they know for certain how art is destined to develop. Yet, should time march on in a different direction, their arrogance can seem preposterous or embarrassing in retrospect.

Other professed lovers of avant-garde art may be more interested in novelty than in quality. For them, the controversy surrounding a new work may be more exciting than the work itself. Of course, newness and controversy have long enlivened all the Western arts, and my friend at the party was surely saying that he saw nothing that he considered really new at Ballet Rambert.

However, to overvalue newness may conceivably make it impossible for an art to develop. Early in the nineteenth century, women revolutionized ballet by dancing on pointe, and Marie Taglioni triumphed as an exemplar of pointe work. Yet, if no one after her had continued to dance on pointe because pointe technique was now familiar, we would never have had *Swan Lake, The Sleeping Beauty*, or Balanchinian abstractions.

In our own time, every few years some former admirer of Balanchine or Cunningham will complain that because these choreographers have not made any recent innovations they are now repeating themselves and, hence, are uninteresting. But to build upon past innovations can be enriching, whereas an endless quest for novelty alone could result in the depletion of an art's resources, since none of the novelties discovered would be further developed.

At present, we live in a pluralistic era of dance, an era that was made possible by one of the theories of our last avant-garde. The Judson choreographers and their sympathizers believed that any movement can function as a dance movement. In the 1960s, this led to a use of "nondance" movement. But, in time, choreographers also drew upon skilled movement from fields other than dance—for instance, athletic movement, and choreographers as various as Molissa Fenley, Karole Armitage, and the Pilobolus collective have delighted in gymnastic proficiency. Yet, if any movement can function as dance movement, that theory also implies that conventional dance movement is still viable.

Many dancers today are familiar with several ways of moving. Modern dancers study ballet, quite a number of ballet dancers have taken at least a few modern classes, and modern dancers such as Twyla Tharp and Laura Dean have created works for ballet companies. Other dancers have explored Oriental dance, martial arts, meditation, physical therapy, clowning, mime, and sign language for the deaf. Geographical as well as stylistic interchanges have also taken place. American choreographers have been acclaimed in Europe, and the presentations of the Brooklyn Academy of Music have made it possible for New York audiences to sample contemporary European dance.

Some contemporary choreographers have staked out particular areas for themselves. Trisha Brown, Lucinda Childs, and Dana Reitz are all, in their own ways, fascinated by structural rigor. Spinning recurs as a leitmotif in Laura Dean's dances. Senta Driver is concerned with weighted movement.

Much present-day choreography remains plotless or abstract. Nevertheless, some recent productions have exhibited a renewed interest in plot, theme, characterization, and, on occasion, social commentary. For instance, the peace movement's return to prominence has prompted several dances expressing horror at the prospect of nuclear war. Curiously enough, most of the choreographers of such pieces have emerged from backgrounds in abstract dance and have had little contact with an earlier era's exponents of dance-drama. Meredith Monk, Kenneth King, and Phoebe Neville have long been interested in thematic works, and in the past few seasons there have been fascinating thematic dances by such choreographers as Johanna Boyce, Tim Miller, Bill T. Jones, and Arnie Zane.

Thus, we can rejoice in variety. However, pluralism, like any other cultural tendency, has its perils. For one thing, it can encourage self-indulgence. Whereas fiercely competitive artistic "schools" may engage in endless squabbling, the existence of such rival "isms" can also force artists to examine ideas seriously and to take carefully considered aesthetic stands.

Moreover, one can fear that pluralism may paradoxically lead to compartmentalization. In order to be noticed, choreographers may decide that they have to possess some stylistic attribute or compositional gimmick that is theirs alone. It would, however, be unfortunate if Dean felt obliged to include spinning in each new dance not because she wished to do so, but because she thought her audience expected it. And would Driver's commitment to heavy movement make her hesitant to incorporate sylphlike lightness into a piece, even when it might be appropriate? Similarly, would Driver ever feel that she could not use spinning because that would be an invasion of Dean's territory?

Yet, even taking these dangers into account, the possibilities of pluralism are enormous. At least in theory, dancers should now be able to investigate any form of new movement they wish without fearing that they are betraying some artistic cause. And they can make use of their legacy of movement from the past without risking the charge of being reactionary.

So, instead of pining for an avant-garde, perhaps we should pray to Terpsichore, "Let there be dance. Let there be different kinds of dance." And maybe we had better add, "O gracious Muse, make all that dance good."

*New York Times*, 5 December 1982

# AN ESSAY

# ON DANCE CRITICISM

We ride a moving earth; we cannot feel  
It move. And yet we know its motion by  *Diversion of Angels*  
The way we count it out in time, and how,  (Graham)  
In time, some kinds of counted things  
    return.  *The Mind Is a*  
The blood flows, the heart beats, the breath  *Muscle* (Rainer)  
Goes in and out. The throat swallows.  
    Eyelids  
Blink. The eye travels. The hand travels.  
What's in the hand moves onward with the  
    hand.  
And what is on the mind moves with the  *How to Pass, Kick,*  
    mind.  *Fall, and Run*  
Listen: the steam moves in the pipes—the  (Cunningham)  
    sound  
Of motion—traffic fades out in the distance,  
Someone hammers on a roof; unseen,  
I know his progress only by his rhythm.  
I fix my gaze upon an empty wall.  
It fills: chains in my eyes float up and  
    down it.  
Smoke drifts, too, from my cigarette, and yet  *Countdown* (Perez)  
I have not smoked in fourteen years:  
    remembered  
Motion. Gauzes rustling in the wind,  
With beating wings an apparition bursts  
Out of the wall: imagined motion, a flight  *La Sylphide*  
Of fancy. How far should I pursue that fancy  (Bournonville)  
As real before I ought to let it fade  
Into the wall again? For if I claim  
This fancy always real, am I not mad?  *Coppélia* (Saint-Léon)

And yet, without such fancies, am I not
    hopeless?
The mind draws things together, gives
    thought flesh,
Makes flesh as protean as thought. Then
    things,
Passed from the light in which they're seen,    *Canfield*
    are past    (Cunningham)
And dark. I stop to polish my glasses or cut
A hangnail: my nervous tics. My glasses
    never
Come clean enough, though I keep wiping
    them.
And here I'm stuck. What is there to say
    next?

(A pause.) I pace. Then I repeat myself:    *Memorandum*
We ride a moving earth, we count things    (Driver)
    out,
And what is on the mind moves with the
    mind.
I bring things back again: old stories, jokes,
Punchlines, taglines, those times we used
    to go
And see whoever it was, our favorite jokes,
A repertory of experiences
Rehearsed, revived to entertain ourselves,    *Junk Dances* (Louis)
Things real and things imagined: the game,
    the sport,
The boast, the lie, the jest, charade,    *Parade* (Massine)
    pretense,
The dressing up, the dressing down, the
    leap

Of faith, the standing firm, the scampering
  off,
The lust for bodies and the lust to travel,
And the What If: thus what, for instance, if
Our faces were not on our faces, but         *Tent* (Nikolais)
Were somewhere else: the face, say, at the
  back
Of the head, in the small of the back, or in
  the navel,
The crotch, the armpit, or the spleen—if so,
How would we look or move, how would we
  face
The world? Inspired, we rush to make      *Insects and Heroes*
  ourselves                                 (Taylor)
All over and all different: godly
Of limb, serene of mind, poised, in full    *Apollo* (Balanchine)
Control, above it all, or freaks—lumpish,
Shuffling, shambling, crouching, slouching,   *A Folk Tale*
  hopping                             (Bournonville)
Witches and trolls of the emotions, unfit
For good society. And yet no matter
What, we do go on.

          There is this hope
(We pause before we dare to speak of it)   *Serenade*
That we, despite our stumbles and mis-steps,    (Balanchine)
Are somehow an ensemble, secretly      *The Sleeping Beauty*
Harmonious, aspiring toward a clear      (Petipa)
Accord we could achieve if we but knew
The way, that in our rises and our falls    *The Bix Pieces*
There is a beat, a pulse, a measure that,     (Tharp)
However faint, joins step to step as words   *Accumulations*
Are joined to words until those words in sum   (Brown)

Transcend themselves as syntax. So
   actions are
More than the gestures out of which
   they're made.
But even as gesture leads to gesture, gesture
Drops back and vanishes. Everything          *Orpheus* (Balanchine)
To which we give a name or value has
Either already happened or it has           *Theatre Events*
Not happened yet. What's happening now is its    (Cunningham)
Going to become the thing we'll think
It is—except, as we go on ourselves,
It, too, may turn out differently, for things
Change even as we think of them: we add
Details, ignore the hard or boring parts,
Forget, or simply fail to focus on
The evidence. And then we later find
Something has changed. When was it that    *Education of the*
   I knew                                     *Girlchild* (Monk)
I didn't like artichokes or opera
(Though I kept thinking that I ought),
   just when
Did it first dawn on me I could not stay
Up late at night as I once did, and when
Did I first weep at Schubert? When did I last?   *Passage in Silence*
Things pass from us, we pass along, all farings   (Neville)
Become farewells, all languages are notings
Of goodbye and gestures of godspeed.        *A New Life* (Waring)


Look at what is, and there may be a dance.
Finding a dance in what we see is finding    *Esplanade* (Taylor)
Time for things before they are forgotten.
To talk of dancing is to talk of what
Once was, of how it moves us now, and what

It means this moment that we talk of it.
Then talking is the new dance, it is the mind's
Dance. And dancing, we think, is what we do
Always, and all creation joins the dance.

*Looking at the Dance*
(Denby)

*Chelsea* 39 (1980): 57–60

# INDEX